Real Estate Institute

InstituteOnline.com

800-995-1700

PASS THE MORTGAGE LOAN ORIGINATOR TEST:

A STUDY GUIDE FOR THE NMLS SAFE EXAM

Second Edition

CONTRIBUTIONS BY PETER CITERA

PASS THE MORTGAGE LOAN ORIGINATOR TEST:

A STUDY GUIDE FOR THE NMLS SAFE EXAM
Second Edition

Printed in the United States of America.

ISBN 978-0-9975621-1-8

∎P1∎

All inquiries should be addressed to:
Real Estate Institute
6203 W. Howard
Niles, IL 60714
(800) 995-1700
InstituteOnline.com

TABLE OF CONTENTS

INTRODUCTION – PREPARING FOR THE NATIONAL COMPONENT EXAMINATION i

CHAPTER ONE – FEDERAL MORTGAGE-RELATED LAWS................................ 1

  A.   REAL ESTATE SETTLEMENT PROCEDURES ACT (RESPA)..............................1

  B.   EQUAL CREDIT OPPORTUNITY ACT (ECOA), REGULATION B 5

  C.   TRUTH IN LENDING ACT (TILA), REGULATION Z...8

      1.   Home Ownership and Equity Protection Act (HOEPA, Section 32)........10

      2.   Higher-Priced Mortgage Loans (HPML, Section 35)............................10

      3.   Loan Originator Compensation 11

  D.   TILA-RESPA INTEGRATED DISCLOSURE RULE (TRID) 12

  E.   OTHER FEDERAL LAWS AND GUIDELINES 20

      1.   Home Mortgage Disclosure Act (HMDA) 20

      2.   Fair Credit Reporting Act (FCRA) 21

      3.   FTC Red Flags Rule 23

      4.   Privacy Protection / Do Not Call 24

      5.   Dodd-Frank...25

      6.   Bank Secrecy Act/Anti-Money Laundering (BSA/AML) 28

      7.   Gramm-Leach-Bliley Act– Privacy and FTC Safeguard Rules 30

      8.   Mortgage Acts and Practices – Advertising (Regulation N) 31

      9.   Electronic Signatures in Global and National Commerce Act (E-SIGN Act) 32

     10.   USA PATRIOT Act 33

     11.   Homeowners Protection Act 34

  F.   REGULATORY AUTHORITY..35

      1.   Consumer Financial Protection Bureau (CFPB).................................35

      2.   Department of Housing and Urban Development 36

CHAPTER TWO – GENERAL MORTGAGE KNOWLEDGE.............................. 37

  A.   QUALIFIED AND NON-QUALIFIED MORTGAGE PROGRAMS 37

      1.   Conventional / Conforming 37

      2.   Government (FHA, VA, USDA)...40

      3.   Conventional / Nonconforming (Jumbo, Alt-A, etc.)...........................46

          a.   Statement on Subprime Lending 47

          b.   Guidance on Nontraditional Mortgage Product Risk 49

          c.   Non-Qualified Mortgages (Non-QMs)......................................50

B. MORTGAGE LOAN PRODUCTS 50

   1. Fixed 50

   2. Adjustable 51

   3. Balloon 54

   4. Reverse Mortgage 54

   5. Home Equity (Fixed and Line of Credit) 56

   6. Construction Loans 56

   7. Interest–Only Loans (First Lien) 57

C. TERMS USED IN THE MORTGAGE INDUSTRY 57

   1. Loan Terms 57

   2. Disclosure Terms 58

   3. Financial Terms 60

   4. General Terms 61

CHAPTER THREE – MORTGAGE LOAN ORIGINATION ACTIVITIES 65

A. APPLICATION INFORMATION AND REQUIREMENTS 65

   1. Application Accuracy and Required Information (e.g., 1003) 65

      a. Borrower 65

      b. Loan Originator 66

      c. Verification and Documentation 66

   2. Suitability of Products and Programs 66

   3. Disclosures 67

      a. Accuracy 68

      b. Timing 68

B. QUALIFICATION: PROCESSING AND UNDERWRITING 70

   1. Borrower Analysis 70

      a. Assets 70

      b. Liabilities 72

      c. Income 73

      d. Credit Report 75

      e. Qualifying Ratios (e.g., Housing, Debt-to-Income, Loan-to-Value) 76

      f. Ability-to-Repay Mortgage Rules 79

      g. Tangible Net Benefit 80

   2. Appraisals 81

   3. Title Report 83

   4. Insurance: Hazard, Flood, and Mortgage 84

C. CLOSING 86

   1. Settlement/Closing Agent 86

    2.   Explanation of Fees 87

    3.   Explanation of Documents 89

    4.   Funding 90

  D. FINANCIAL CALCULATIONS USED IN MORTGAGE LENDING....................91

    1.   Period Interest...91

    2.   Payments (Principal, Interest, Taxes, and Insurance; Mortgage Insurance, If Applicable) 91

    3.   Down Payment...93

    4.   Loan-to-Value (Loan-To-Value, Combined Loan-to-Value, Total Loan-to-Value)..94

    5.   Debt-to-Income Ratios...95

    6.   Temporary and Fixed Interest Rate Buy-Down (Discount Points) 97

    7.   Closing Costs and Prepaid Items...97

    8.   ARMs (e.g., Fully Indexed Rate) 98

    9.   Qualified Mortgage Monthly Payment Calculations...........................99

CHAPTER FOUR – ETHICS 101

  A. ETHICAL ISSUES RELATED TO FEDERAL LAWS 101

    1.   Violations of Federal Law...101

    2.   Prohibited Acts 101

    3.   Fairness in Lending...102

    4.   Fraud Detection 104

    5.   Mortgage Fraud Categories and Red Flags 105

    6.   Advertising..107

    7.   Predatory Lending and Steering 108

  B. ETHICAL BEHAVIOR RELATED TO LOAN ORIGINATION ACTIVITIES.........108

    1.   Financial Responsibility 108

    2.   Handling Consumer Complaints 109

    3.   Company Compliance..110

    4.   Relationships With Consumers, Your Company and Investors 110

    5.   Truth in Marketing and Advertising 112

    6.   Consumer Education..112

    7.   General Business Ethics 113

CHAPTER FIVE – UNIFORM STATE CONTENT 115

  A. SAFE ACT AND CSBS/AARMR MODEL STATE LAW 115

    1.   State Mortgage Regulatory Agencies....................................115

      a.   Regulatory Authority...116

      b.   Responsibilities and Limitations 117

2. State Law and Regulation Definitions 117
3. License Law and Regulation 119
    a. Persons Required to Be Licensed 119
    b. Licensee Qualifications and Application Process 124
    c. Grounds For Denying a License 125
    d. License Maintenance 126
    e. NMLS Requirements 127
    f. Temporary Authority to Operate 127
4. Compliance 129
    a. Prohibited Conduct and Practices 129
    b. Required Conduct 130
    c. Advertising 130

PRACTICE EXAM A 131

PRACTICE EXAM B 143

PRACTICE EXAM C 155

PRACTICE EXAM ANSWER KEYS 167

GLOSSARY 169

QUICK REFERENCE CHARTS AND LINKS 187

A. Disclosure Requirements and Timeline 187

B. Triggering Events and Timeline 188

C. Maximum Penalties and Implementing/Enforcing Agencies 189

D. Benchmark Debt-to-Income Ratios (Front / Back) 190

E. Loan Estimate Fees and Tolerances 190

F. Helpful Links and Reference Tools 191

INTRODUCTION – PREPARING FOR THE NATIONAL COMPONENT EXAMINATION

The Secure and Fair Enforcement for Mortgage Lending Act of 2008 (the *SAFE Act*) was enacted by Congress in 2008 and set forth requirements for the licensing and registration of all mortgage loan originators. Loan originators who work for an insured depository or its owned or controlled subsidiary are required to become registered. All other loan originators are to be licensed by the states.

These state-licensed loan originators must pass a written examination, including a National Component and (depending on state rules and prior licensure) a State-Specific Component for each state where they wish to be licensed. The creation and administration of the entire examination is overseen by the Nationwide Multistate Licensing System and Registry (NMLS-R) – formerly called the Nationwide Mortgage Licensing System.

The NMLS-R has provided an outline of the content included in the National Component of the examination. The examination consists of 125 multiple-choice questions and is divided into five major content areas, each with a number of subtopics.

Based on the NMLS-R National Component content outline, the number of test questions allocated to each of the five major content areas will be as follows:

- ❑ Federal mortgage-related laws (Chapter 1 of this study guide) – 23%
- ❑ General mortgage knowledge (Chapter 2) – 23%
- ❑ Mortgage loan origination activities (Chapter 3) – 25%
- ❑ Ethics (Chapter 4) – 16%
- ❑ Uniform state content (Chapter 5) – 13%

Throughout the study guide, you will find definitions and concepts that you will need to recall in order to pass the examination. Learning and committing to memory the specific definitions and lists of points in this guide will greatly increase your chances of passing the examination.

Note, however, that these materials are intended only as a specific review of the points in the content outline and are only meant to better prepare you for the examination. The study guide is not a replacement for complete training materials or review of actual laws and regulations when beginning a career as a residential mortgage loan originator.

When taking the examination, it will help to remember the following tips:

- ❑ Do not spend unnecessary time on a difficult question. You should first answer all of the questions that you know the answer to.
- ❑ Thoroughly read EVERY question and EVERY answer before making a choice, even for the questions you feel certain about. Make certain you are answering the question they are asking you, not the question you THINK they're asking you.

- Before reading each question, stop, sit up straight and take your hand off the mouse and the keyboard. This will help you focus on the question and answers and will break the "read/click/advance" rhythm that your mind naturally wants to get itself into. Humans thrive on repetitive tasks; don't let this tendency hurt your score!

- If you are in doubt about the answer to a question, move on to another one and come back to it later.

- When you are unsure between two or more choices, you should choose one and return to the question later.

- When you believe there are actually two correct choices, you should look for small differences that make one a better choice or read the question again.

- If you have selected one answer but are thinking about choosing another one, only switch away from your first choice if you are certain that the second choice is correct. You will find that your first choice is usually the right one.

- Never leave a question unanswered. Unanswered questions are scored as incorrect.

CHAPTER ONE –
FEDERAL MORTGAGE-RELATED LAWS

A. REAL ESTATE SETTLEMENT PROCEDURES ACT (RESPA)

The Real Estate Settlement Procedures Act (RESPA) allows borrowers to receive pertinent and timely disclosure regarding the nature and costs of the real estate settlement (closing) process. Enacted in 1974, the law was originally proposed to add more transparency to costs associated with certain real estate transactions and to eliminate abusive practices – such as kickbacks – that artificially increased the cost of settlement services.

In general, mortgage professionals must obey RESPA when a loan is a **federally related mortgage loan** secured by a one-to-four-unit residential property. Over time, the definition of *federally related* has expanded to encompass most loans made by depository and non-depository lenders. The law does not apply to loans secured by commercial properties, vacant land (unless a dwelling is intended to be constructed on the land within two years) or properties containing 25 or more acres. Temporary financing, such as bridge loans and construction loans, are also exempt. Regarding residential (one-to-four-family) rental properties, RESPA applies generally when the *purpose of the credit itself* is consumer-related but does NOT apply when the loan is for business purposes. The law applies whether a covered loan is being originated by a lender OR a mortgage broker. RESPA defines a *mortgage broker* as "a person (other than an employee of a lender) that renders origination services and serves as an intermediary between a borrower and a lender... including a person that closes the loan in its own name in a **table-funded transaction**.

For example, if an individual were purchasing a two-unit building and planned to rent both units to others for profit, this WOULD NOT be covered by RESPA. However, a refinancing loan on a residential rental property where the proceeds are going to pay off personal credit card debt WOULD be covered by RESPA, as the purpose of the credit itself is consumer-related.

The rules for complying with RESPA are found in **Regulation X**. Those rules are promulgated and enforced at the federal level by the Consumer Financial Protection Bureau (CFPB). Failure to comply with RESPA can result in stiff financial and criminal penalties. In addition, state regulatory agencies may suspend or revoke a mortgage loan originator's license for RESPA violations.

Prohibiting Kickbacks – RESPA Section 8

RESPA prohibits kickbacks or unearned fees. A **kickback** is generally defined as providing a *thing of value* to a third party in return for the referral of **settlement service business**. For example, a loan originator paying a fee to a real estate agent for each closed loan that was referred by the agent would be providing a kickback. A violator may be fined up to $10,000 and/or imprisoned for up to one year for providing kickbacks, and both the provider and the recipient may be liable.

Keep in mind that a "thing of value" includes gift cards, sports tickets, advertising space, marketing materials bearing a real estate agent's information to give to his/her clients, and donations to a real estate agent's favorite charity, among others.

Despite prohibiting kickbacks, RESPA does NOT prohibit the payment of fair market value for goods or services that were actually received or performed. Nor does it prohibit a mortgage originator from passing out promotional material bearing the originator's information, logo, etc. in a real estate agent's office. RESPA also does not prohibit joint marketing efforts on the part of loan originators and real estate agents, so long as all parties pay for their fair share of the marketing space. The CFPB takes the "fair share" rule seriously, such that if a mortgage company and a real estate company share space on a billboard advertisement and the mortgage company has 62% of the available billboard space, the mortgage company would need to cover 62% of the cost, and the real estate company would need to cover the remaining 38%. A 50/50 split of costs in this case would connote a kickback and violate Section 8 of RESPA.

Regulation of Escrow Accounts – RESPA Section 10

Under RESPA, the lender cannot require the borrower to deposit into an escrow account a sum in excess of the estimated payment of taxes, insurance premiums or other charges with respect to the property. The installment payment cannot be more than 1/12 of the total annual amount, plus such an amount as is necessary to maintain an additional cushion balance which cannot exceed 1/6 (two months) of the estimated totals. Remember, <u>the maximum cushion on escrow accounts is TWO MONTHS (1/6 of a year) of taxes and insurance payments over the maximum amount needed to satisfy these charges when they become due.</u>

When a loan has an escrow account for property taxes and insurance, <u>lenders are required to provide borrowers with a summary of the account at closing and once per year for as long as the escrow account is in force</u>. This summary form shows payments into and disbursements from the account. The one provided at closing is referred to as the **Initial Escrow Statement**, and the annual disclosure and statement is sometimes referred to as the **Notice of Escrow Analysis**.

The "Required Use" Provision Barring Mandatory Use of a Title Company - RESPA Section 9

Title insurance is a type of insurance that protects against defects in title that were not listed in a title report. An owner's policy of title insurance does more than just report on the condition of title (outstanding liens, etc.); it protects the owner from claims against his/her ownership interest. A lender's policy of title insurance protects the lender from claims that may jeopardize the validity or priority of the lender's mortgage lien. Under RESPA, it is illegal for a property seller to require the buyer to use a particular title insurance company, and violation of this provision can result in what is referred to as **treble damages**. That is, those who violate this provision of RESPA can be held liable for three times the cost of the title services that were improperly required – in addition to the standard RESPA maximum penalties described above.

Servicing Concerns

Servicing a loan encompasses all of the things necessary to collect and track a borrower's payments, send periodic loan statements as required and respond to borrower inquiries on an ongoing loan. In unfortunate cases when borrowers become delinquent, the servicer also must handle loss mitigation and foreclosure proceedings in accordance with federal law. RESPA establishes guidelines for lenders to respond to borrower inquires about their loans as well as rules that balance the interests of borrowers and creditors in the foreclosure process.

The "Qualified Written Request"

When borrowers have a question about anything to do with the servicing of their loan (an escrow account issue, potential misapplication of a payment or a late fee, for example), they have the ability to file what is called a Qualified Written Request (or QWR) under Section 6 of RESPA. In order to receive the full protections afforded under the law, this should be done in writing and sent to the address that the servicer maintains for that purpose, which may be different from the address to which payments are mailed. The servicer generally must confirm receipt of the QWR letter within five business days of receipt and respond with an answer within 30 days.

RESPA Disclosure Requirements

In certain cases, lenders must provide several documents to borrowers within three business days of receiving or preparing a loan application unless the application is denied during that time period. Under RESPA, these documents are as follows and will be explained later in this section:

- Good Faith Estimate (GFE) – used ONLY for reverse mortgages today.

- Mortgage Loan Servicing Disclosure.

- The CFPB's Home Loan Toolkit – required on purchase transactions only.

When determining the required delivery date for these early disclosures, be aware that a **business day** is defined to be "any date on which the creditor is open to the public for carrying on substantially all of the creditor's business functions." There are multiple definitions of a business day that affect disclosures that we must send, and knowing which definition applies to which disclosure is *crucial* to passing the NMLS exam.

In many cases, the three-day clock for providing these documents will begin long before the signing of any paperwork. For the purposes of both RESPA and TILA, you have an application (and the disclosure clock starts ticking) when you know the following six pieces of information:

- The borrower's name.

- The borrower's Social Security number.

- The address of the subject property (the property that is being financed).

- The borrower's monthly income.

- The borrower's estimate of value of the property (NOT an appraisal).

- The loan amount.

If it helps, you may want to remember these items with the acronym ANVILS (Address, Name, Value, Income, Loan Amount, SSN)

Good Faith Estimate

The **Good Faith Estimate (GFE)** is the required disclosure of the known or anticipated fees, charges or settlement costs that the mortgage applicant is likely to incur at the settlement (closing) of the loan. Each such estimate must be made in good faith and bear a reasonable relationship to the charge a borrower is likely to pay at closing. It must be delivered within three business days of receiving or preparing an application.

The GFE is closely related to the **Uniform Settlement Statement** – commonly referred to as the *HUD-1* settlement statement. The HUD-1 sets forth a complete list of the actual settlement costs that will be charged at the closing, and it must be made available for review, if requested by the borrowers, at least one business day prior to settlement.

IMPORTANT NOTE: On October 3, 2015, with the implementation of the **TILA-RESPA Integrated Disclosure Rule** (TRID), the GFE and HUD-1 were replaced by two new forms called the *Loan Estimate* and the *Closing Disclosure* for the vast majority of real estate loans in the United States. However, the old disclosure forms continue to be used on reverse mortgages.

You will read much more about the Loan Estimate and the Closing Disclosure later in this study guide, as they are requirements under Regulation Z, not Regulation X.

Mortgage Loan Servicing Disclosure

The **Mortgage Loan Servicing Disclosure** provides notice on what the lender intends to do with the servicing of the loan after it is closed – whether it will service the loan itself or transfer servicing to another entity – and it must be provided to the borrower within three business days of the loan application. Note that the Mortgage Loan Servicing Disclosure is NOT the same document as the Servicing Transfer Statement, which informs the borrower that his/her loan has been transferred to another servicer and is provided *after* closing.

Other RESPA Disclosures

In addition to the disclosures already mentioned, RESPA requires that the following disclosures be made to consumers:

- Affiliated Business Arrangement Disclosure (AfBA).
- Servicing Transfer Statement.

The **Affiliated Business Arrangement Disclosure (AfBA)** informs mortgage applicants of any service providers that may be used in the loan transaction that are affiliated with the lender. An *affiliated business arrangement* exists when the referring party has a greater than 1% ownership interest in the business receiving the referral. Although it is commonplace for most companies that use affiliated businesses to include this disclosure with their standard disclosure package, the letter of the law states that this disclosure must be provided to the borrower no later than the time the referral to the affiliated business is made. In many cases, this occurs after the initial three-business-day period. It is simply good practice to issue the disclosure within three business days of loan application if referrals are made to an affiliated business as a standard practice. Note that in cases where the lender *requires* the use of a particular affiliated business (generally tax service companies and/or flood certification providers), disclosure must be made at the time of application. Lenders are generally prohibited from requiring the borrower to use a specific title insurance company, although most refinance borrowers elect to use a lender's recommended provider, whether or not there is an affiliated relationship.

The **Servicing Transfer Statement** is required to be provided to the borrower by the servicer no later than 15 days BEFORE servicing rights are transferred to a new institution. It gives the borrower details on the servicing transfer, including the new address(es) for payments or inquiries on the loan. This disclosure is often referred to as a *goodbye letter* in industry jargon. New servicers are required to send the borrower a notice (also known as a *welcome letter*) containing the same information no later than 15 days AFTER the transfer of servicing takes place. Note that the requirements for both the existing and new servicer can be combined into one notice as long as that notice is provided to the borrower 15 days before the transfer.

There is also a statutory 60-day "grace period" during which any payment mistakenly made to the old servicer must be forwarded by that company to the new servicer and, as long as the old servicer receives the payment in a timely manner, no late fee can be assessed. This is true even if the new servicer receives the payment after a date on which a late fee would ordinarily be assessed.

Can an MLO also act as a real estate broker/agent? This is one of the most common questions in the business, and the answer is, in most cases, yes although it is not considered ethical by many real estate trade associations. If this "dual relationship" is going to exist, it MUST be disclosed to the borrower(s) before signing any application documents, and they must consent to the arrangement. Note that this practice is *strictly prohibited* on all transactions using FHA financing.

B. EQUAL CREDIT OPPORTUNITY ACT (ECOA), REGULATION B

The **Equal Credit Opportunity Act (ECOA)** prohibits discrimination in the granting of all types of credit on the basis of:

- Race.
- Color.
- Religion.
- National origin.
- Sex.
- Marital status.
- Age (provided that the applicant has the capacity to enter into a legally binding contract).
- Receipt of income from public assistance benefits.
- The fact that the applicant has exercised any right, in good faith, under the Consumer Credit Protection Act.

Regulation B is the federal regulation that implements ECOA. Rulemaking and enforcement power regarding ECOA belongs to the Consumer Financial Protection Bureau (CFPB).

It is worth noting that while ECOA prohibits lenders from denying credit on the basis of receipt of income from public assistance benefits, lenders are permitted to deny credit on the basis of a borrower's income level being unstable or unlikely to continue.

In order to ensure compliance with ECOA, lenders and mortgage loan originators should refrain from asking any questions that may be construed as discriminatory. For example, a loan originator should never ask a borrower directly whether any portion of his/her income is derived from alimony, child support or spousal maintenance. ECOA allows for those forms of income to be used (as long as they meet the requirements for continuity), but only if the borrower elects to disclose them. If borrowers do not wish to use such income as a basis for qualification, they may leave those sources undisclosed. An example of an appropriate non-discriminatory question that a loan originator may ask is, "Are there any other sources of income you wish to disclose to me?"

Note that although it is considered discriminatory to ask if an applicant *receives* income from alimony, child support or spousal maintenance, it is NOT considered discriminatory to ask if an applicant has been mandated by a court to <u>pay</u> alimony, child support or other maintenance. In fact, loan originators should ask this question, as those payments are treated as liabilities and must be disclosed on the loan application.

It is also permissible to ask the applicant(s) their marital status, as this may have an impact on the documents that the lender will require to be executed at closing. However, if an applicant is not legally married, it is NOT permissible to ask if he/she is divorced, widowed, etc. Thus, the only three choices on the application regarding marital status are: married, unmarried and separated. Additionally, one should never ask applicants how many children they have (or plan to have). Rather, the proper question is, "How many <u>dependents </u>do you have?"

If an applicant wishes to apply for individual credit (in his or her name only), a creditor cannot require the addition of a co-borrower to the loan application. In the case where adding a co-borrower may improve the chances of loan approval, the creditor may inform the applicant of this fact but may NOT suggest who the potential co-applicant should be. For example, asking a borrower if "anyone else may be willing to serve as a co-borrower" is OK but asking a borrower "if their spouse might be willing to serve as a co-borrower" is NOT OK.

In addition to outlawing discrimination in the granting of credit, ECOA defines the procedures for applicant notification. Lenders must notify all residential loan applicants of action taken on their loans within <u>30 days</u> after receiving a completed loan application (a completed application here includes any required documentation and is not the same as the six pieces of information found in RESPA and TILA). If there is adverse action taken against an application (the application is denied, or the lender issues a counteroffer on different terms than those applied for), *all applicants* must receive written notification called an "adverse action notice." This notice must disclose the actual reason(s) that the denial or counteroffer occurred. If the applicant's credit profile factored into the adverse action, the lender must provide the applicant with the name, address and toll-free phone number of the credit reporting agency that provided the credit report used in making the decision. Should the applicant not submit all information necessary for a complete application within a 30-day period, creditors may send a *notice of incompleteness* telling the applicant what information is missing and providing a deadline for submission, after which the application will be withdrawn or denied if the required information is not received.

ECOA and Appraisals

ECOA also mandates that an applicant for a first-lien mortgage loan secured by a dwelling receive a copy of the appraisal report or *any written valuation* used in conjunction with rendering the credit decision. The applicant must be informed of this right via disclosure made within three business days of application. A copy of all valuations must be provided promptly upon receipt by the creditor but in no case can the applicant receive it fewer than three business days prior to loan closing. An applicant may elect to waive the "prompt delivery" requirement but *cannot* waive the requirement to receive the copy at least three business days prior to loan closing.

Identifying Discrimination

There are three separate legal theories that the CFPB has indicated are valid ways to identify discrimination in lending under ECOA:

- Overt discrimination.
- Disparate treatment.
- Disparate impact.

Overt Discrimination

Overt discrimination is discrimination that is explicit or obvious. An example would be advertising that indicates that members of a protected class are not welcome at the institution. Alternatively, overt discrimination might exist if there is a widespread understanding in the community that members of a protected class will not be served by an institution.

Disparate Treatment

Disparate treatment is discrimination that is defined by differences in the way members of a protected class are served by the institution. For example, an individual may be engaging in disparate treatment by shaking the hand of members of one race or gender and not following the same procedure with members of another race or gender. Disparate treatment can also occur if members of a protected class are charged higher rates and/or fees than similarly situated members of a non-protected class.

Disparate Impact

Disparate impact is a method of identifying discrimination through statistical analysis. It occurs when a practice or policy that appears to be non-discriminatory on its face has a disproportionately negative effect on members of a particular race, gender or other protected class. Unlike other forms of discrimination, discrimination identified via disparate impact is often illegal <u>even if the discrimination is unintentional</u>. For example, one of the largest fair-lending settlements based on disparate impact theory alleged that a creditor's minimum credit score policies resulted in a disproportionate number of minority applicants receiving FHA loans instead of less expensive conventional loans.

C. TRUTH IN LENDING ACT (TILA), REGULATION Z

The purpose of the **Truth in Lending Act (TILA)** is to promote the informed use of consumer credit (i.e., credit to a consumer primarily for personal, family or household purposes) by requiring disclosure about its terms and cost. TILA is actually Title I of a broader piece of legislation called the *Consumer Credit Protection Act of 1968*, and it does not apply to loans for commercial or business purposes. When dealing with residential mortgage loans, the test as to whether TILA applies to a particular transaction is based on the purpose of the credit itself – NOT the occupancy of the property – similar to the test under RESPA described earlier in this text.

Disclosure under TILA is important because it helps the consumer compare costs (including rates and fees) when shopping for a mortgage loan. Comparison shopping is considered the best means by which a consumer can avoid abusive lending practices.

Regulation Z is the federal regulation that implements TILA. Rulemaking and enforcement power under TILA are handled by the Consumer Financial Protection Bureau.

CHARM Booklets

Some disclosures under TILA are specific to adjustable-rate mortgage loans (ARMs). An **adjustable-rate mortgage** loan is a mortgage loan with an interest rate that can change at any point during the life of the loan. TILA requires that lenders offering ARMs furnish an additional written disclosure, called the **ARM Disclosure,** that provides historical information about ARM loans similar to the one that the borrower has applied for, as well as the **CHARM (Consumer Handbook on Adjustable Rate Mortgages) booklet**, which provides general information on, and covers risks associated with, the ARM product. These disclosures must be provided within the same three-business-day period as the Loan Estimate, which we will cover in detail elsewhere.

Advertising and Trigger Terms

Regulation Z provides that when certain loan terms, called **trigger terms**, are set forth in an advertisement, a number of other terms must be disclosed as well. Trigger terms are as follows:

- The amount or percentage of down payment.
- The number of payments or period of repayment.
- The amount of any payment.
- The amount of any finance charge.

When trigger terms are used, the advertisement must also state all of the following terms:

- The amount or percentage of the down payment.
- The terms of repayment.
- The annual percentage rate.

Further, TILA makes it clear that, when advertising an interest rate on a loan, creditors must also advertise the APR. In a print advertisement, this must be done in close proximity to the interest rate and must be in at least the same font size and identical typeface as the interest rate. APR, however, is allowed to stand alone when not advertised with any of the trigger terms above; no interest rate is needed when the advertisement contains only the APR as it measures the total cost of the loan (including the finance charge) and not just the cost of interest.

Transfer of Ownership Disclosure

TILA requires entities that purchase or acquire mortgage loans to notify the borrower(s) and provide the name, address and phone number of the new owner of the mortgage, as well as the location where the transfer of ownership in the mortgage loan is recorded, within 30 days after acquisition. This requirement applies only to loans secured by a borrower's primary residence. (Do NOT confuse this requirement, which applies to a transfer of ownership of the loan, with the RESPA mandate that a borrower be notified 15 days before a transfer of servicing occurs.) The owner of the loan and the servicer are frequently separate entities.

TILA Right of Rescission

Under Regulation Z, borrowers have the right to cancel certain credit transactions for a period _after_ closing/settlement. This is called the **right of rescission**.

The right of rescission applies ONLY to **refinance transactions** on a principal residence. (In a refinance transaction, the borrower is paying off an existing obligation with a new loan or converting equity into cash by obtaining a new loan on a property that does not currently have an outstanding obligation).

The right of rescission extends for three business days from the later of:

- Closing on the transaction (signing loan documents) OR
- Delivery of all material disclosures OR
- Delivery of two copies of a "notice of right to cancel" to everyone with the right to rescind.

NOTE: Typically, all of the above events occur on the same day.

Under TILA, when calculating the right of rescission, the definition of a business day includes any day except Sundays and federal holidays. Thus, Saturday can be included in the day count, but Sunday and legal holidays cannot.

The day of signing is NOT included in the three-day calculation. Therefore, if each of the three events described above happens on a Monday, the three-day rescission period lasts through Thursday at 11:59 p.m. The first opportunity to fund the loan would be Friday.

Note that the right to rescind a refinance transaction on a principal residence applies to anyone appearing on title to the property (not just borrowers), and everyone with rescission rights must receive two copies of the required rescission notice. There does not need to be agreement between parties when rescission occurs. Thus, if one individual exercises his or her right to rescind, the transaction is cancelled even if others wish for it to continue to funding.

When a loan is rescinded, the creditor must refund to the borrower all monies collected within 20 calendar days of rescission occurring, regardless of whether those funds have been spent. For example, the creditor is required to refund the borrower an appraisal fee that was paid, even if the appraisal has been completed and the appraiser paid.

1. Home Ownership and Equity Protection Act (HOEPA, Section 32)

As a result of TILA and the **Home Ownership and Equity Protection Act (HOEPA)**, additional disclosures and limitations on loan terms apply to certain loans with high interest rates and/or high loan fees. For example, a loan that is subject to HOEPA cannot feature a balloon payment within the first five years of the loan, negative amortization or a prepayment penalty. A loan subject to HOEPA can also not be refinanced by the original creditor within one year unless doing so would create a clear and tangible benefit for the consumer.

The restrictions mentioned above regarding HOEPA apply to **high-cost mortgage loans** (sometimes referred to as *Section 32 loans*). In order to figure out whether a loan is a high-cost loan, we must compare our loan's APR against the Average Prime Offer Rate (APOR) as published weekly on the Consumer Financial Protection Bureau's (CFPB) website. A loan will be considered a high-cost home loan if its APR exceeds the APOR by more than 6.5% for a first lien or 8.5% for a subordinate lien OR when the total points and fees payable in conjunction with the loan exceed 5% of the loan amount (the points and fee threshold is the lesser of 8% of the loan amount or $1,099 for loans of $21,980 or less; these figures are adjusted annually by the CFPB).

Be careful not to confuse high-cost mortgage loans with *higher-priced loans*, Higher-priced loans will be explained in the next section.

For many years, HOEPA only applied to refinances of primary residences. Since 2013, however, coverage has expanded to encompass all purchase, refinance, closed-end home equity loans and HELOCs secured by a borrower's principal residence. HOEPA does not apply to reverse mortgages, true construction loans and those loans originated by a Housing Finance Agency (HFA).

2. Higher-Priced Mortgage Loans (HPML, Section 35)

TILA/HOEPA was amended in 2009 to create a new category of loans called *higher-priced mortgage loans*, sometimes known as *HPMLs* or *Section 35 loans*. Should a loan be deemed a HPML, the borrower must escrow property tax and insurance payments (on first liens only) for a minimum of five years, and the lender is prohibited from charging a prepayment penalty if the loan's interest rate can adjust in the first four years of the loan term. Additionally, lenders must verify the borrower's ability to repay all higher-priced mortgage loans by looking at the borrower's income, assets, credit and debt and by calculating a debt-to-income ratio.

A loan is considered a higher-priced mortgage loan if its APR exceeds the Average Prime Offer Rate (APOR) published weekly by the Consumer

Financial Protection Bureau (CFPB) by 1.5% for first-lien loans, 2.5% for jumbo first-lien loans and 3.5% for subordinate liens.

3. **Loan Originator Compensation**

In 2011, the Federal Reserve Board issued a rule changing the way that mortgage loan originators could be paid. Specifically, this version of the rule prohibited **dual compensation**; that is, it restricted an originator to being paid from either the borrower OR the lender on a given transaction, but not both. Additionally, the rule eliminated the form of compensation known as **yield-spread premium (YSP),** in which mortgage brokers and originators were able to increase their compensation by providing the borrower an interest rate higher than that for which they qualified. Since the effective date of the compensation rule, <u>MLOs have been prohibited from being compensated based on the terms or conditions of a mortgage loan</u> (other than a percentage of the loan amount), and YSP has been replaced for mortgage brokers by **lender-paid compensation (LPC)**, which is essentially a fixed percentage of the loan amount that does not vary based on loan characteristics (other than the loan amount). Borrowers can choose, however, to pay a higher interest rate in exchange for lower closing costs. In this case, the borrower must receive a closing cost credit for all of the increased yield on a transaction resulting from the higher rate.

In 2014, the CFPB modified the MLO compensation rule to provide some clarification and expanded compensation guidelines. Here is a summary of the MLO compensation rule as it currently stands:

Types/Terms of Compensation Prohibited

- Interest rate on the loan (YSP).

- Sales of services from an affiliated business (i.e. title insurance), although the OWNER of the affiliated business can legally be paid on its profits.

- Any term or condition of the loan, or proxy for a term or condition of the loan (i.e. a point bank allowing an MLO to retain yield overage on a file to be credited to a future file that may be short on yield).

- Steering a consumer into a loan that results in higher compensation, unless clearly in the best interest of the consumer.

Permissible Types/Terms of Compensation

- Salary.

- Commission based on dollar volume of loans or number of loans closed, so long as that compensation does not vary based on the terms or conditions of a given loan or does not become a proxy for the terms or conditions. Most common is *basis points (bps) compensation.* where the MLO receives the same percentage of the loan amount on every loan originated. MLOs may also receive a higher percentage of the loan amount on each loan when their total originations exceed an aggregate volume threshold.

- Participation in a tax advantaged/defined benefit retirement plan, like a 401(k), stock ownership plan, bonus, etc.

- Participation in an undefined, non-tax advantaged bonus plan, as long as the total bonus paid does not exceed 10% of the MLO's total compensation for the year/reporting period.

Finally, MLOs generally cannot REDUCE their compensation on a given transaction to assist the borrower unless there is an unforeseen change in circumstance that affects the settlement costs on a transaction. It is not permissible for MLOs to reduce their compensation due to a mistake on their part. To put it simply, MLOs generally must receive their exact amount of compensation on every file that is closed and funded, except in unforeseen circumstances.

D. TILA-RESPA INTEGRATED DISCLOSURE RULE (TRID)

Prior to October 3, 2015, borrowers received two cost-related disclosure forms at the time of application and potentially two more similar forms at the time of closing. The similar forms (called the Good Faith Estimate and Truth in Lending disclosure) contained overlapping information, which presented challenges to consumers and creditors alike. For borrowers, the overlapping forms created confusion and hindered a consumer's understanding of the lending process. For creditors, having multiple forms with similar information complicated compliance and distracted professionals from other important business.

In response to those problems, the Dodd-Frank Act called on the Consumer Financial Protection Bureau to combine some of the disclosures required by RESPA and TILA and issue rules governing their proper use. By integrating some of the disclosure forms and making other related changes, the government hoped to make it easier for consumers to understand the terms of their loans.

The CFPB addressed the integration of the RESPA and TILA disclosures by finalizing what has become known as the *TILA-RESPA Integrated Disclosure Rule*. The rule contains two newly integrated disclosure forms and instructions on how to use them. Note that even though these disclosures are referred to as *TRID* or *TILA/RESPA Integrated Disclosures*, the actual requirements for providing them to applicants are now contained entirely in Regulation Z.

Specifics regarding the newly integrated forms will be discussed in greater detail over the next few pages. However, the basics are as follows:

- The Good Faith Estimate and the initial Truth in Lending disclosure form were combined into one disclosure form known as the **Loan Estimate**. This form discloses the cost of the credit itself, as well as settlement cost information based on the information known at the time of application.

- The HUD-1 Settlement Statement and the final Truth in Lending disclosure form were combined into one disclosure form known as the **Closing Disclosure**, which discloses actual cost information at the time of closing/settlement/consummation of the loan.

The contents of the TILA-RESPA Integrated Disclosure Rule (including the requirements pertaining to the two new disclosure forms) apply in credit transactions involving a wide range of mortgage loans. The rule applies to practically every kind of closed-end credit transaction that is secured by real property. Credit provided to certain trusts for tax-planning purposes is covered by the new rule, too.

Even some loans that have been exempt from former RESPA requirements (including the provision of a Good Faith Estimate) need to be compliant with the new rule. For example, the rule applies to short-term construction loans and loans that are secured either by vacant land or by 25 or more acres, all of which were formerly exempt from disclosure requirements under RESPA/Regulation X.

As with any rule, however, there are some exceptions. The TRID rule doesn't apply to the following types of mortgage loans:

- Home-equity lines of credit (HELOCs).

- Reverse mortgages.

- Mortgages for mobile homes not secured by real estate.

- Loans from anyone who funds no more than five loans in a calendar year (typically sellers assisting in financing properties that they are selling).

Reverse mortgages continue to use the GFE, HUD-1 and TIL disclosure forms, and HELOCs now use something called the important terms disclosure.

Now that you know the basics of the two new disclosures, let's go into more detail on each.

Loan Estimate

The new Loan Estimate (or *LE*) form replaces the Good Faith Estimate required by RESPA and the initial Truth in Lending disclosure form required by TILA. The purpose of the new form is to help applicants obtain an early understanding of various features, costs and risks that are associated with a potential mortgage loan.

Records of Loan Estimates must be kept by creditors for at least three years after the loan has been consummated.

Intent to Proceed

In addition to providing essential information to potential borrowers, the Loan Estimate is an important disclosure form because creditors are prohibited from performing certain acts until the form is received and the borrowers have indicated their **intent to proceed** with the transaction presented.

The borrower can indicate an intent to proceed with the transaction in any way that he or she chooses, unless the creditor requires a specific kind of communication. The intent to proceed might be provided orally in a face-to-face or phone conversation or in some written format. However, a creditor cannot interpret a borrower's silence as an intent to proceed with the transaction.

Until the borrower has received the Loan Estimate and indicated an intent to proceed, a creditor is generally forbidden from charging any fees. Prohibited fees in this early stage of the transaction include (but are not limited to) application fees, appraisal fees and underwriting fees. The only fee that can be charged prior to delivery of the Loan Estimate and receipt of the borrower's intent to proceed is a fee for obtaining the borrower's credit report. In cases where the creditor is not charging an advance fee for the credit report, the regulation specifically prohibits taking any credit card information or collecting a check before receiving the applicant's intent to proceed, even if the card is not charged or the check is not cashed.

Delivering the Loan Estimate

The creditor is required to provide the Loan Estimate to a borrower or place it in the mail no later than three business days after taking the borrower's application. The form does not need to be given or mailed to the borrower if the borrower withdraws the application during that three-day period or if the application is denied by the creditor during that period.

The three-day clock for providing the Loan Estimate begins when a creditor receives an *application*. For purposes of complying with the TILA-RESPA Integrated Disclosure Rule, an application is considered to have been received when the creditor has obtained the following six pieces (and ONLY these six pieces) of information from the applicant:

- Name.
- Income.
- Social Security number.
- Property address.
- Estimated value of property.
- Loan amount.

The application is considered to be taken when the creditor has the sixth and final piece of information, even if that information is taken verbally from the applicant.

Be aware that although mortgage brokers may provide the Loan Estimate to borrowers, <u>the creditor is ultimately responsible for its accuracy and delivery</u>. If a violation occurs by a mortgage broker, it is the *creditor* who is held liable.

Loan Estimates and Business Days

Since the Loan Estimate must be provided within three business days of a creditor receiving an application, it is important to understand the definition of a *business day*.

Within the context of the deadline for providing the initial Loan Estimate, a business day is any day on which a creditor is open to the public for the purpose of conducting its regular business activities.

The definition of *business day* can be tricky because it isn't identical in all federal mortgage laws and rules. For example, the term has a different meaning when it is used in regard to any revised Loan Estimates and the Closing Disclosure form. You'll learn more about this other form later in this study guide.

The day that the creditor receives the sixth piece of information is considered "day zero." Thus, the three-day period begins on the business day AFTER the application has been triggered. For example, if the creditor triggers the application on Monday (by obtaining the last required piece of information), Tuesday would be day one, Wednesday would be day two and the Loan Estimate would have to be delivered to the borrower (or placed in the mail) no later than midnight on THURSDAY.

Completing the Loan Estimate

Since the Loan Estimate, in part, replaced the Good Faith Estimate, it's not surprising that the figures contained on the LE must be based on an honest assessment of settlement costs that the applicant is likely to pay. We refer to this as holding the creditor to a *good faith standard* when putting together the disclosure. This standard requires the amounts listed on the form to be generated from the best information that is reasonably available to the creditor at the time of issuance. A creditor or mortgage broker who does not exercise due diligence when completing the form is not acting in good faith and is in violation of the rule.

A creditor will be deemed not to have acted in good faith if amounts charged to the borrower end up exceeding the amounts on the Loan Estimate by more than the prescribed tolerances, which we'll discuss shortly. The presumption of bad faith will occur even if the underestimates are the result of mere miscalculations or unintentionally poor estimates.

Tolerances

In some cases, the amounts actually charged to borrowers at settlement can exceed the amounts listed on the Loan Estimate. This is particularly true in regard to charges from third-party service providers for which the borrower is permitted to shop. However, even these charges might have a limit to how much they can differ from the amounts on the Loan Estimate. The amount that a particular charge can exceed the amount listed on the Loan Estimate is known as the charge's *tolerance*.

Some charges and fees on the Loan Estimate have "zero tolerance." In other words, the borrower cannot be charged more than the amount listed on the LE at closing.

The following items have a zero-tolerance standard, and the charges cannot increase between the LE and the Closing Disclosure without a valid "changed circumstance," which we'll discuss in a bit:

- Origination fees and discount points paid to a creditor and fees paid to a mortgage broker.
- The cost of third-party services that the borrower is not allowed to shop for (typically appraisal, credit report, tax service, flood certification, etc.).
- Transfer taxes.

Third-party services for which the borrower is permitted to shop for a provider have a cumulative tolerance of 10%, as do recording fees paid to a unit of government for recording the mortgage in the public record. Although any one of these third-party service charges can exceed the corresponding charge listed on the Loan Estimate by any amount (even above 10%), the aggregate amount listed on the Closing Disclosure for these items cannot exceed the amount disclosed on the Loan Estimate by more than 10%.

The 10% tolerance is cumulative (figured upon the sum total of all such costs) and applies to the following charges and fees:

- Recording fees.

- Fees to third-party service providers that the borrower is allowed to shop for (typically title services, termite inspections, etc.) if the borrower elects to use a provider listed on the creditor's recommended provider list.

Note that if a borrower is allowed to choose a third-party service provider and selects a provider who is NOT on the creditor's recommended provider list (which must be provided to the applicant within three business days of application), the cost of the service will not be subject to any tolerance and may increase from the amount listed on the Loan Estimate without limit.

Final charges and fees that are greater than those listed on the Loan Estimate and exceed their allowed tolerances <u>must be refunded to the borrower within 60 days after consummation</u> or a TILA violation has occurred.

Revised Loan Estimates / Changed Circumstances

When the creditor relies upon data provided by the applicant to issue the initial Loan Estimate that proves to be inaccurate, or becomes inaccurate during the processing of the loan, the creditor is permitted to issue a revised LE for the purposes of resetting the tolerance calculations. This is called a **changed circumstance.**

Generally speaking, when a revised Loan Estimate is used, the amounts on the revised form are the ones that will be compared to the final settlement costs to evaluate the good faith standard. <u>Any amounts on the original form will no longer apply unless the creditor has issued a revised LE where the settlement charges have been reduced.</u> In this case, creditors are now permitted to compare the final charges on the Closing Disclosure to those disclosed on the *initial* Loan Estimate for the purpose of determining whether there is a tolerance issue that needs to be resolved.

If a revised Loan Estimate is issued, it will need to be mailed or given to the borrower no later than three business days after the creditor learns of the changed circumstance, and the creditor is only permitted to revise the charges that are directly affected by whatever the changed circumstance is. For example, if the borrower's income proves to be different than what was originally disclosed to the creditor, the creditor may reissue the LE and make changes to the discount points, interest rate or loan program as necessary. However, the creditor would NOT be able to add or adjust transfer tax in this case, as borrower income has no bearing on transfer tax.

Note that, in all cases, a revised Loan Estimate CANNOT be received by the applicant on or after the day the Closing Disclosure is received. If any changed circumstance occurs after the Closing Disclosure has been delivered. the creditor must use a revised Closing Disclosure – NOT a Loan Estimate – to reset the tolerances. Thus, in practice, the latest the applicant can receive a revised Loan Estimate is four days prior to closing (as the Closing Disclosure must be given to the borrower no more than three business days prior to closing).

Generally speaking, there are three broad categories of changed circumstances:

- An extraordinary or unexpected event that could not have been reasonably foreseen by the creditor.

- A change in the information that was reasonably relied on by the creditor when making the Loan Estimate.

- New information that impacts the settlement costs or the borrower's eligibility for the loan.

Common changed circumstances include the following:

- The borrower requests changes to the credit terms or the settlement.

- A previously floating interest rate is locked after the original Loan Estimate was given or mailed to the borrower.

- A Loan Estimate has already been given or mailed to the borrower, and the borrower has gone more than 10 business days without indicating an intent to proceed. (All terms on the initial LE, other than the interest rate and discount points, are required to be honored by the creditor for 10 business days from the date the LE is issued.)

- The loan is a construction loan, and settlement is expected to occur more than 60 days after the Loan Estimate has been given or mailed to the borrower. (On construction loans, the creditor is permitted to revise the LE as necessary for any reason until 60 days prior to loan consummation.)

- The appraisal reveals that the borrower overestimated the value of the property.

Less common examples of a changed circumstance are:

- The title insurance company goes out of business.

- A natural disaster damages the property.

Key Terms Appearing on the Loan Estimate

The **Annual Percentage Rate (APR)** is the total cost of credit over the life of the loan, expressed as an effective annual interest rate. It includes any interest, discount points, origination fees, mortgage insurance premiums and other costs of borrowing money.

The **Total Interest Percentage** (TIP) discloses to borrowers the total amount of interest that they will pay over the life of the loan, expressed as a percentage of the original loan amount. Note that this figure is accurate only when borrowers make just the minimum monthly payment due for each billing period over the entire term of the loan. Prepaying any portion of the principal amount effectively lowers the loan's TIP.

Waiting Periods After the Loan Estimate

A transaction cannot be consummated until seven business days after the provision of the Loan Estimate. This seven-day period starts when the creditor delivers or mails the form (in other words, not necessarily when the borrower actually receives it).

The definition of *business day* for the purpose of this waiting period differs from the definition that lenders use to determine the deadline for providing the Loan Estimate. For purposes of the seven-day waiting period, a business day is not merely any day on which a creditor is open to the public to conduct regular business. Instead, it is any day except Sundays and federal holidays.

A borrower can waive the seven-day waiting period in the event of a *bona fide personal financial emergency*. For instance, a borrower might want to eliminate or shorten the waiting period if the loan is needed right away in order to prevent a property from being sold at a foreclosure proceeding.

Regardless of the specific situation, a borrower who wants to waive or reduce the waiting period must give the creditor a signed handwritten statement that explains the issue and specifically requests the elimination or reduction of the waiting period. No pre-printed waiver forms are allowed. In practice, many creditors will not allow borrowers to waive the waiting period under any circumstances, even though the law does make this allowance.

The Home Loan Toolkit

This booklet, which is required under TRID, is also required to be provided to residential mortgage loan applicants within three business days of application (following the same definition of "business day" as is used in providing the Loan Estimate) – on purchase transactions only. The booklet, which replaced the old HUD Special Information Booklet, is designed to be used in conjunction with the Loan Estimate and Closing Disclosure to help borrowers understand the transaction. Like the Special Information Booklet, creditors are permitted to place their logo on the cover and translate it into other languages, but they may NOT change any of the wording in the booklet.

Closing Disclosure

Now that you know the specifics of the Loan Estimate form, let's go over the details of the other major form related to the TILA-RESPA Integrated Disclosure Rule.

The Closing Disclosure (or CD) replaces the HUD-1 Settlement Statement and final Truth in Lending disclosure that was provided to borrowers at closing. The new form is used to help consumers understand the final costs and terms of the transaction. It must be provided in all transactions that require the issuance of a Loan Estimate and have reached the closing stage.

Copies of the Closing Disclosure (and all documents related to it) must be kept by the creditor for at least five years. If the creditor sells the loan or transfers servicing to another entity, the other entity must receive a copy of the form. At that point, both the creditor, the new owner and/or the new servicer must keep their copies for at least five years from the time of consummation.

Delivering the Closing Disclosure

Creditors are ultimately responsible for giving the Closing Disclosure to the borrower no later than three business days before consummation.

Once again, it is important for us to understand the definition of business day within its proper context. The Closing Disclosure must be given to the borrower no later than three business days prior to consummation. For the purposes of this deadline, a business day is all days except Sundays and federal holidays. Remember, this definition is not the same as the one used to determine timely delivery of the Loan Estimate form.

The Closing Disclosure can be provided to the borrower in person, or it can be mailed physically or electronically. If it is mailed, the borrower is deemed to have received it three business days after the mailing date. If it is sent electronically (email), the consumer is deemed to have received it three business days after electronic delivery. When a transaction is rescindable under Regulation Z, a copy of the Closing Disclosure must be provided separately to every consumer who has the right to rescind. For non-rescindable transactions, the CD only needs to be provided to one consumer with primary obligation on the loan.

The requirement to provide the Closing Disclosure at least three business days before closing creates a potential waiting period that could temporarily prevent a transaction from moving forward. Like the waiting periods associated with the Loan Estimate, the three-day requirement for the Closing Disclosure can be waived by the borrower (and the loan can be consummated) if there is a bona fide personal emergency. Similar to the waiver requirements for the Loan Estimate, the borrower would need to give the creditor a written and signed explanation of the emergency.

The Role of Settlement Agents

Creditors might utilize settlement agents (these may be title companies, escrow companies, attorney offices or real estate broker offices depending upon the state) in order to complete certain tasks or monitor the status of a transaction. For example, settlement agents might ensure that all necessary documents have been signed by consumers and that all fees, charges and other kinds of payments have been made prior to the end of a transaction. Settlement agents also typically provide important disclosures to borrowers.

The TILA-RESPA Integrated Disclosure rule allows creditors to use settlement agents for the purpose of completing and/or delivering the Closing Disclosure. However, the creditor is responsible for the accuracy of the form and ensuring that it is delivered in a timely manner. The creditor will be held liable for any violations committed by the settlement agent in providing the closing disclosure to the borrower(s). Settlement agents are responsible for the CDs provided to seller(s) in a purchase transaction.

Revised Closing Disclosures

When changes result in different amounts being charged than what appeared on the initial Closing Disclosure, a revised form must be provided to the borrower. The deadline for providing a revised form will depend on the type of change and on the time it occurs. In some cases, the issuance of a corrected Closing Disclosure might temporarily delay the transaction.

If any of the following changes occur after the issuance of the Closing Disclosure but prior to consummation, the creditor must provide a corrected Closing Disclosure to the borrower no later than three days before the consummation (in other words, a reset of the three-day waiting period is required):

- An increase in the APR by more than 0.125% (for most loans) or 0.25% (for "irregular" loans with nontraditional payments or periods, such as reverse mortgages and construction loans).

- A change in the loan product.

- The addition of a prepayment penalty.

Other changes that occur prior to consummation must still be disclosed on a corrected form, but those changes are less likely to delay the transaction. For changes that do not require a new waiting period, the corrected form must be given to the borrower no later than at or before consummation.

If a change occurs within 30 calendar days after consummation, the creditor will have 30 calendar days to deliver or mail a revised Closing Disclosure. An example of this kind of change would be an underestimated recording fee. However, a change in taxes or in other costs that aren't related to settlement doesn't require a new disclosure after consummation.

Some instances require a corrected Closing Disclosure within 60 calendar days after consummation. This requirement will apply in cases where a clerical error has occurred. For example, a borrower would be entitled to a new Closing Disclosure within 60 calendar days after consummation if the original form were to contain the incorrect name of a third-party service provider.

We mentioned tolerances earlier in this study guide and how creditors might be required to reimburse borrowers if certain costs on the Loan Estimate form are lower than the borrower's actual costs. If a creditor reimburses a borrower for this reason, the reimbursement will be noted on a new Closing Disclosure. This, too, must be given within 60 calendar days after consummation.

E. OTHER FEDERAL LAWS AND GUIDELINES

1. Home Mortgage Disclosure Act (HMDA)

Adopted by Congress in 1975, the **Home Mortgage Disclosure Act (HMDA)** was written as a response to public concerns that lenders were *redlining*. **Redlining** is the arbitrary denial of real estate loan applications in certain geographic areas without considering individual applicant qualification.

HMDA does not expressly prohibit redlining nor require that a certain number of loans be made in certain neighborhoods. Instead, lenders subject to HMDA must compile certain data, provide the data in a certain format to government agencies and make available to the public a disclosure statement regarding that institution's lending activities. The log of applications that a creditor must keep and provide to the federal government is called a **Loan Application Register** (or LAR).

The data to be compiled by lenders pursuant to HMDA includes the following key information regarding each loan (and additional information not covered here):

- Application date.
- Loan type (e.g., conventional, FHA, VA) and loan term.
- Loan purpose (e.g., purchase or refinance).
- Preapproval request (indicates whether a preapproval was requested by the borrower).
- Occupancy type and lien position.
- Loan amount, loan-to-value and combined loan-to-value ratios.
- Action taken on the loan application and date.
- Property address and value (as used in the loan transaction).
- Property location (county and census tract information).

- Borrower ethnicity, race, sex and age.

- Borrower gross income, credit score and debt-to-income ratio,

- The *rate spread* (the difference between the loan's APR and the Average Prime Offer Rate on the date the rate was locked).

- The NMLS number of the MLO originating the loan.

For HMDA, the information above must be kept on all dwelling-related loans. The definition of dwelling under HMDA is much more expansive than under other laws we discuss in this guide and includes "any residential structure, whether or not it is attached to real property." Thus, a loan on a mobile home that is not affixed to real estate *would* be reportable under HMDA but *would not* be subject to the requirements of RESPA or the TRID rule under TILA.

A lender must accept the loan application from the borrower even if he/she refuses to provide information (for example, ethnicity or race) requested pursuant to HMDA. In fact, if the borrower elects not to provide race and sex information, the mortgage loan originator is required to record a guess (for applications taken face-to-face only). That guess can legally be based only on visual observation or surname (last name). As of January 1, 2018, creditors are required to provide applicants with a HMDA form that allows them to disclose their race and ethnicity in a *disaggregated fashion.* This means that applicants can disclose their race as, for example, "Thai" or "Japanese" instead of the more traditional (and *aggregated*) "Asian." When borrowers do not wish to furnish such data and creditors are required to guess as described above, they must only guess in an aggregate manner. That is, they can simply select "American Indian or Alaska Native" and are not required to attempt to guess whether an applicant is, for example, Cherokee or Sioux.

The data provided in the LAR is used by federal and state regulators to monitor creditors for risk factors and warning signs of discrimination. If warning signs are present, a fair lending examination may be undertaken by the CFPB (under the Equal Credit Opportunity Act), HUD (under the Fair Housing Act) and/or by state regulators.

Regulation C is the federal regulation that implements HMDA. The Consumer Financial Protection Bureau has primary rulemaking and enforcement authority over this regulation.

2. Fair Credit Reporting Act (FCRA)

The Fair Credit Reporting Act (FCRA) regulates the users and use of consumer credit information, ensuring accurate information is used when decisions are made based upon data in a consumer's credit report. Most requirements of the law are implemented and enforced by the Consumer Financial Protection Bureau.

The Fair Credit Reporting Act primarily impacts credit reporting agencies and how credit information is obtained; however, it also sets some rules for lenders:

- Lenders can only request credit information for those applicants who have applied for loans and who have provided the appropriate authorization.

- If a lender turns down an application as a result of information provided on the credit report, the lender must notify the applicant in writing of this fact and provide the name, address and toll-free phone number of the reporting credit bureau. Turning down an application is an example of an <u>adverse action</u>. Under the FCRA, an **adverse action** is an unfavorable decision against a consumer that is made (in whole or in part) on the basis of credit information. Whereas ECOA requires a written notice when adverse action is taken for *any* reason, FCRA requires notice only when the adverse action is related in some way to credit information.

The Fair Credit Reporting Act requires each of the nationwide **consumer reporting agencies** (also known as *credit bureaus*, these agencies are Equifax, Experian and TransUnion) to provide an individual with his/her credit report upon request and at no charge, once <u>every 12 months</u>. Individuals may also request their credit score from the credit bureaus, but the bureaus are permitted to charge a fee for this additional information.

The website where individuals may obtain the free reports mandated by the FCRA is www.annualcreditreport.com.

The Fair Credit Reporting Act defines the <u>permissible purposes</u> for which a consumer's credit report may be accessed. They include:

- Making a decision on a credit transaction.

- For employment reasons.

- In insurance underwriting.

- For a subpoena or to enforce financial responsibility laws.

- In relation to a *legitimate business need*.

In order for the information to be lawfully disclosed for the purpose of a **legitimate business need**, the disclosure must relate to a business transaction that was initiated by the consumer. Alternatively, it must be intended to help a creditor review an account in order to determine whether a consumer continues to meet the terms of that account.

Accessing a credit report for a consumer without any of the above permissible purposes is a violation of the law. Note that a loan originator may not provide a credit report to a real estate agent for the purpose of pre-screening a tenant for the agent's rental property. This is prohibited even with the permission of the individual whose report is being accessed because the loan originator does not have a permissible purpose.

The Fair Credit Reporting Act states that most adverse items of information regarding a consumer may only be retained on a consumer credit report for <u>seven years</u>. Bankruptcies may remain on the credit report for <u>10 years from the filing date</u>, and unpaid federal tax liens may be retained on credit reports forever.

Individuals who have identified incomplete or inaccurate information in their credit file may report it to the consumer reporting agency, and the agency must investigate unless the dispute is frivolous. Inaccurate, incomplete or unverifiable information must be removed or corrected by the agency, usually within <u>30 days of receipt of a dispute</u>.

Additionally, the FCRA and its 2003 amendment, the Fair and Accurate Credit Transactions Act (FACTA), provides for the placing of **fraud alerts** on an individual's credit file. There are three kinds of alerts, and when a creditor encounters one on a file it is required to address and clear it *before extending credit to the borrower* in order to ensure that it is not facilitating identity theft. The three types of fraud alerts are:

- One-call fraud alert – remains on the file for *one year* and can be placed by anyone who thinks their personal information has been compromised.
- Extended alert – remains on the file for *seven years* and can only be placed with actual evidence of identity theft (a police report, for example).
- Active duty alert – can only be placed by active duty military members being deployed. Lasts for *one year* but can be renewed for the length of the deployment.

The FCRA/FACTA also provides for an individual's ability to place a **credit freeze** on a credit report. Doing this makes the report inaccessible to lenders unless the individual specifically requests that the freeze be lifted. Recent amendments to FACTA prohibit consumer reporting agencies from charging individuals a fee to place or lift a credit freeze on their reports.

Finally, mortgage companies are required to provide all applicants for residential mortgage credit with the National Credit Score Disclosure Form at application. This disclosure shows the consumer his/her credit scores as received by the mortgage company and lists reasons why those scores were not higher. If the lender is going to then offer the consumer credit on terms materially less favorable than those offered to the most creditworthy applicants, the lender must indicate this by providing a *risk-based pricing notice* to the applicant informing them of this fact.

3. <u>FTC Red Flags Rule</u>

According to official government estimates, as many as 12 million Americans have their identities stolen each year. Under the Fair and Accurate Credit Transactions Act of 2003 (the *FACT Act* or *FACTA*), **identity theft** means a fraud, committed or attempted, using the identifying information of another person without authority. Identifying information may include name, Social Security number, date of birth or numerous other forms of identification.

The Red Flags Rule was created as a result of the FACT Act and requires many businesses and organizations to implement a written **identity theft prevention program**, which is designed to detect the warning signs, or **red flags**, of identity theft in day-to-day operations. The Red Flags Rule is the only section of the FCRA/FACTA to be implemented and enforced by the Federal Trade Commission.

Entities subject to the Red Flags Rule, which include banks, mortgage lenders and mortgage brokers among many others, must take steps to prevent identity theft and mitigate the damage it inflicts. By identifying red flags in advance, a business will be better equipped to spot suspicious patterns when they arise and may be able to prevent a red flag from escalating into a costly episode of identity theft.

An identity theft prevention program must be maintained by each covered firm. A company's program must include reasonable policies and procedures to identify the red flags of identity theft that it may encounter in the day-to-day operation of its business. Red flags may include any of the following:

- Alerts, notifications and warnings from a credit reporting company.
- Suspicious documents.
- Suspicious personally identifying information.
- Suspicious account activity.
- Notice from other sources, including a customer, a victim of identity theft or a law enforcement official.

The program must be designed to detect the red flags that have been identified by the business. For example, if fake identification has been identified as a red flag that the business might encounter, the business must have procedures in place to detect possible fake, forged or altered identification.

The program must define appropriate actions to be taken when red flags are detected.

The program must set forth a method through which the business will re-evaluate the program periodically to reflect new risks from identity theft.

4. Privacy Protection / Do Not Call

Many mortgage professionals have successfully forged new business relationships by "cold-calling" prospects; however, loan originators must exercise particular care in order to avoid violating restrictions on telemarketing.

The Federal Trade Commission, Federal Communications Commission and the states enforce the **National Do Not Call Registry**. Sellers of goods or services (including loan origination services) by phone are required to search the registry every 31 days and delete from their call lists those phone numbers that are in the registry.

It is illegal for any telemarketer to call a number on the registry unless:

- The seller has received express written permission to call the consumer; or

- An *established business relationship* (or *EBR*) exists between the seller and the consumer. EBRs are considered to exist for <u>18 months</u> from the date of the consumer's most recent purchase, delivery or payment (in the case of mortgage originations, this would be 18 months from the date of closing on a completed transaction). EBRs also extend for <u>three months</u> from the date a non-customer has inquired about the seller's services or submitted an application to the company.

The consequences of violating Do Not Call regulations are severe: A violator may be subject to a fine of up to <u>$42,530 per violation.</u>

There are also rules in place in situations when telemarketing is permitted. For example, even when a number is not on the Do Not Call list, it may not be called before 8:00 AM or after 9:00 PM in the customer's local time zone. Also, companies must maintain an internal Do Not Call list and must add consumers to that list when they specifically request not to receive calls from that company; this applies even if the consumer's number does not appear on the national list, and the internal list is also subject to the same 31-day removal requirement described above.

The Federal Trade Commission is responsible for rulemaking and enforcement of the National Do Not Call Registry Act. Companies must retain all telemarketing records for two years and produce them upon request.

5. Dodd-Frank

Signed into law on July 20, 2010, the **Dodd-Frank Act** fundamentally changed consumer financial protection and regulation in the United States. This law has had a significant impact on mortgage businesses. It addresses several issues, including the following topics:

- Loan originator compensation.

- Anti-steering provisions.

- Risk retention requirements.

- Ability-to-repay provisions.

- Prepayment penalty restrictions.

Loan Originator Compensation

The Dodd-Frank Act expressly prohibits compensating a mortgage loan originator based on the terms or conditions of a mortgage loan. More information about the law's impact on loan originator compensation appears in an earlier section of this study guide. Although the original LO Compensation Rule was written by the Federal Reserve Board, because of Dodd-Frank provisions, enforcement and rulemaking authority for this rule now lies with the CFPB.

Anti-Steering Provisions

The Dodd-Frank Act also contains language designed to eliminate *steering* in mortgage lending. **Steering** occurs when a loan originator, whether at the company level or the individual loan originator level, directs a borrower to a given loan or loan product to increase compensation when that loan is "not in the consumer's interest."

The Dodd-Frank Act tells us that there are three distinct ways to comply with the anti-steering provisions of the law:

- Show that the transaction is "in the consumer's interest."

- Show that the compensation involved with the transaction/loan is no greater than what the originator would have made on any other transaction/loan for the borrower's situation.

- Satisfy the safe-harbor provisions. (NOTE: This is the method that most loan originators use to comply. Following the processes established in the safe harbor will automatically insulate the originator from legal action claiming that the originator engaged in steering.) In order to satisfy the safe-harbor provisions, ALL of the following must occur on a loan:

  - The loan originator must present loan options for each type of loan in which the consumer expressed an interest.

  - At minimum, the loan options presented must include the following:

    - The loan with the lowest interest rate.

    - The loan with the lowest interest rate and no "risky features," such as negative amortization or a prepayment penalty.

    - The loan with the lowest cost in terms of points and fees.

  - The loan originator must have a reasonable belief that the consumer will qualify for all of the options presented.

  - A mortgage broker must present the consumer with loan options from a number of different creditors with whom it does business.

Risk Retention Requirements

Dodd-Frank imposes certain mandates on entities that securitize loans (i.e. pool loans together and sell mortgage-backed securities or *mortgage bonds*, which pay investors a fixed rate of return, the money for which is provided by individual homeowners making payments on the mortgage loans contained in the pool). Securitizers must retain at least 5% of the risk on the loans they securitize unless those loans are deemed a *qualified residential mortgage (QRM)*. By "retaining risk", we mean that the securitizer cannot transfer the entire loan and must retain a level of ownership in the loans that go into a given pool.

Essentially, these provisions are designed to ensure that entities that securitize loans have some "skin in the game;" the thought being that the overall quality of loans ending up in these pools will be higher and have better underwriting than they otherwise would if the securitizer was not forced to retain risk on the loans.

Ability to Repay (ATR) and Qualified Mortgages (QM)

Section 1411 of Dodd-Frank requires mortgage lenders to verify a borrower's ability to repay a loan before extending credit. Essentially, this section establishes minimum underwriting standards for residential mortgages. This requirement applies to all *consumer-purpose mortgages* except home-equity lines of credit (HELOCs), reverse mortgages, timeshare loans or temporary financing. Loans made for business purposes are also exempt from this requirement. This rule carries with it a *private right of action*, which means that borrowers can sue creditors individually if they find they cannot afford their loans and feel their ability to repay was not properly vetted by the creditor. In fact, borrowers are specifically allowed to assert a violation of the ability-to-repay rule as a defense to foreclosure for the life of the loan.

The ability-to-repay provision requires creditors to make a "reasonable and good faith determination" based on verified and documented information that, at the time the loan is consummated, the consumer has a reasonable ability to repay the loan according to its terms, as well as all applicable taxes, insurance (including mortgage insurance), and assessments. The following items must be included in the underwriting analysis:

- Credit history.

- Current and reasonably expected income.

- Current liabilities/obligations.

- Debt-to-income ratio or residual income.

- The monthly payment for any other mortgage(s) on the property.

- If the loan is an ARM or has negative amortization, the loan must be underwritten to the fully indexed rate for a fully amortizing loan.

A safe harbor provision was also added to TILA in the form of a **qualified mortgage (QM).** (NOTE: Do NOT confuse QMs with qualified residential mortgages [QRMs]. The QM deals with a consumer's ability to repay. The QRM deals with risk retention and focuses on the secondary market.) In essence, if a mortgage loan fulfills all of the requirements to be a QM, the institution is deemed to have complied with the ability-to-repay requirements. This is an important distinction because loans that meet the QM standards insulate the lender from potential legal action as described above. If the QM loan in question is a higher-priced mortgage loan, the creditor receives legal protection called a *rebuttable presumption of compliance* that is slightly less complete than a safe harbor. Borrowers do have some limited legal recourse on rebuttable presumption transactions.

The requirements for a QM are, in general:

- No negative amortization.

- No balloon payments (except for *small creditors*, defined by the CFPB as institutions that make no more than 500 first-lien mortgage transactions per year and have less than $2 billion in assets).

- Income and financial resources must be verified and documented.

- For ARMs - must be underwritten as a fully amortizing loan at the maximum interest rate that the loan can adjust to in the first five years.

- Maximum loan term of 30 years.

- Maximum total debt-to-income ratio of 43%. (This requirement DOES NOT apply to loans eligible for sale to Fannie Mae and Freddie Mac [through 2020], or those insured by the VA or guaranteed by FHA. Loans held in portfolio by "small creditors," as defined above, are also exempt from the 43% ratio requirement).

- A maximum of 3% of the loan amount in "points and fees."

- For a small creditor, any loan that it makes and holds in its portfolio will be considered a QM as long as the borrower's debt-to-income ratio was verified.

Again, violations of the ability-to-repay provisions provide the consumer with a <u>life-of-loan</u> defense to foreclosure. In other words, mortgagors in foreclosure can assert that the lender did not properly verify their ability to repay the loan and seek damages as long as the loan remains in force. In practice, a consumer that goes into foreclosure in year 29 of a 30-year loan can assert that the lender did not act properly when originating the loan 29 years prior as a defense against that foreclosure proceeding. This makes the QM definition critical, as loans that fall into this category will carry maximum protection for the lender.

Prepayment Penalty Restrictions

In conjunction with the ability-to-repay provisions, the Dodd-Frank Act also set limits on prepayment penalties. Prepayment penalties are prohibited on the following loans:

- ARM loans.

- Loans with an APR exceeding the average prime offer rate by 1.5% for first-lien conforming loan amounts, 2.5% for first-lien jumbo loans and 3.5% for subordinate-lien loans (also known as *higher-priced mortgage loans*).

- Loans that do not otherwise meet the QM definition.

Prepayment penalties, when legally permissible, are limited to 3% of the outstanding balance of the loan in the first year, 2% in the second year and 1% in the third year. No prepayment penalty may last beyond <u>three years</u>.

6. <u>Bank Secrecy Act/Anti-Money Laundering (BSA/AML)</u>

The **Bank Secrecy Act (BSA)** requires that financial institutions (including residential mortgage loan origination businesses) take steps to prevent and report cases of money laundering. In general, **money laundering** involves bringing illegally obtained funds into and out of the financial system in a manner that evades law enforcement. Laundered funds are often linked to such serious crimes as terrorism, arms smuggling and drug trafficking.

Entities that are subject to the BSA must implement an anti-money laundering (AML) program. The AML program should be designed to identify, detect and report possible red flags (or warning signs) of money laundering. The complexity and specifics of an AML program must reflect the type and level of risk that the financial institution faces in regard to money laundering. Therefore, no two AML programs are likely to be exactly the same.

As part of the AML program, a business must train its originators so that they know how anti-money laundering laws apply to them, are aware of red flags and are filing proper reports with the federal government. In a manner similar to the business's overall AML program, the training must reflect the kind and level of risk that the trained person is likely to encounter. Therefore, training for different kinds of workers should not be exactly the same.

Although businesses have the freedom to tailor an AML program in ways that reflect their unique needs and risk factors, the program must be tested periodically by a third party to ensure its effectiveness.

Businesses that are required to have an AML program must also have a designated compliance officer. The compliance officer has the following responsibilities, among other duties:

- Serving as a company resource for any information related to the BSA and anti-money laundering issues.

- Filing and updating management about suspicious activity reports (SARs) that are filed with the Financial Crimes Enforcement Network.

- Remaining up to date concerning BSA requirements.

The Financial Crimes Enforcement Network (FinCEN) is the federal agency charged with monitoring BSA compliance. The agency operates under Department of Homeland Security oversight and is responsible for the following tasks:

- Maintaining databases filled with information obtained from various anti-money laundering endeavors.

- Facilitating communication among financial institutions and law enforcement in order to conduct investigations of potential wrongdoing.

- Overseeing an electronic network that allows different entities to access and share consumers' account information with proper permission.

Under the BSA, loan origination mortgage companies (including mortgage brokers) must file **suspicious activity reports** (SARs) under certain circumstances. These reports must be filed with the Treasury Department whenever a person engages in suspicious mortgage transactions of $5,000 or more. SARs must also be filed whenever a financial institution suspects an insider of conducting an illegal transaction of any amount and whenever transactions seem to be designed to evade the $5,000 reporting requirement.

Do not confuse the SAR with the Currency Transaction Report, which must be filed whenever a cash transaction involves more than $10,000. That report will likely not come into play in the day-to-day lives of most mortgage loan originators.

The government requires financial institutions to file SARs within <u>30 days</u> of detecting suspicious activity if the perpetrator is an identifiable person or within <u>60 days</u> of initial detection if the perpetrator cannot be identified. Copies of reports must be kept for at least five years.

A financial institution cannot alert customers to the fact that a report has been filed against them, and individuals at the institution cannot discuss the existence of a report unless they are obligated to do so by law or by their position within the business, such as when a person reports a suspect to FinCEN or when a compliance officer reports SARs to upper management. Note that filing a SAR and reporting to management as required does not relieve the financial institution from other requirements to protect confidential consumer information.

7. Gramm-Leach-Bliley Act- Privacy and FTC Safeguard Rules

The Financial Modernization Act of 1999, also known as the **Gramm-Leach-Bliley Act (GLBA)**, includes provisions to protect individuals' personal financial information held by financial institutions. Some of the issues pertaining to GLBA compliance include financial privacy rules, safeguard rules and pretexting rules.

Financial Privacy Rule

The GLBA requires financial institutions to give their customers **privacy policies** that explain the financial institution's information collection and sharing practices. The privacy notice must include the categories of *non-public personal information* that the institution collects and describe how that information is shared. The notice must be given to the customer either in writing or, if the customer agrees, electronically. It is NOT permissible to give notice to the customer orally, either in person or over the telephone. This notice is required to be given at three distinct times:

- When the "consumer" becomes a "customer."

- Annually, for as long as the individual remains a "customer."

- When the institution's privacy practices change (while the individual is a "customer").

In turn, customers have the right to limit some sharing of their information. The customer's right to limit the sharing of information to non-affiliated third parties is called the **opt-out right.**

A short form of the privacy policy must be available to consumers (not customers) in an easily accessible place, such as on the company's website.

Generally speaking, one is considered a *consumer* if the person has a one-off transactional relationship with a covered business. One is a *customer* if the relationship is ongoing. For example, a mortgage broker will likely be dealing with *consumers* under this rule, as the relationship stops after closing. However, mortgage servicers will generally have *customers*, as loan servicing is an ongoing process.

Safeguards Rule

The GLBA requires financial institutions to have a written security plan to protect the confidentiality and integrity of confidential consumer financial information. This security plan must describe the measures that the firm is taking to protect data, and employees should be trained on the requirements of the plan. Your plan may, for example, require you to lock up all borrower data at the end of the workday, change your computer passwords every so often and shred documents containing confidential borrower information when they are no longer needed. Also, please remember that it is illegal to share personal information on a loan application, including credit and approval status, with anyone not party to the application unless you have received explicit permission to share such information from the applicants or are required by law to share it.

Responsibility for writing/changing rules and enforcing the Safeguards Rule remain with the Federal Trade Commission even though responsibility for most of the GLBA's other provisions have been transferred to the CFPB.

Pretexting Provisions

The GLBA prohibits the use of false pretenses, including fraudulent statements and impersonation (pretexting) to obtain consumers' personal financial information, such as bank balances. For example, loan officers calling a borrower's bank to obtain information would be guilty of pretexting if they were impersonating the borrower to get that information. No pretexting occurs if individuals are forthright with who they are, what they are attempting to do and why.

8. Mortgage Acts and Practices – Advertising (Regulation N)

Regulation N was issued by the Consumer Financial Protection Bureau in order to prohibit false or misleading advertising of mortgage products. It applies to any *commercial communication* designed to produce a sale or to create interest in mortgage products or services. Note that the definition of "commercial communication" is very broad and includes promotional items and Web pages, sales scripts and "on hold" content and emails (as well as more traditional forms of advertising).

Social media accounts are also a big source of regulatory scrutiny under Regulation N (and Regulation Z). MLOs need to be very careful that any posts or updates they make on their pages conform to advertising guidelines if they are business related. Additionally, if you are going to create any social media content or posts that mention loan origination, it is imperative that your name and NMLS number, your company name and NMLS number, business address and phone number are easily found on your page, whether it be in the post itself or under the "about me" section of the account if one exists.

Advertisements for mortgage products and services cannot contain any material misrepresentations, whether they are stated (expressed) or implied. A fact is *material* if knowledge of the truth would lead reasonable consumers to consider an alternative option in accomplishing their goals. In order to avoid confusing the public, mortgage professionals should be particularly careful when their advertising mentions the following topics:

- Any type of interest rate.

- Fees or costs to the consumer.

- Taxes and insurance.

- Prepayment penalties.

- Whether the loan product is fully amortizing.

- Amount of credit or cash that will be received as part of a mortgage credit transaction.

- Number, amount or timing of required payments.

- Potential for default.

- Eliminating or reducing a consumer's debts.

- Government loan programs, federal agencies or any connection (or lack thereof) to the federal government.

- Eligibility for loan products or loan programs.

- Credit counseling services.

For example, advertising that you have a "five-year fixed rate loan" when, in fact, you are offering an adjustable-rate loan with an initial rate period of five years would be considered deceptive and is a violation of both Regulation N and Regulation Z unless the ad clearly states that the product is a variable or adjustable rate *before* using the word "fixed". Additionally, information about the loan program and potential payment changes would certainly be considered "material."

In accordance with Regulation N, copies of all advertisements must be kept for at least two years.

9. Electronic Signatures in Global and National Commerce Act (E-SIGN Act)

The Electronic Signatures in Global and National Commerce Act, also known as the *E-Sign Act*, was passed in 2000 in order to address the validity of electronic signatures and the use of electronic disclosures.

In general, the law clarifies that a contract or signature cannot be considered invalid or unenforceable simply because it is in an electronic format.

The law also sets requirements for businesses and other entities that want to provide documents to consumers in an electronic format rather than on paper. In order for required documents to be sent to a consumer solely in an electronic format, the entity that is required to provide the documents must first obtain the consumer's consent and disclose the following information:

- The consumer's right to withdraw his or her consent (and the consequences, if any, of doing so).

- The consumer's right, if any, to obtain a non-electronic version of the documents and how to obtain it.

- Whether the consumer's consent will apply to other transactions.

- Procedures for withdrawing consent.

- Procedures for updating the consumer's contact information.

- Any hardware or software requirements for viewing electronic documents. (If the hardware and software requirements change and there is a reasonable risk that the consumer will no longer be able to access an electronic document, the consumer must be informed of the change and given the opportunity to receive a non-electronic version free of charge.)

Institutions utilizing e-signatures must also take steps to verify the identity of the consumer(s) that are signing documents electronically. There are a number of ways to do this, from requiring electronic validation of a government-issued ID to the more common password or PIN methods.

The E-Sign Act contains exemptions for certain records that still might need to be provided on paper. For example, some provisions of the law don't apply to notices of default, acceleration, repossession, foreclosure or eviction involving a primary residence.

A financial institution is also required to maintain electronic records accurately. These records must reflect the information contained in applicable contracts, notices or disclosures and must remain accessible to all persons legally entitled to access the records for the period required by law and all e-signed forms must be capable of being accurately reproduced from the stored data.

10. USA PATRIOT Act

The USA Patriot Act is intended to help the federal government respond to potential terrorist threats and monitor suspicious activity. Among other things, the law:

- Imposes minimum standards for verifying customers' identities on financial institutions subject to the law.

- Establishes guidelines for sharing customer financial transaction and records information with law enforcement during an investigation of a terrorism and/or money laundering case, subject to certain oversight (Section 314(a) sharing).

- Establishes a framework for financial institutions to share confidential consumer financial information with one another in order to identify and report money laundering or terrorist activity after first notifying the Department of the Treasury that the sharing is going to occur (Section 314(b) sharing).

- Requires (along with the BSA) the establishment of anti-money laundering programs, which are meant to identify and address financial crimes.

All financial institutions subject to the requirements of the USA Patriot Act must maintain a written **Customer Identification Program** (CIP) that describes, in depth, the methods that will be taken to verify the identities of individuals (and all beneficial owners of companies) seeking to open accounts with the institution. Before opening a new account, a financial institution must take reasonable steps to verify the customer's identity through *documentary* or *non-documentary* means and must confirm that the customer is not on a government list of known or suspected terrorists. The definition of financial institution under this law is very broad and covers depository and non-depository financial companies, including mortgage banks and mortgage brokers.

Mortgage companies generally use the documentary method of verifying identity, obtaining a copy of a valid government-issued photo ID from all borrowers before the transaction closes. Some companies that operate exclusively online may use the non-documentary method by, for example, requiring borrowers to answer questions about data contained in a report from a consumer reporting agency to confirm their identities. Regardless of the method employed, institutions need to maintain records of the information that was used as part of this process, including the customer's name, address and date of birth. Documentary methods also require capturing the number, issuing agency, issuing date and expiration date appearing on the IDs used.

Requirements for anti-money laundering programs can be found elsewhere in this study guide.

11. Homeowners Protection Act

Under the **Homeowners Protection Act (HPA)**, mortgage insurance on a loan for a borrower's primary residence must be automatically cancelled when the loan-to value ratio (LTV) reaches 78% or less of the original value of the property and the borrower is not delinquent. This is referred to as *automatic termination*, and there will be no appraisal done by the servicer.

Homeowners may *request* cancellation of private mortgage insurance (PMI) when the loan balance reaches 80% of original value and the borrower has a good payment history. This means that no payment was 30 days or more past due in the previous 12 months and no payment was 60 days or more past due in the previous 24 months. *Original value* for refinanced mortgages is whatever appraised value the lender relied on in the specific loan refinance transaction. This is referred to as *borrower-requested cancellation,* and the lender will generally complete an appraisal or other valuation to ensure that the property has not declined in value since the transaction closed. The borrower will be required to pay for this valuation, and borrowers must receive a copy of any valuation done.

For loans with borrower-paid mortgage insurance (BPMI), the lender or servicer must provide a disclosure to the homeowner at or before settlement describing these cancellation rights. In addition, the lender or servicer must disclose this information annually to the homeowner. Borrowers also must receive a written notice when automatic termination has occurred, and servicers cannot require the borrower to pay any further premiums beyond 30 days from that date.

For loans with lender-paid mortgage insurance (LPMI), the PMI disclosure must be provided at or before the loan commitment is issued. Unlike BPMI, LPMI does not terminate and will remain in effect until the loan is paid off.

The HPA does not apply to government loans (like FHA). All FHA loan programs require their own kind of mortgage insurance, called *mortgage insurance premium* or MIP. FHA mortgage insurance protects the lender or investor against default by the borrower for the life of the loan, and premiums may need to be paid for the entire period, depending upon other loan characteristics. Additionally, loans on second homes and investment properties are not subject to HPA requirements.

F. REGULATORY AUTHORITY

1. Consumer Financial Protection Bureau (CFPB)

The Dodd-Frank Act created the new federal "super-regulator" called the **Consumer Financial Protection Bureau**, or CFPB. The CFPB has been tasked with rulemaking and enforcement for the vast majority of federal mortgage laws. In addition to its rulemaking and enforcement powers, the CFPB also is the primary federal regulator for all non-depository financial institutions, which include state-licensed mortgage banks and mortgage brokers. It also has primary oversight responsibility for any *systemically important financial institution*, which is defined as any depository institution with total assets over $10 billion. In order to maintain its independence, the CFPB is funded through the Federal Reserve, not via congressional appropriations like other federal agencies. As part of its supervisory function, the CFPB can perform examinations/audits of any financial institution it regulates, reviewing their operations and files to ensure compliance with relevant federal consumer financial law. The agency uses a risk-based approach to determine which companies it will examine, focusing more on larger entities and those that have generated a disproportionate number of consumer complaints. Consumers can file complaints about any regulated institution at https://www.consumerfinance.gov/complaint/.

Note that applicable state regulators still have authority over non-bank originators at the state level.

2. Department of Housing and Urban Development

The U.S. Department of Housing and Urban Development (HUD) is a federal Cabinet-level department charged with strengthening the housing market in ways that aid the economy and protect consumers. In recent years, many of HUD's rulemaking and enforcement responsibilities have been transferred to the Consumer Financial Protection Bureau. However, HUD still plays a major role in several aspects of mortgage lending. For example, HUD continues to approve lenders that want to make FHA-insured loans and continues to enforce the Fair Housing Act. It is also responsible for administering federal housing programs such as the Section 8 assistance program and other grant programs.

The Fair Housing Act prohibits discrimination in most residential real estate transactions if it is based on any of the following factors:

- Race.

- Color.

- Religion.

- National origin.

- Gender.

- Physical or mental disability.

- Familial status (the fact that an adult has a child 18 or younger living with him or her).

CHAPTER TWO –
GENERAL MORTGAGE KNOWLEDGE

A. QUALIFIED AND NON-QUALIFIED MORTGAGE PROGRAMS

1. Conventional / Conforming

The **secondary market** is where existing mortgage loans (and the right to collect borrower payments) are bought and sold.

There are many benefits to having a secondary market for mortgage loans. Perhaps most importantly, the secondary market provides liquidity so that a primary mortgage lender (a lender making a loan directly to a borrower) or secondary market investor can buy or sell mortgage loans at any time. The liquidity permits a lender to obtain cash required to fund new loans or meet other obligations. Similarly, investors are more likely to invest in mortgage loans if they know that the loans can be readily sold at a later date.

The secondary market also permits management of interest-rate risk by allowing a lender or investor to readily diversify its portfolio of loans. An investor may invest in loans with different interest rates and spanning diverse geographic locations. (This also mitigates the risk of being overexposed to economic conditions prevalent in one area of the country.)

An additional benefit of the secondary market is the way in which it promotes standardization and uniformity in regard to credit requirements, loan types and loan documents. The major institutions, government-sponsored enterprises and federal agencies that invest in the secondary market create industry standards for the types of loans that they purchase.

Without the secondary market, the 30-year fixed rate mortgage likely would not exist, and certainly not at the rates being provided through today's mortgage originations.

There are several important entities operating in the secondary market. Those investors include the following entities:

- Fannie Mae.

- Freddie Mac.

- Ginnie Mae.

- The Federal Home Loan Bank System.

- Private investors.

Fannie Mae

Created in 1938 to purchase FHA loans as a means to assist the housing sector in the midst of the Great Depression, **Fannie Mae** is a **government-sponsored enterprise** (GSE) that acts as a quasi-governmental agency for the purpose of making a secondary market for mortgages. Today, Fannie Mae, along with its close cousin, Freddie Mac, purchases many different types of loans. Fannie's full and formal name is the Federal National Mortgage Association (which sometimes appears in abbreviated form as *FNMA*).

Fannie Mae is the nation's largest mortgage investor. To be eligible for purchase, mortgages must meet very specific program requirements and guidelines.

Through a process known as **securitization**, Fannie Mae "pools" the loans it purchases into investment vehicles called **mortgage-backed securities (MBS)**. Also referred to as *mortgage bonds*, these securities are offered for sale to the public and are often purchased by pension funds, state governments and foreign sovereign entities in addition to individual investors and investment management funds. It is through the purchase of these bonds that Fannie Mae receives money to purchase more loans and keep the secondary market's liquidity cycle running. Investors that purchase mortgage bonds receive fixed interest payments on their bond until it is sold or matures. The money to pay interest to investors comes from individuals making their mortgage payments each month.

Lenders selling loans to Fannie Mae must complete a formal approval process to ensure that they meet specific criteria, such as a minimum net worth, volume, quality of loans, etc. Each lender has its own contract with Fannie Mae, and that contract is reviewed and renewed on a regular basis.

Fannie Mae was a government agency from 1938 to 1968, at which point it was converted into a shareholder-owned private company. In 2008, with the coming of the mortgage crisis, Fannie Mae was essentially re-nationalized, and the federal government has been the controlling shareholder ever since, holding the company in conservatorship.

Freddie Mac

Freddie Mac is the second major GSE. Its full name is the Federal Home Loan Mortgage Corporation (which sometimes appears in abbreviated form as *FHLMC*).

Freddie Mac was created by Congress in 1970 to provide a secondary market for mortgages originated by savings and loan associations and establish competition for Fannie Mae. Though the entities can work very closely together, Freddie Mac is regarded as Fannie Mae's largest competitor. Like Fannie Mae, Freddie Mac exists in the secondary market and securitizes the loans it purchases and issues mortgage bonds. In fact, in 2019 Fannie Mae and Freddie Mac began issuing a single mortgage-backed security containing loans purchased by both entities.

Ginnie Mae

Ginnie Mae does not purchase or sell loans on the secondary market. Rather, Ginnie Mae issues guarantees on bond pools that are comprised exclusively of government-backed (FHA/VA/USDA) loans. The Ginnie Mae guarantee on the bond ensures that the investors who purchase the bonds receive their interest payments even if the underlying loan pool experiences a high level of borrower defaults.

Created by Congress in 1968, Ginnie Mae is now part of the Department of Housing and Urban Development (HUD). Its full name is the Government National Mortgage Association (sometimes abbreviated as *GNMA*).

Federal Home Loan Bank System

The **Federal Home Loan Bank (FHLB) system** is owned by over 8,000 community financial institutions and provides advances to financial institutions in order for those institutions to make residential mortgage loans. The Federal Home Loan Banks were originally designed to spur lending in local communities through their member banks, and they still have that goal today, although many of the nation's largest banks and insurance companies have become members of the system in recent years. Like Fannie Mae and Freddie Mac, the Federal Home Loan Banks are GSEs.

There are 11 independent FHLBs throughout the United States, and each of them has programs designed to facilitate liquidity in the community lending space.

Private Investors

In addition to the above government and government-related investors, the secondary market has had many private investors, including Wall Street companies and large financial institutions.

As we mentioned earlier, one of the major functions of secondary market investors is to turn large groups of mortgages into mortgage bonds (or mortgage-backed securities) that the public can invest in. The process by which individual loans are pooled together and converted to investible assets is called *securitization*. Investors receive payments from these bonds on a regular basis at a fixed rate of return. These payments to investors are funded by the payments made by borrowers on the underlying mortgages. However, since the housing crisis of 2007 and 2008, mortgage-backed securities from the private sector have become less common, leaving Fannie Mae, Freddie Mac and Ginnie Mae to shoulder the majority of secondary market functions.

Conventional and Conforming Loans in the Secondary Market

The ability to sell certain loans to a particular entity in the secondary market will depend greatly on whether the loans are conventional conforming, conventional non-conforming or government loans. Any loan that is <u>not</u> insured or guaranteed by the federal government is called a **conventional loan.** This includes private loans sold to Fannie Mae and Freddie Mac or loans sold to other secondary market purchasers. Conversely, a loan that is insured or guaranteed by the federal government is referred to as a *government loan*. Government loans also might be sold to Fannie Mae or Freddie Mac.

Conventional loans sold to Fannie Mae and Freddie Mac are also referred to as **conforming loans** because they meet (conform to) a uniform set of credit standards, program parameters and loan amount limits. Among other standards, qualifying ratios for conforming loans are determined by Fannie Mae and Freddie Mac.

A private loan that does not satisfy the standards of Fannie Mae or Freddie Mac is considered to be a **non-conforming loan**. There are many factors that may make a conventional loan non-conforming, such as loan amount (jumbo loans are non-conforming) and credit score (*subprime loans* are also non-conforming). Non-conforming conventional loans are typically either retained in portfolio by the funding lender or sold to a private secondary-market investor/securitizer (not Fannie Mae or Freddie Mac).

Among the qualifying standards set by Fannie Mae and Freddie Mac are maximum loan-to-value ratios on loans eligible for purchase. Fannie and Freddie generally require a 5% down payment from the applicant (95% LTV) on a one-unit primary residence, however, both GSEs have exceptions for their affordable housing loan programs that are designed to serve low-to-moderate income borrowers. These loans (Fannie Mae refers to its program as *HomeReady* and Freddie Mac's is *HomePossible*) allow for a reduced down payment of 3% (97% LTV) and will also allow various forms of grants and second mortgages to cover the down payment and closing costs associated with the transaction. These grants and second mortgages are generally provided by government entities or nonprofit institutions and enable the borrower to finance up to a combined 105% of the purchase price in a purchase transaction. In order to be eligible for the HomeReady or HomePossible products, the borrower qualifying income cannot exceed 80% of the *Area Median Income* (AMI) established annually by the American Community Survey (run by the census bureau).

As referenced elsewhere in this guide, Fannie and Freddie also set benchmark debt-to-income ratios on loans to be eligible for sale.

2. <u>Government (FHA, VA, USDA)</u>

In the previous section, we discussed mortgage loans that are either insured by or guaranteed by the federal government. There are three types of government-related loans that are integral parts of the mortgage industry:

- Federal Housing Administration (FHA) loans.
- Veterans Affairs (VA) loans.
- United States Department of Agriculture (USDA) rural-development loans.

FHA loans <u>insure</u> lenders in the event of borrower default, and VA and USDA loans provide a <u>guaranty/guarantee</u> to lenders in the event of borrower default. VA loans provide a partial guaranty, which is <u>generally 25% of the loan amount</u> while <u>USDA loans provide a 90% guarantee.</u> (VA uses the term *guaranty* while USDA refers to a *guarantee*, thus both terms appear here.)

FHA Loans

FHA loans are made by banks, mortgage companies or any other primary lending entity authorized by the Department of Housing and Urban Development (HUD) as an approved mortgagee/lender.

The FHA insures these residential mortgage loans under one of three mortgage insurance funds. If the borrower defaults on an FHA loan and the lender forecloses, these insurance funds will cover the lender's loss (if any) after the property is sold at a foreclosure sale.

FHA-Eligible Properties

For purchases involving an FHA loan, the property must be an owner-occupied, one-to-four-unit residence, and the buyer (borrower) must meet a 3.5% minimum investment (minimum down payment) requirement. Because FHA purchase loans are only made on owner-occupied properties, the borrower must occupy the property within 60 days after closing to be compliant with the terms of the note and mortgage and must continue to occupy the property for a minimum of one year.

All properties must meet HUD's minimum property requirements (MPR), which are designed to ensure that FHA-insured loans are only made on properties that are safe for occupancy as well as structurally and mechanically sound.

Loan-to-Value Limits and Property Qualifications

FHA's maximum loan-to-value on purchase transactions is 96.5% (3.5% down payment).

FHA's maximum loan-to-value on rate/term refinances is 97.75%, and on cash-out refinances, it is 80%.

FHA Loan Limits

Each state and territory under HUD's jurisdiction is provided with statutory loan limits based on local residential real estate prices in each county. These maximum loan limits are applied to the base loan amount before adding any financed mortgage insurance premium.

FHA Mortgage Insurance Premiums (MIP)

All FHA loan programs require mortgage insurance. FHA mortgage insurance protects the lender or investor against default by the borrower for the life of the loan. There are two types of mortgage insurance premiums:

- Upfront mortgage insurance premiums (UFMIP).

- Monthly mortgage insurance premiums (monthly MIP).

The **upfront mortgage insurance premium (UFMIP)** is calculated by multiplying the loan amount by a factor and then collecting that amount at closing. It can be paid by the borrower or the seller (for the borrower). The FHA UFMIP is currently 1.75% of the loan amount for ALL forward mortgages and 2.0% of the maximum claim amount for HECM (reverse) mortgage transactions. The UFMIP can always be financed if the borrower so chooses, even if it results in the total loan amount exceeding the maximum loan-to-value for the product.

Monthly MIP is calculated by multiplying the base loan amount by a factor, then dividing by 12. The borrower pays the MIP as part of the monthly mortgage payment, along with principal, interest, taxes and insurance (PITI).

Standard FHA loan programs require both UFMIP and monthly MIP. For standard forward mortgages, the annual MIP (paid monthly) follows the following chart:

LOAN AMOUNT	LOAN TERM	LTV	ANNUAL MIP
$625,500 or less	Greater than 15 years	95% or less	0.80%
$625,500 or less	Greater than 15 years	More than 95%	0.85%
More than $625,500	Greater than 15 years	95% or less	1.00%
More than $625,500	Greater than 15 years	More than 95%	1.05%
$625,500 or less	15 years or less	90% or less	0.45%
$625,500 or less	15 years or less	Greater than 90%	0.70%
More than $625,500	15 years or less	78% or less	0.45%
More than $625,500	15 years or less	Between 78% and 90%	0.70%
More than $625,500	15 years or less	Greater than 90%	0.95%

(Gray shading indicates the most common FHA loan scenarios.)

The annual MIP for all FHA forward mortgages with at-closing LTVs exceeding 90% will remain in effect for the term of the mortgage. Annual MIP for all FHA forward mortgages with at-closing LTVs less than or equal to 90% will be paid by the borrower for 11 years. Annual MIP for HECM reverse mortgages is 0.50%.

FHA Qualifying Ratios

In general, in order to obtain an FHA loan, the monthly mortgage payment cannot exceed 31% of the borrower's income. Similarly, a qualified borrower generally must have total monthly debt obligations of no more than 43% of his or her income. These ratios are less strict than the qualifying ratios for conforming conventional loans, and even these looser standards aren't always adhered to in cases where a borrower makes a large down payment or has other compensating factors, such as a very strong credit profile. Although you should know the 31%/43% benchmark ratios and be able to work with them in an exam scenario, in practice, an automated underwriting system (AUS) will often recommend approval for loans that exceed these figures.

FHA loans are also **assumable**. That is, a new buyer may take over the payments of the existing mortgage holder, subject to approval of the loan servicer and HUD credit guidelines. The process of releasing the original borrower and substituting the new mortgagor is known as **novation.**

VA Loans

VA loans are made to owner-occupant veterans by private lenders such as banks, thrifts and mortgage companies. To obtain a loan, the veteran applies directly to a lender. If the loan is approved, the VA guarantees a percentage of the loan amount after closing. The guaranty protects the lender against loss if the borrower defaults in repaying the loan and is provided through what is referred to as the **VA entitlement** that all eligible veterans receive as a result of their service. The only reliable proof of a veteran's eligibility and remaining entitlement is a **Certificate of Eligibility** (COE) issued by the VA. In order to obtain this certificate, lenders will need to obtain the veteran's DD-214 (Certificate of Release or Discharge) if he/she has been separated from service. If the veteran is still serving in the armed forces, a *Statement of Service* replaces the need for the DD-214.

A **veteran** is defined as a person who is currently serving in the U.S. Army, Navy, Air Force, Marine Corps or Coast Guard, or who has been discharged from those services and has served a sufficient amount of time to be eligible for the VA mortgage program. Reservists and members of the National Guard are also eligible (although they have different qualifying guidelines for time in service) as are unmarried surviving spouses of veterans who were killed in action or who died as a direct result of a service-connected disability.

Term of Service

Regular veterans who serve during wartime (as defined by the Department of Defense) are required to serve a minimum of 90 days of active duty before becoming eligible for benefits. Regular veterans who serve during peacetime are required to serve a minimum of 181 days of active duty before becoming eligible for benefits. Regardless of whether they served in wartime or peacetime, discharged veterans must have served a two-year term.

Reservists or members of the National Guard must serve six years in order to become eligible for the VA loan program.

VA Loan Limits

The Department of Veterans Affairs does not specify a maximum dollar loan limit. Thus, the maximum loan amount depends upon the property value as well as the requirements of secondary market investors. In practice, the VA guaranty will generally be limited to 25% of the loan amount. However, in cases where the veteran does not have full entitlement because of an outstanding VA loan or prior default, the guaranty will be limited to 25% of the loan amount or the *county loan limit* (typically $510,400, but higher in some "high-cost" areas), whichever is less; in this case, the veteran must also have sufficient entitlement remaining to cover the guaranty necessary.

On purchase transactions, the loan amount is generally limited to the purchase price + VA funding fee (an uncommon exception exists that allows some borrowers to finance energy efficient property improvements, but that is not of relevance in this guide).

The loan amount may be further limited to the VA's determination of the reasonable value of the property obtained through a VA appraisal, which is also called a **Certificate of Reasonable Value (CRV)**.

VA Funding Fee

Unlike an FHA-insured loan, there is no minimum investment or down payment required for VA loans. A VA-guaranteed loan may have a loan-to-value ratio of up to 100%. (The **loan-to-value ratio** equals the loan amount divided by the lesser of the purchase price or appraised value of the property.)

While the veteran does not necessarily have to make a down payment, the veteran will be required to pay a **VA funding fee** to the VA to help defray the costs of the VA home loan program; this fee may be financed in the loan and may result in the total loan amount (with the financed funding fee) exceeding 100% of the value of the property. The amount of the funding fee is a percentage of the loan amount and is based on the veteran's particular circumstances. The funding fee may also be refundable depending on circumstances. The size of the funding fee will depend on the following factors:

- Whether the loan is for a purchase or refinance transaction.

- The loan-to-value ratio.

- The number of times the borrower has obtained a VA loan.

NOTE: Active duty veterans who have received the Purple Heart, veterans with a service-connected disability, spouses of servicemembers who died as a direct result of their service and spouses of prisoners of war are exempt from paying the funding fee.

Assumption of VA Loans

Unlike most conventional loans, a VA-guaranteed loan may be assumed by a purchaser of the subject property, and the interest rate will remain intact. The purchaser is not required to be a veteran in order to assume the loan, although the purchaser must meet minimum creditworthiness standards. However, if the purchaser is not a veteran, the selling veteran's entitlement will not be restored when the loan is assumed, and that veteran would, therefore, likely not be eligible for a new VA loan until the existing loan has been paid in full.

VA Qualification

Unlike other loans, VA loans require the originator to perform two different qualification calculations– one on debt-to-income ratio and one on **residual income.** Residual income is the amount that is left over to purchase necessities like food and gasoline after all other expenses are paid. We use the figure to determine whether veterans will have enough money left over to support themselves.

VA is the only major loan product with a residual income requirement, and it mandates that the lender take the gross monthly income and deduct:

- Income taxes withheld.

- All minimum monthly debt payments, including the mortgage.

- Maintenance costs on the property (calculated at 14 cents per square foot of the property per month).

- Childcare costs if necessary for the adult household members to work.

The remaining amount is then compared to the required residual income chart published by the VA, which takes into account family size and the region of the country in which the property is located.

Regarding debt-ratio qualification, the VA uses one benchmark qualifying ratio of 41% covering all of the veteran's debts. (The VA does not have a housing ratio benchmark.) Regarding residual income qualification, the originator must fill out the VA Loan Analysis form to determine whether the residual family income meets the requirements, which vary based on family size and region of the country in which the property is located.

USDA Loans

Also called *rural development" loans*, these mortgages are overseen by the United States Department of Agriculture (USDA) under the Housing and Community Facilities Programs (HCFP). There are two types of USDA loans that we will discuss here:

- USDA guaranteed loans.

- USDA direct loans.

USDA Guaranteed Loans

USDA guaranteed loans are made by private institutions that receive a USDA guarantee against loss after a foreclosure proceeding. They are available to individuals with *low-to-moderate income* (defined as a household income no greater than 115% of the area median income) and who may have difficulty finding affordable conventional credit.

All USDA-guaranteed home loans are limited to owner-occupied, single-family homes (no multi-units) located in an eligible area (typically open country or towns with no more than 35,000 people). The borrower pays a *USDA guarantee fee* to the USDA to obtain the guarantee. The upfront fee (which can be financed) is currently 1.0% of the loan amount, and the annual fee (paid monthly) is 0.35%.

The maximum loan-to-value on a USDA guaranteed loan is 100% before any financed upfront guarantee fee (101% with the financed fee), and the benchmark debt-to-income ratios are 29/41.

USDA Direct Loans

USDA direct loans are made directly by the USDA to *low and very low income* borrowers who lack alternative housing options and who may need additional flexibility in qualifying, such as accommodation of higher debt ratios and terms up to 38 years.

3. Conventional / Nonconforming (Jumbo, Alt-A, etc.)

Conventional (non-government) loans that do not meet Fannie Mae and Freddie Mac standards or program parameters are called non-conforming because they do not meet (conform to) those standards or parameters.

Non-conforming loans may be originated for a particular portfolio lender or may be sold to institutional investors in accordance with any loan product guidelines published by those investors. For example, the investor may set forth qualifying ratio guidelines for particular non-conforming loans that it proposes to purchase from an originating lender. Non-conforming loans include, among other things, *jumbo loans*, *Alt-A loans* and *subprime mortgages*.

Jumbo Loans

Loan amounts higher than the Fannie Mae and Freddie Mac limits are referred to as **jumbo loans**. The current Fannie and Freddie loan limit for a one-unit property in the continental United States is $510,400, although in limited areas designated as *high-cost areas*, it can be as high as $765,600 in the highest-cost areas of the country. The maximum high-cost area loan limit is typically set at 150% of the standard conforming loan limit.

Alt-A Loans

Alt-A loans are non-conforming as a result of the credit risk associated with the borrower. Unlike a jumbo loan, where the loan is non-conforming because of the size of the loan, an Alt-A loan represents increased risk to the lender because the borrower is unable to meet underwriting standards for a conforming loan, generally related to documentation requirements. During the housing bubble, many Alt-A loans required less verification of income and assets than many other loans. Examples of these kinds of loans at the time included the following:

- Loans where the income on the application was not verified by the underwriter *(stated-income loans)*.

- Loans where no income was disclosed on the loan application, meaning that qualifying ratios could not be calculated *(no-ratio loans)*.

- Loans where income and assets were disclosed on the application but neither were verified *(stated-income/stated-asset loans)*.

- Loans where income, assets and employment were not disclosed, and the applicant was qualified on little more than credit score *(no-documentation / no-doc / "NINJA" loans)*.

Most of these loan types are no longer offered in today's mortgage market, although stated-income loans have returned in limited form in the "non-QM" sector. Unlike the stated-income loans of the housing bubble, they do generally require a substantial down payment and verified assets and are more common in the investment property space.

Subprime Loans

When a mortgage applicant's credit history reflects significant derogatory issues or the loan is otherwise ineligible for sale to Fannie Mae, Freddie Mac or other prime investors because of a combination of credit and documentation issues, the loan is classified as a **subprime loan** and carries a higher degree of risk. With a subprime loan, the lender (and ultimately, the investor) incurs relatively greater risk of a borrower default, so the interest rate is raised to compensate the lender for taking that risk. During the housing bubble, these loans were often originated as adjustable-rate mortgages with a large rate increase coming in two or three years and also at very high loan-to-value ratios. Today's non-QM sector has begun to originate loans that would likely be considered *subprime*, although the loan-to-value guidelines are much more strict, the initial rate changes less volatile and the first rate adjustment (if any) coming later in the loan term.

a. Statement on Subprime Lending

Multiple federal banking regulators publicly released a *Statement on Subprime Mortgage Lending* in June of 2007. These agencies developed the statement to address emerging risks associated with certain subprime mortgage products and lending practices. This statement was directed only to institutions regulated by the specific agencies.

Concerned that the statement equally applied to mortgage brokers and loan originators that were not regulated by the federal agencies, the Conference of State Bank Supervisors (CSBS), the American Association of Residential Mortgage Regulators (AARMR) and the National Association of Consumer Credit Administrators (NACCA) issued a parallel Statement on Subprime Mortgage Lending (the *Subprime Statement*), intended to guide state-chartered lending institutions and state-licensed mortgage professionals.

The Subprime Statement specifically expresses concern regarding adjustable-rate mortgage (ARM) products typically offered to subprime borrowers that have one or more of the following characteristics:

- Low initial payments based on an introductory teaser rate that expires after a short period and then adjusts based on the index rate plus a margin for the remaining term of the loan.

- Very high or no limits on how much the payment amount or the interest rate may increase on adjustment dates.

- Limited or no documentation of borrowers' income.

- Product features likely to result in frequent refinancing to maintain an affordable monthly payment.

- Substantial prepayment penalties and/or prepayment penalties that extend beyond the initial fixed interest rate period.

Products with one or more of the above characteristics can cause *payment shock* for the borrower, as the borrower may encounter a significant increase in the amount of the monthly payment when the interest rate adjusts to the fully indexed basis. Loan providers may also be negatively affected by such loans, as they may incur unwarranted levels of credit, legal, compliance, reputation and liquidity risks due to the elevated risks inherent in the products.

The Subprime Statement sets forth guidelines for risk management practices that loan providers should follow in order to mitigate these risks.

First, providers should ensure that they do not engage in predatory lending practices involving one of the following elements:

- Making loans based predominantly on the foreclosure or liquidation value of a borrower's collateral rather than on the borrower's ability to repay the loan according to its terms.

- Inducing a borrower to repeatedly refinance a loan in order to charge high points and fees each time the loan is refinanced. This practice is referred to as *loan flipping*.

- Engaging in fraud or deception to conceal the true nature of the mortgage loan obligation or ancillary products from an unsuspecting or unsophisticated borrower.

The Subprime Statement expressly requires that real estate loans reflect all relevant credit factors, including the capacity of the borrower to adequately service the debt. Note that this issue was addressed in greater detail by the Dodd-Frank Act and its accompanying rules. For more information about Dodd-Frank, including its corresponding *ability-to-repay* requirements, see the first chapter of this study guide.

Finally, the Subprime Statement emphasizes that communications with consumers, including advertisements, oral statements and promotional materials, should provide clear and balanced information about the relative benefits and risks of the products. Consumers should receive clear explanations of the risk of payment shock and the ramifications of prepayment penalties, balloon payments and any lack of escrow for taxes and insurance. Such information should allow consumers to better budget and plan regarding their homeownership expenses.

In order to ensure that these types of protections are provided, the loan providers must develop strong control systems to monitor whether actual practices match intended policies and procedures. Important controls include establishing appropriate processes for hiring and training loan personnel and working with third parties.

b. Guidance on Nontraditional Mortgage Product Risk

In a manner similar to the Subprime Statement, CSBS and AARMR also issued a joint statement of *Guidance on Nontraditional Mortgage Product Risks*. The Guidance recognized increased risks associated with the use of mortgage products that allow borrowers to defer payment of principal (and sometimes interest), whether or not the borrower is a subprime borrower.

The Guidance, issued in 2006, recognized that lending standards that long had been conservative were becoming looser and looser, particularly for products referred to as *nontraditional mortgage loans*. Nontraditional mortgage loans may include interest-only mortgages where a borrower pays no loan principal for the first few years of the loan and *payment option ARMs*, where a borrower has flexible payment options with the potential for negative amortization.

The Guidance advised state agencies to expect loan providers to effectively assess and manage the risks associated with nontraditional mortgage loan products. Such risk management can only be achieved by applying sound underwriting and quality control regarding these products. The following are some of the specific steps recommended to loan providers:

- Underwriting standards should address the effect of a substantial payment increase on the borrower's capacity to repay when loan amortization begins. If the borrower won't be able to repay at that time, the loan probably should not be made at all.

- Analysis of repayment capacity should avoid over-reliance on credit scores as a substitute for income verification in the underwriting process.

- Avoid the use of loan terms and underwriting practices that heighten the need for a borrower to rely on the sale or refinancing of the property once amortization begins.

- Recognize that higher pricing does not replace the need for sound underwriting.

- Consider limiting the spread (difference) between the initial interest rate and the fully indexed rate in order to minimize payment shock and negative amortization.

- Establish quality control procedures that include a regular review of a sample of nontraditional mortgage loans to confirm that policies are being followed. Hold business managers accountable for correcting deficiencies in a timely manner.

- Communicate clear and balanced information to consumers at a time early enough to allow the consumer to make a reasoned decision regarding the loan product. In order to be truly helpful, this information should be communicated earlier than upon submission of an application or at consummation of the loan.

- Continue to communicate clear information about the product through monthly statements that explain the effect of negative amortization and any upcoming changes in rates.

- Avoid obscuring significant risks to the consumer. If a loan provider markets the benefits of lower initial payments, it should also emphasize the risks associated with future rate changes.

Remember the guidelines for qualified mortgages (QMs) as discussed in Chapter One. You should be able to identify characteristics of such mortgages. Remember that all loans eligible for sale to FNMA and FHLMC are, by definition, qualified mortgages through 2020 as long as the total points and fees do not exceed the 3% cap.

c. Non-Qualified Mortgages (Non-QMs)

Any residential mortgage loan that contains one or more of the prohibited features as described in Chapter One cannot attain the status of *qualified mortgage*. To review, here are some of the disqualifying features:

- Potential negative amortization.

- Interest-only payments.

- Total debt-to-income ratio exceeding 43% (not applicable for FNMA/FHLMC/FHA/VA/USDA loans).

- Total points and fees exceeding 3% of the loan amount.

- Prepayment penalties (on non-fixed-rate loans OR fixed-rate loans that are also higher-priced loans). Fixed-rate, non-higher-priced loans can have prepayment penalties that don't exceed 3% in year one, 2% in year two and 1% in year three.

Lenders are not prohibited in any way from making non-qualified mortgages. However, should a lender elect to do so, that loan will not receive any special protection from borrower-initiated lawsuits alleging violations of the Ability-to-Repay (ATR) rule. Additionally, non-QMs, by definition, do not meet the criteria of *Qualified Residential Mortgages*. Thus, any mortgage bonds issued and backed by such loans would require the issuer to retain 5% of the risk in those securities.

B. MORTGAGE LOAN PRODUCTS

1. Fixed

A **fixed-rate mortgage** (sometimes referred to as an *FRM*) is a type of mortgage loan in which the interest rate and payments (principal and interest) remain the same for the life of the loan. The most common loan terms are generally 15 or 30 years, although in today's mortgage market it is possible to obtain a loan with any term from 10 to 30 years (a 26-year mortgage, for example). Odd-year terms help borrowers who wish to refinance to take advantage of lower interest rates but do not wish to add years back onto the loan term. Terms greater than 30 years were widely available prior to the 2008 crash but have become very uncommon today, largely due to the QM cap of 30 years on a loan term. These loans are usually paid on a monthly basis, although biweekly payment schedules may also be offered.

A borrower may prefer a fixed-rate mortgage loan because it eliminates any risk of rising interest rates during the life of the loan. The rate will never change as a result of any corresponding change to an index or Treasury rates. Therefore, the principal and interest payment remains static for the life of the loan, although the total payment may change if the borrower escrows (pays property taxes and/or insurance with the loan) and those charges change. For example, if a borrower has private mortgage insurance on a loan and the policy terminates according to the guidelines in the Homeowner's Protection Act, the borrower's payment will decrease on a fixed-rate loan. Similarly, an increase in property tax on a borrower's property will result in a payment increase on a FRM.

2. Adjustable

An adjustable-rate mortgage (ARM) is a type of mortgage instrument in which the interest rate periodically adjusts up or down according to a specific index and pre-determined margin.

Interest Rates for ARMs

The steps involved with calculating an ARM's interest rate can differ depending on whether the ARM has just been issued and any caps that have been included as part of the lending agreement. At adjustment, interest rates for ARMs are generally calculated by adding the ARM's index value to the lender's margin.

An **index** is an economic measurement that is used to make periodic interest adjustments for an adjustable-rate mortgage. The most common indexes in use today are:

- The London Interbank Offered Rate (LIBOR), which measures the average rates that international banks in London lend each other U.S. dollars for either six months or one year. This index will cease to exist in 2021.

- The Cost of Funds Index (COFI), which measures the average interest rates that banks pay on deposits. Often measured in the Western region / 11th Federal Home Loan Bank District.

- The Constant Maturity Treasury (CMT), which takes the average yield on a basket of U.S. Treasury securities and adjusts them to a standardized maturity period of one year.

- The Secured Overnight Financing Rate (SOFR), which measures the average rates that banks are paying to borrow U.S. dollars overnight to meet required cash reserve thresholds. This is the index likely to replace LIBOR for many loans in 2021.

Lenders may offer ARM loans tied to any of these indexes to borrowers. Note, however, that the lender has no control over what the measurement of the index is at any given time.

The **margin** is the number that a lender adds to an index to determine the interest rate of an ARM. Usually, the margin is measured in *basis points*. Each basis point equals 1/100 of 1%. (For example, a margin of 350 basis points would require adding 3.5% to the index to determine the interest rate.) The margin does not change during the life of the loan, and you may want to think of it as the lender's profit on a given loan. Higher margins result in higher rates when the loan adjusts.

By adding the index to the margin, lenders calculate the **fully indexed rate**, which is the rate that is typically charged at each adjustment period. The interest rate on an ARM loan at closing is called the **introductory rate**, and it will be in effect for a period of time ranging from one month to 10 years, depending upon the loan product. The introductory rate is also known as the *start rate* or *initial rate*. When the introductory rate is lower than the fully indexed rate at the time of closing, it is known as a **teaser rate**. All introductory rates, whether teaser or not, are set by the lender. When the initial rate expires, the loan will undergo the first of several **adjustment periods**, during which a new interest rate will be in effect. At adjustment, the interest rate will adjust to the fully indexed rate (sometimes rounded to the nearest 0.125%) unless a rate cap limits the change. Like the initial rate, the rate for the adjustment period can last anywhere from several months to several years until it is re-calculated.

When the interest rate being calculated for an ARM's adjustment period doesn't match the fully indexed rate, it is probably because of a rate cap, rate floor or rate ceiling.

Rate Caps

A **rate cap** is a limitation on the amount that an interest rate may increase or decrease at a given adjustment or over the lifetime of the loan. These may also be referred to as *adjustment caps*.

There are three types of rate caps on most ARM loans:

- The **initial cap** applies only to the first rate adjustment period and indicates the number of percentage points that a rate may increase over the start rate.

- The **periodic cap** applies to all subsequent adjustment periods and indicates the number of percentage points that a rate may increase or decrease from the rate that was in effect immediately prior to the adjustment.

- The **life cap** sets a maximum number of percentage points that the rate can increase over the start rate for the life of the loan.

On a lender's rate sheet or guideline document, these caps are expressed as a series of three numbers with slashes between them. For example,

"Caps=5/2/5." In this scenario, the loan could adjust 5% at the FIRST adjustment period, 2% at every adjustment period thereafter, and could only adjust 5% total over the life of the loan. For loans where the initial cap and the periodic cap are identical, two numbers are sometimes used. For example, a loan with a 2% initial cap, a 2% periodic cap and a 6% life cap could be expressed as "2/2/6" OR "2/6." Remember that the numbers here indicate maximum *percentages of change,* NOT maximum interest rates. Also remember that caps are not guarantees of rate increases or decreases. The interest rate will adjust to the fully indexed rate UNLESS that rate is higher than the rate allowed by the cap, in which case the cap will be triggered and the borrower will be assessed the capped rate for the period of time until the next potential rate change.

Rate Floor

Although rate caps generally protect the borrower, a **rate floor** is sometimes included in a lending agreement in order to protect the lender. The rate floor is the lowest interest rate to which an ARM may adjust. For loans sold to Fannie Mae or Freddie Mac, this is usually identical to the margin, such that if the value of the index goes to 0 (or below), the lender will still make its margin on the loan. The periodic cap also can benefit the lender if rates are decreasing, as it will limit the amount of decrease, just as it protects the borrower by limiting the amount of increase in a rising rate environment.

Payment Caps and Negative Amortization

Some ARM products have a feature that limits the amount that a borrower's payment may increase at a given adjustment period, regardless of the increase in the interest rate. Although this feature can help prevent borrowers from needing to pay unpredictably high monthly payments, it causes a potentially unfavorable occurrence known as **negative amortization**.

Negative amortization occurs when the interest payment due from the borrower is less than the amount of interest that actually accrued on the loan in the prior month. The difference between what is paid and what is due is added back to the loan principal for that month, causing it to increase rather than decrease. In effect, this can force the borrower to eventually make bigger payments (or payments for a longer period of time) in order to retire the debt.

Describing ARMs

On ARM loans, we generally use two numbers with a forward slash in between them to describe the characteristics of the product. The first number represents the number of years that the initial rate will be in effect with no change. The second number represents how often the rate will adjust when the changes start. For example, a 5/1 ARM describes a loan where the initial rate will be in effect for five years and then the rate will adjust once per year thereafter. Generally speaking, a 1 in the second position indicates a loan that will adjust annually, and a 6 in the second position indicates a loan that will adjust every six months (semiannually).

Thus, a 3/6 ARM is a loan where the initial rate will be in effect for three years and will then adjust every six months.

The most common types of ARM loans today are called *hybrid ARMs* because they exhibit characteristics of both ARMs and fixed-rate loans. A hybrid ARM is a loan where the initial rate is in effect for a period greater than one year before any possible rate change.

Disclosing Rate Adjustments to the Borrower

Because it's important that borrowers understand what's happening with their loan, Regulation Z imposes upon servicers the responsibility to notify borrowers in advance of upcoming potential adjustments to their interest rate. For hybrid ARMs, there are two change disclosures:

- The *Initial Interest Rate Adjustment Disclosure* is required to be provided to borrowers between 210 and 240 days before the FIRST adjustment on their loan and notifies them of the potential for a rate change. They will only receive this disclosure once.

- The *Ongoing Interest Rate Adjustment Disclosure* is required to be provided to borrowers at ALL adjustments (including the first) and will inform them what their actual rate and payment will be at adjustment. This form must be provided between 60 and 120 days before the first payment is due at the new interest rate.

3. Balloon

A **balloon mortgage** is a type of fixed-rate mortgage loan with monthly payments based on a longer amortization period than the loan term. For example, the loan's amortization schedule may be based over 30 years while the term may only be five, seven, 10 or 15 years. This allows the borrower to make lower monthly payments for that shorter period of time, with a large payment of the full remaining principal balance and interest due at the maturity date. The final payment due is called a *balloon*. An example of a common balloon loan is a 360/180 loan, in which a borrower is required to make payments based on a 30-year payment schedule for 15 years. Then, after those 15 years, the remaining loan balance would be due. Since the minimum payments on a balloon mortgage *do* reduce the principal balance but do not extinguish the balance by the end of the loan term, we call balloons *partially amortizing loans*.

4. Reverse Mortgage

On a **reverse mortgage**, there are no mandatory principal and interest payments due from the borrower (although the borrower will still be responsible for property tax and insurance payments). In fact, in many cases the lender will actually make periodic payments to the borrower that come from the borrower's equity in the home. This product is often used to provide income to retirees or elderly borrowers based upon their existing home equity. The loan accrues interest each month just as a standard forward mortgage does, and the balance becomes due in full (with accrued interest) when the last remaining borrower dies, the last remaining borrower moves into a nursing home for a period of 12 months, or the property is sold. <u>In order to qualify for a reverse mortgage, all individuals on title must be 62 years of age or older</u>, although non-borrowing spouses who are not on title are allowed to occupy the property after the borrower's death as long as they were disclosed to the lender at application and have remained married to the borrower for the life of the loan.

Reverse mortgages may also be referred to as *reverse annuity mortgages (RAM)* or *home-equity conversion mortgages (HECM)*. HECM is the FHA's reverse mortgage program and is the most common program available today. The amount that an applicant may borrow is based on the age of the youngest borrower, the value of the property and the expected interest rate on the loan. Although for many years, it was not necessary for an applicant to demonstrate income or assets in order to obtain a reverse mortgage, FHA added basic qualification requirements in 2014 as a response to some elderly individuals losing their homes due to unpaid property taxes. Additionally, lenders are now prohibited from advertising that a reverse mortgage has "no payments" because of the borrower's need to remain current on taxes and insurance.

Today, individuals must demonstrate their ability to make property tax and homeowners insurance payments. If they are unable to do so, FHA now requires that the lender establish a **life expectancy set-aside** (**LESA**) to assist the applicant in making such payments when they come due. This resembles an escrow account, although it is different in that the money is segregated from the available applicant funds upfront.

Finally, for most HECM loans, HUD now limits the amount that a borrower can take as a disbursement from the proceeds of the loan to 60% of the total available principal limit in the first year. This is to reduce the number of people who make poor choices and spend all of the capital in a short timeframe.

Reverse Mortgage Loan Maturity

A reverse mortgage loan will mature – that is, the entire outstanding balance will become due and payable – in the following situations:

- The last remaining borrower or non-borrowing spouse dies.

- The property is sold.

- The last remaining borrower or non-borrowing spouse moves into a nursing home, and the subject property ceases to be the borrower's primary residence for 12 consecutive months.

In the first situation above (which is the most common), the property will pass to the borrower's heirs who will then have six months to either sell the property or pay the loan off in cash or with a refinance; they may also receive an additional six-month extension if the property is being marketed. The heirs may also elect to allow the property to go through the foreclosure process if they do not wish to do any of the things above. In this case, any money gained via the foreclosure sale process above and beyond the outstanding balance due will be returned to the heirs/estate of the deceased. Reverse mortgages are *non-recourse loans,* which means that the lender cannot attempt to recover any shortage after a foreclosure sale from any other assets that the borrower or heirs possess. Similarly, heirs will not be responsible for any foreclosure proceeding and the foreclosure will not be reflected on the credit report of the heirs because they did not incur the obligation.

5. Home Equity (Fixed and Line of Credit)

A **subordinate lien** is any mortgage or other lien that has priority lower than that of the first mortgage. Such a lien is also referred to as a *junior lien*. Loans secured by subordinate liens are referred to as **subordinate financing**.

A subordinate loan is not necessarily a second mortgage. There may be multiple subordinate encumbrances on a property (e.g., a mechanics lien placed by a contractor who was not paid, a judgment that has attached to the property, a third mortgage, etc.). Each lien is subordinate to those with higher lien priority. Liens are assigned priority by the date they are recorded with the county clerk or recorder of deeds in the county in which the property is located. The oldest lien on a property is the first lien, the second oldest is the second lien, and so forth. However, some government liens – like property tax liens, for example, may be considered *priority liens* by operation of law and move to the front of the line.

Home Equity Line of Credit (HELOC)

The most common form of subordinate financing in residential lending is the **home equity line of credit (HELOC)**. A HELOC is a revolving mortgage loan that allows the borrower to take advances at his/her discretion up to an approved limit that represents a percentage of the borrower's equity in a property. The minimum payments are generally interest-only for the period of time that the borrower can access the funds (called the *draw period*). Some HELOCs also have an amortizing period that follows where the borrower can no longer access the funds but is reducing principal with each payment (called the *repayment period*). During the draw period, if the borrower makes payments towards the loan's principal, that money becomes eligible to be accessed again until the draw period is complete.

Fixed Home Equity Loans

Home equity loans (HELs) are always disbursed in one fixed sum and repaid in accordance with a defined amortizing payment schedule. Unlike with a HELOC, the borrower is not permitted to re-borrow any portion of the principal amount of the loan once it has been repaid to the lender.

6. Construction Loans

A **construction loan** is provided to facilitate the new construction of improvements at a property. Typically, a construction lender will require a low loan-to-value ratio and will only release funds as it receives evidence of actual completion of construction. The release of funds from a lender to the contractor is referred to as a *draw*. Generally, construction loans provide for repayment of interest-only on the outstanding balance. (Remember, the balance will grow as draws are disbursed to the contractor(s) by the lender.) Many construction loans also have a requirement to pay off the principal balance within a limited time period following completion of the construction. The most common terms for construction loans are six to nine months. Some construction products automatically convert to long-term, closed-end loans after construction is complete. These are called *construction-to-permanent loans*. While true short-term construction loans are exempt from many RESPA and TILA requirements, construction-to-permanent loans do not receive that same exemption, as they do convert to closed-end, permanent loans.

7. Interest-Only Loans (First Lien)

An **interest-only loan** is a type of mortgage that allows the borrower to pay only the interest that has accrued each month on the mortgage for a period of years, after which the loan generally becomes fully amortizing. Today, the most common interest-only period is 10 years. Thus, on a 30-year, fixed rate, interest-only loan, the borrower is only required to pay the interest accrued in any given month for the first 10 years, after which time the loan converts to an amortizing loan with the full balance to be paid over the remaining 20 years of the loan term. The borrower is allowed to pay down the principal during the interest-only period by paying more than the minimum due. If the borrower elects to do so, that can result in a significantly lower payment after the interest-only period expires and the loan **recasts** to fully amortize over the remaining term. Interest-only loans may have either fixed or adjustable rates.

The formula used to calculate an interest-only payment is:

(Loan Amount x Interest Rate) ÷ 12

C. TERMS USED IN THE MORTGAGE INDUSTRY

In order to engage in proper conduct and pass your licensing exams, you must be familiar with several mortgage-related definitions. Although key terms can be found throughout this study guide, those included in this section deserve special attention.

1. Loan Terms

When evaluating a loan applicant, it is important to consider the five "C"s of underwriting:

- Capacity.
- Capital.
- Credit.
- Collateral.
- Character.

Capacity refers to the borrower's ability to repay the loan (and service other debts and obligations) based upon sufficient income. The underwriter relies on the loan processor to verify the income information set forth by the borrower in the loan application. The borrower's capacity to repay a loan is determined, in part, by calculating and evaluating a debt-to-income ratio.

Capital refers to the borrower's ability to make a down payment, pay for closing costs and fund any escrows or reserves required at closing. It is important that the Uniform Residential Loan Application (URLA/Form 1003) indicates clearly the source of funds that the applicant will use to close the mortgage loan because these funds must be verified in the file. In some cases, a lender will require that a borrower have enough **reserves** (liquid assets left over after closing) to pay a certain number of mortgage payments. For example, it is common for lenders to require that borrowers have two months of mortgage payments in reserve on primary residence transactions and six months in reserve on a loan secured by an investment property. The applicant's capital is generally evaluated by looking at the last two months of bank statements and/or quarterly investment account statements.

Credit is evaluated by looking at the credit report. While the borrower's FICO credit score is very important, there are other items that can affect the evaluation of the applicant's creditworthiness. For example, outstanding judgments or tax liens can certainly cause issues, even for an applicant with an acceptable FICO score. Oftentimes, if there is an isolated period of unsatisfactory credit in an otherwise satisfactory report, these are due to circumstances beyond the borrower's control, such as job loss or the death of a family member. These are called **extenuating circumstances** and may be able to be accommodated in underwriting. Finally, we look to the credit report as one means of establishing minimum payments on applicant debt in calculating a debt-to-income ratio.

Collateral refers to the property being mortgaged as security for the loan. The value of that property is established by a property appraisal performed by a licensed appraiser. Although value is certainly very important, the appraisal also provides a description of all property characteristics, such as the number of bedrooms and bathrooms, the condition of the property, square footage, zoning, etc. There are many issues on an appraisal besides insufficient value that could result in the denial of a mortgage loan.

Character refers to the borrower's willingness to repay the debt, as distinguished from the borrower's *ability* to repay the debt. Credit history can help to provide an indication of a borrower's willingness to repay, and evaluation of extenuating circumstances (as mentioned above) factors in as a measure of character, especially in loans that are manually underwritten.

2. <u>Disclosure Terms</u>

Some important terms must be understood in order for you to make proper disclosures to consumers.

Annual Percentage Rate

The annual percentage rate (APR) is a measurement of the total cost of the credit, expressed as an annual rate. The APR includes specific costs of financing, both those paid at the time of closing and those paid over the term of the loan. Charges that affect a loan's APR are called **finance charges** because they are incurred as a direct result of the credit obligation. The largest finance charge in any loan is interest, and we disclose this cost to the borrower in both the interest rate itself and as the biggest component of the APR. In regard to fees, the general rule is that a fee *is* a finance charge (and will be included in the APR) if that fee would *not* be paid in a comparable transaction done without a loan – that is, one completed entirely with cash.

On a fixed-rate loan, the APR is higher than the interest rate because it includes all items that are included in the finance charge. For example:

- Interest.

- Discount points.

- Mortgage insurance premiums.

- Administrative fees (origination fees, discount points, processing, underwriting, etc.).

Mortgage professionals have several disclosure-related responsibilities regarding a loan's APR. For a review of these requirements, please review Chapter One of this study guide.

Yield Spread Premium / Premium Pricing

A yield spread premium (YSP) is an amount paid by a creditor to a mortgage broker at closing to compensate the broker for making a loan at an interest rate which is higher than the interest rate that the investor would have accepted for that loan.

Due to the Dodd-Frank Act and its accompanying rules, it is illegal for a loan originator to be paid different amounts based on the terms or conditions of a loan. In other words, YSPs have effectively been banned. However, it is acceptable for a borrower to accept a higher rate – which would result in a higher premium (called *premium pricing*) – as long as any premium that exceeds the broker's standard compensation be credited back to the borrower to cover closing costs.

Lender-Paid Compensation

Effective with the enactment of the rules referenced above, lender-paid compensation has replaced the YSP. This is compensation paid to a broker from a lender, and it does NOT vary based on the terms or conditions of a loan. Rather, the broker makes the same fixed compensation (generally a percentage of the loan amount) on every loan originated and funded through a given lender EXCEPT loans on which the broker is paid directly by the borrower (called *borrower-paid compensation* loans).

Service Release Premium

Service release premium (SRP) is paid by an investor to a *banker* only. The investor is purchasing the rights to service (collect payments on) the loan after closing, and the amount of the compensation is dependent upon the value of those rights. Although similar to YSP in that higher-rate loans generally attract higher service release premiums, SRP is a *secondary market* transaction (paid *after* closing) and does not appear on the Loan Estimate or Closing Disclosure provided to the applicant. SRPs are not prohibited by the Dodd-Frank Act.

3. Financial Terms

Negative Amortization

Negative amortization occurs when the interest payment due does not cover all of the interest accrued for the period. Any unpaid interest is added to the loan's outstanding principal balance, causing it to grow.

Positive Amortization

Positive amortization occurs when a portion of each payment is applied to principal, thereby reducing the outstanding balance. On positively amortizing loans, the interest portion of each payment decreases, and the principal portion increases over time, such that the first payment consists almost entirely of interest, while payments late in the loan term consist almost exclusively of principal.

Fully Amortizing Loans

A loan is fully amortizing when the regular monthly payments result in the principal balance being extinguished at the end of the loan term. Most fixed-rate loans are fully amortizing.

Partially Amortizing Loans

A loan where a portion of the principal is repaid with regular monthly payments but the balance is not fully extinguished at the end of the loan term (resulting in a large payment to satisfy the remaining balance) is called a *partially amortizing loan*. Balloon loans are partially amortizing loans.

Bridge Financing

A **bridge loan** is sometimes used when buyers wish to finalize the purchase of a new home before their current home is sold. Bridge loans are short-term cash-out loans made on the equity in the applicant's current property in order to allow them to close on the purchase of a new transaction. They are paid back either through the sale of the current property or, if the applicant elects to retain the property, through a subsequent mortgage loan.

Refinancing Cost Recapture

When refinancing, the borrower will incur certain closing costs. Whether these closing costs are paid in cash at closing or rolled into the principal amount of the new, refinanced loan, the borrower will want to determine the period over which those costs are "recaptured" via savings achieved through the refinanced loan.

In order to determine the amount of time in which the refinancing costs will be recaptured, we must determine the difference between the amount of the monthly payment under the new loan and under the pre-existing loan.

Once we have the difference between the new and old monthly principal and interest payments, we can divide the amount of the refinancing costs by that difference to determine the number of months after which that cost will be "recaptured." After that period of time, the borrower begins to achieve true savings as a result of the lower monthly payment.

As an example:

- Suppose that total refinancing costs equal $1,650. These costs may include loan fees, title insurance premiums, closing costs, etc.

- The total monthly principal, interest and mortgage insurance payment under the existing loan was $1,900 per month.

- The monthly principal, interest and mortgage insurance payment under the new loan is $1,600 per month.

- As a result, the difference between the two monthly payments is $300 per month.

- The $1,650 of refinancing costs will be recaptured by the end of 5 1/2 months ($1,650 divided by $300 equals 5 1/2).

If the borrower believes that he/she will sell the mortgaged property or refinance again within the recapture period (in the example above, over the 5 ½ months after the closing of the refinance), then the borrower should not refinance since the closing costs would not be recaptured until after that time period. The borrower would be incurring refinance costs without the benefit of any real-dollar savings.

NOTE: The VA program refers to this concept as *recoupment* and mandates that all costs be recouped with payment savings in the first 36 months of a refinance using the Interest Rate Reduction Refinancing Loan (IRRRL) program. This is essentially a streamline refinance for an existing VA loan into a new VA loan that does not require verification of income, assets, liabilities or appraised value.

4. General Terms

Wholesale Lending

Wholesale lenders purchase and sell loans that have been originated by third parties, such as mortgage bankers or brokers.

Wholesale lenders may purchase loans with the intent to package the loans for sale to secondary market investors; or they may purchase loans in order to hold and service the loans themselves. A wholesale lender servicing loans (i.e., interfacing with and collecting payments from borrowers) may be referred to as a **servicer**.

Retail Lending

Retail lending refers to direct lending to borrowers. Many different parties participate in retail lending, including:

- Mortgage brokers.
- Mortgage bankers.
- Commercial banks.
- Thrifts.
- Credit unions.

Mortgage Brokers

A **mortgage broker** is a firm that, for a commission, matches borrowers and lenders. A mortgage broker does not retain servicing, does not use its own funds and is not a lender. In fact, state laws prohibit firms licensed as brokers from engaging in any loan ownership, sale or servicing.

Mortgage Bankers

A **mortgage banker** originates, funds and sells loans secured by mortgages on real property. Mortgage bankers generally act as intermediaries between investors and borrowers. They fund loans with money that they control (typically off of a line of credit from a depository institution, also called a **warehouse line of credit**) and usually then sell the loan in the secondary market to repay the warehouse line funds. Mortgage bankers may also service loans, although that tends not to be their primary function. Some states actually require a separate license or endorsement to allow a mortgage banker to engage in the act of servicing loans.

Commercial Banks

A **commercial bank** is a financial institution organized to accumulate funds primarily through time and demand deposits and to make those funds available to finance the nation's commerce and industry through business lending and depository facilities. Commercial banks also participate in residential mortgage lending. They may be chartered by the federal government or a state government.

Thrifts

A **thrift** (also known as a *savings and loan*) is a banking institution regulated by the Office of the Comptroller of the Currency. Thrifts can be state-chartered or federally chartered but must invest a certain percentage (currently 65%) of their deposits in residential mortgage loans and similar assets.

Credit Unions

A **credit union** is a financial institution operating somewhat differently than other banking institutions. Credit unions are not-for-profit organizations where the account holders (called *members*) have some common characteristic. For example, a credit union may be setup to serve employees of one company and their families. After deducting operating expenses and reserves, credit unions return their earnings to their members.

Price Protection Options

A few key terms are used to describe consumer-friendly features regarding interest rates.

Rate Lock

A **rate lock** agreement between the borrower and lender details a specified period of time in which the lender will keep a specific interest rate and fee combination available for the borrower. Some lenders may charge a fee (called a **rate lock fee)** in order to dissuade the borrower from switching to a different lender in the event of a decrease in market interest rates before closing.

Floating Rate

An interest rate that has not been locked by agreement between the applicant and lender is referred to as a **floating rate**. Floating the rate will benefit the borrower if interest rates drop between the time of application and closing but will have an adverse impact on the borrower if rates move higher. The floating rate is ultimately "locked in" sometime prior to closing.

Real Estate Contract

The **real estate contract** (also referred to as a *purchase and sale agreement* or a *sales contract*) is a written contract between a buyer and seller of real property, setting forth the price and the terms of the sale. This contractual agreement contains all the terms and conditions upon which the seller agrees to sell and the buyer agrees to buy.

As a loan originator, it is very important to review the terms of the real estate contract, as they contain information that can have a direct impact on your financing transaction. For example, you need to know if the seller or real estate agent is contributing any funds toward the buyer's closing costs, which will be spelled out in the contract.

Additionally, there are some important dates that you need to take notice of. The **financing contingency date** (or simply *contingency date* or *commitment date*) contractually dictates when the borrower's financing must be in place. In most states, this means that the applicant must have a clear commitment, which means that the loan must be clear to close by the contingency date. The closing date on the contract is the day that the documents will be signed and the deed transferred from the seller to the buyer.

NOTE: If the file will not be clear to close by the contingency date, or a delay results in a missed closing date, you MUST let the applicant, real estate agent and/or any attorneys involved in the transaction know as soon as you suspect that a delay may occur. Failing to meet these deadlines without getting a mutually agreed-upon extension in writing can put the buyer's purchase and any earnest money deposit in jeopardy.

Foreclosure

Residential mortgage loan payments are due on the first day of each month, with a grace period through the fifteenth day of each month. Payments made after the fifteenth may incur a late charge. Payments which are more than 30 days past due will be reported by the lender as delinquent to the credit bureaus.

Failure to make payments can ultimately lead to foreclosure. A **foreclosure** is a proceeding to extinguish all rights, title and interest of the owner of a property in order to sell the property and satisfy a lien against it. According to federal servicing regulations, borrowers must be at least 120 days delinquent on their payments in order for a lender to start the foreclosure process. The foreclosure process is different from state to state. For example, some states require court action to complete the process (**judicial foreclosure**), and some require only administrative action (**non-judicial foreclosure**).

During a **redemption period**, the borrower may pay off the loan in full in order to avoid a foreclosure sale of the property. States that have redemption periods that expire prior to or at the time of a judicial sale of a property have the **equitable right of redemption.** Other states allow the right of redemption to exist even after a judicial sale has occurred. This is called the **statutory right of redemption.**

A judicial sale generally occurs once the lender has obtained a judgment of foreclosure. The borrower's rights in the property are extinguished upon sale (except in states that have the statutory right of redemption), and the borrower must vacate the property.

In some states, if a lender fails to recoup all of the outstanding principal, interest and fees through the foreclosure process, it may take legal action individually against the borrowers for the shortage, resulting in something called a *deficiency judgment*. States that allow for deficiency judgments are called *recourse states* and states that do not allow this practice are considered *non-recourse states*.

CHAPTER THREE –
MORTGAGE LOAN ORIGINATION ACTIVITIES

A. APPLICATION INFORMATION AND REQUIREMENTS

1. Application Accuracy and Required Information (e.g., 1003)

Once a purchase agreement is executed (or once a decision is made to refinance), the loan originator and the borrower meet to complete a loan application (or complete one over the phone or the Internet). The application is referred to as the **Uniform Residential Loan Application (URLA)** - also called *the 1003*, as it is Fannie Mae's form number 1003.

A good real estate loan application presents a complete and accurate financial picture of the borrower as of the date on the application. After reviewing the application and credit report (and automated underwriting system findings, if applicable), an **underwriter** should be able to make an initial credit decision, then review documentation validating the application information to support that decision.

The lender/creditor is responsible for the accuracy of the application information through the entire origination process and will be held responsible by the end investor for all inaccuracies, even if they occurred as a result of a data change after loan approval but before the actual closing (i.e. borrower loss of employment).

For conventional conforming loans (and many government loans as well), the underwriter will be reviewing recommendations made by the two largest AUS systems: Fannie Mae's **Desktop Underwriter (DU)** and Freddie Mac's **Loan Product Advisor (LPA)**. If the AUS recommendation on the file was "Approve," underwriters typically just must verify that the information on the 1003 submitted to the AUS matches the actual loan documentation. If the recommendation on the file was "Refer," the underwriter must actually make a manual credit decision on whether the applicant's risk factors meet Fannie and Freddie's underwriting criteria.

a. Borrower

The customer is obligated to provide accurate and truthful information and supporting documentation. As part of the loan process, the loan originator must review the application for any inconsistencies or warning signs suggesting that the information provided is not truthful (called *misrepresentation*). Other individuals, such as the processor and the underwriter, also perform consistency checks on the application and supporting documentation. Intentionally concealing, adjusting or withholding any material facts that may affect the application constitutes mortgage fraud. Unintentional misrepresentation constitutes negligence. A fact is considered *material* if knowledge of that fact would lead a lender to consider a different course of action on the application.

b. Loan Originator

There are many things that a loan originator can do ahead of time to enhance the loan application process. The loan originator should let the applicant know how much time the procedure will take and advise the borrower to bring all required information, documentation and funds (for fees payable at the time of application).

The core of the mortgage loan originator's job is to obtain a complete and accurate 1003 supported by documentation from the borrower. The application is designed to be completed by the borrower, with the loan originator assisting in data input. The MLO should have the applicant sign the loan application and any other required disclosure documents.

c. Verification and Documentation

The job of a loan **processor** is to assist the loan originator by reviewing the submitted documents and ensuring the file is ready for underwriting. Processors are also responsible for obtaining verification on certain borrower-provided documentation. Often, such verification comes directly from the third party listed on the application – for example, the applicant's employer may need to assist the processor by completing a **verification of employment (VOE)**, and the bank statements may need to be supported by a **verification of deposit (VOD)**. These third-party verifications ensure that the documentation provided is in fact authentic and without misrepresentation. Fraud prevention is of paramount importance in the modern lending environment.

2. Suitability of Products and Programs

The loan originator must understand the borrower's goals in the financing transaction. For example:

- Understand the borrower's concerns regarding the choice between homeownership and renting.

- Understand the benefits that the borrower may receive by refinancing an existing loan.

- Appreciate the borrower's timeline objectives.

- Determine the applicant's tolerance for risk and comfort with the proposed monthly payment.

By understanding those goals, the loan originator will be able to offer products that adequately match the borrower's needs and successfully lay the groundwork for future business opportunities.

In addition, the loan originator must learn the differences between loan programs offered by investors. By understanding both the investor and the borrower, the loan originator can make proper recommendations and fully explain the loan products to the borrower.

The loan originator is more than a clerk filling the borrower's order; the loan originator must analyze the borrower's circumstances and be prepared to make suggestions regarding appropriate loan products upon borrower request. <u>While the final decision on loan product rests with the borrower</u>, the loan originator must keep the borrower's best interests in mind when preparing options and qualifying the applicant(s) for the loan. Failure to do so or proposing a loan option with a payment that cannot reasonably be repaid by the borrower is a form of predatory lending.

3. **Disclosures**

Federal law requires that certain disclosures be delivered by loan originators. Although these disclosures are explained in greater detail in Chapter One, they are important enough to be summarized here as well:

- The Loan Estimate (TILA requirement).

- The Mortgage Loan Servicing Disclosure (RESPA requirement).

- The CFPB Home Loan Toolkit (referred to in both TILA and RESPA).

- A list of settlement service providers that the originating company will use for services that the applicant can shop for (title, etc.) (TILA requirement).

- The Affiliated Business Arrangement Disclosure (AfBA), if the creditor has an ownership of 1% or more of a settlement service provider to which it refers business. (RESPA requirement).

- The Adjustable Rate Mortgage Disclosure (if the loan is an ARM) (TILA requirement).

- The Consumer Handbook on Adjustable-Rate Mortgages – CHARM Booklet (if the loan is an ARM) (TILA requirement).

- The Homeownership Counseling Disclosure (TILA requirement).

Loan Estimate

The Loan Estimate is the required disclosure of the known or anticipated fees, charges or settlement costs that the mortgage applicant is likely to incur at the settlement (closing) of the loan. Each such estimate must be made in good faith and bear a reasonable relationship to the charge a borrower is likely to pay at closing. It must be delivered within <u>three business days</u> of receiving an application (defined as the six pieces of information required under RESPA and TILA and discussed in Chapter One.)

Mortgage Loan Servicing Disclosure

The Mortgage Loan Servicing Disclosure provides notice regarding the lender's intent to transfer or retain the servicing of the loan. Servicing refers to the process of collecting the principal, interest and escrow account payments on the loan. The Mortgage Loan Servicing Disclosure must be provided to the borrower within <u>three business days</u> of the loan application. Note that the Mortgage Loan Servicing Disclosure is NOT the same document as the Servicing Transfer Disclosure, which informs the borrower that his/her loan has been transferred to another servicer.

The Home Loan Toolkit

The CFPB's informational booklet known as the **Home Loan Toolkit** must be provided to all borrowers on purchase transactions only. The booklet sets forth general information regarding the loan process – from application to closing – with a concentration on fees and charges. It must be provided within three business days of the loan application. The loan originator can translate the booklet into different languages and can make changes to the cover to suit his/her business needs (as long as the booklet title does not change). However, the originator cannot change any of the content of the booklet.

The Adjustable-Rate Mortgage Disclosure

On all ARM loans, the borrower must receive a disclosure detailing how the interest rate will be calculated, when the loan will adjust and a historical reference of index values on the index to which that loan's rate will be tied. Borrowers need to be provided information on the loan program for which they are actually applying, although lenders may elect to provide an ARM disclosure containing information on all ARM products that they currently offer. Like the CHARM booklet detailed below, the lender's ARM disclosure must also be delivered within three business days of application for ARM loans only.

CHARM Booklets

Some disclosures under TILA are specific to adjustable-rate mortgage loans (ARMs). An adjustable rate mortgage loan is a mortgage loan with an interest rate that can go up or down during the life of the loan. TILA requires that lenders offering ARMs furnish a CHARM (Consumer Handbook on Adjustable Rate Mortgages) booklet issued by the Federal Reserve to the consumer within three business days of application.

a. Accuracy

We know that the Closing Disclosure must be made to the applicant at least three business days before closing. However, if the APR on the initial disclosure is understated by more than 1/8% for a regular loan or by more than 1/4% for an irregular loan (a loan with multiple advances, such as a construction loan, or a loan with irregular repayment periods – quarterly payments, for example) after the initial disclosure is issued, the creditor must issue a new disclosure with the accurate APR and wait an ADDITIONAL three business days before consummating the loan. Keep in mind that, for the Loan Estimate and Closing Disclosure, there are limits (called tolerances) on the amount that fees can increase. These are discussed in detail in Chapter One and should be reviewed.

b. Timing

The Real Estate Settlement Procedures Act (RESPA) requires that lenders provide specific disclosures to mortgage applicants within three business days of application. Disclosures required by RESPA include the Mortgage

Servicing Disclosure and Affiliated Business Arrangement Disclosure (when applicable).

Again, in many cases, a legal application has been taken well before the 1003 is signed. According to RESPA and TILA, an application is considered to have been taken if the loan originator has gathered the following six pieces of information:

- Borrower's name.

- The address of the subject property.

- Borrower's income.

- Borrower's estimate of value of the subject property (NOT an actual appraised value).

- Borrower's Social Security number.

- Loan amount.

"3-7-3 Rule" Under TILA and the Mortgage Disclosure Improvement Act (MDIA) of 2008

Similarly, the Truth in Lending Act (TILA) requires that the lender provide certain disclosures within <u>three business days</u> of receipt of a mortgage application. These include the Loan Estimate, Home Loan Toolkit and Homeownership Counseling Disclosure (which lists the 10 HUD-approved counseling agencies closest to the applicant's address). Also required within three business days of application on ARM loans are the CHARM booklet and the ARM Disclosure.

Once the Loan Estimate has been delivered to the borrower or placed in the mail, <u>the earliest the loan can close is on the seventh business day</u> after the LE has been provided or mailed. (The Closing Disclosure can be provided to the applicant during this waiting period if it is ready to be sent.)

Regardless of when the Closing Disclosure is issued, should the APR on the loan become inaccurate by more than 1/8% after delivery, the form must be re-disclosed, and an ADDITIONAL <u>three-business-day waiting period is required</u> before consummation.

To reiterate, there are two different definitions of the term *business day* in use as regards these disclosures. For all RESPA disclosures as well as the initial Loan Estimate and HUD Counseling Disclosure, we use the definition "any day that the creditor is open for business to carry on substantially all of its business." This may or may not include Saturdays, Sundays and certain holidays. For revised Loan Estimates (issued when a changed circumstance occurs), the Closing Disclosure and most other TILA requirements, we follow the more straightforward definition of "any day except Sundays and federal holidays."

c. Delivery Method

How the creditor elects to deliver the required disclosures to the applicant has a direct impact on when the applicant is deemed to have received those disclosures. For example:

- If disclosures such as the Loan Estimate and Closing Disclosure are *mailed* to the applicant, they are deemed received on the third business day after they are placed in the mail. This is called the **mailbox rule**.

- If the Closing Disclosure is provided to the applicant via email (with the applicant's permission), it follows the same three-day rule as it would if placed in regular U.S. Mail *unless* the applicant sends the creditor a return message indicating that the document was received. In that case only, an email disclosure would be deemed received when the return message was sent.

- Disclosures sent via fax are deemed to be received the day after they are successfully transmitted.

- Disclosures delivered in person, logically, are deemed received when presented to the borrower.

B. QUALIFICATION: PROCESSING AND UNDERWRITING

1. Borrower Analysis

Between the time of application and the making of an underwriting decision, the loan processor works to verify and validate the accuracy of the application information obtained from the applicant. Although the specific process flow may vary from lender to lender, the loan processor should be able to do the following tasks:

- Immediately read all of the information on the loan application.

- Quickly complete the data entry into the lender's electronic loan origination system.

- Be able to prepare and deliver the initial disclosures required by law to the borrower within the required timeframe (<u>three business days</u> after receipt of the loan application).

- Submit the information to the credit bureau and/or automated underwriting system.

- Submit the file to the underwriter for analysis and issuance of the loan decision.

After the loan application is approved and a loan commitment is issued by the lender, the loan processor is then responsible for obtaining any additional required documentation, coordinating communication among the interested parties and clearing the loan approval conditions contained in the loan commitment and required for closing.

a. Assets

In practically all cases, a borrower must have some assets in order to satisfy a down payment and complete a mortgage transaction. It is important that the application clearly indicate the source of funds that the applicant will use to close the mortgage loan because these funds must be verified in the file. Some sources of funds include:

- Cash in the bank.
- Sale of current residence.
- Gift funds.
- Sale of other assets.
- Secured borrowed funds.
- Cash on hand.

Cash in the Bank

If the applicant indicates on the application that he or she will use cash currently on deposit in the bank to close the loan, then the loan originator can easily verify this by asking for the last two or three months' bank statements.

Two months' statements must be obtained because investors want to see **seasoned funds** (funds that have been in the account for a minimum length of time). If the bank statements reveal any large deposits, the applicants must provide a written explanation of the source of those funds along with supporting documentation like a cancelled check. A large deposit, as defined by Fannie Mae, is any deposit that exceeds 50% of the monthly qualifying income for the loan. If it is obvious from the bank statement where the funds came from (i.e. a direct deposit from employer payroll), further documentation may not be necessary.

Sale of Current Residence

In this case, the applicant must supply a copy of the Closing Disclosure from the sale transaction, verifying that the property has been sold and that the applicant received sufficient proceeds to close the new loan.

Gift Funds

The donor(s) must complete a gift letter indicating the amount of the gift and the donor's relationship to the applicant. The relationship must be acceptable to the investor. Typically, the donor must be a family member, nonprofit organization or employer.

The gift letter must state that no repayment of the funds is required, and the creditor must verify that the funds have been given; this is generally done with a copy of a cancelled check. On FHA loans, donors must also prove that they have the financial ability to gift the money, which is done by providing a copy of a bank statement from which the funds were transferred.

Sale of Other Assets

Some of the items often sold for cash to close a real estate transaction include cars, boats, RVs, guns, artwork, antiques, jewelry and coin collections. In the case of an asset sale, the applicant must prove ownership of the asset that was sold, provide a market value for that asset (i.e. a Blue Book value for cars or an appraisal for jewelry) and show the bill of sale and proof of payment.

Borrowed Funds

Unsecured borrowed funds, such as from a credit card advance, are NOT an acceptable source of down payment. All borrowed funds must be secured by an asset of the borrower, such as a 401(k), to be acceptable for use in the mortgage transaction.

Cash on Hand

Some applicants do not use or trust commercial banks and keep their cash at home. This is referred to as *unverified cash* or *cash on hand*.

Investors generally do not allow cash on hand to be used as a source of down payment or closing costs.

b. Liabilities

Liabilities, including various credit-related obligations, must be considered in order to determine the likelihood of repayment. Most lenders require that the borrower's monthly mortgage payment plus other liabilities not exceed a certain percentage of the person's income. But in order to determine how a liability will impact this debt-to-income qualifying ratio, we first need to know more about the liability itself.

Revolving Accounts (e.g., Credit Cards)

For credit cards and other revolving accounts, the payment that will be used in the calculation of the borrower's debt-to-income ratio is the minimum monthly payment shown on the credit report. If a credit report does not show a minimum monthly payment and one cannot be established, the underwriter will use 5% of the unpaid balance as a payment when calculating the ratios.

Installment Loans

At the discretion of the underwriter, monthly payments for installment loans (such as auto loans) with 10 or fewer payments remaining may be excluded when calculating qualifying ratios. Installment loans can also be paid off or paid down to 10 or fewer payments in order to help an applicant qualify for a loan.

Auto Leases

Monthly auto lease payments are always included in the qualifying ratios regardless of the balance remaining on the lease (as compared to auto loans, which may be excluded if 10 or fewer payments remain).

Student Loans

If payment on a student loan is deferred, Fannie Mae and Freddie Mac both require that the underwriter include a payment in calculating the borrower's debt ratio for qualification purposes. Generally, this is done by obtaining a payment letter from the institution holding/servicing the student loan (e.g. Sallie Mae). If no payment letter can be obtained, the lender must use 1% of the unpaid balance as a payment for loans being sold to Fannie Mae or

Freddie Mac unless the borrower is on an income-based repayment plan and the creditor can verify the income-based plan's payment is $0.

Contingent Liabilities

A borrower has a **contingent liability** when he or she has co-signed for another person's installment debt, but the actual payments are being made by the primary obligor. An example of this would be a parent signing as a co-signer on a child's student loans. Such liabilities do NOT have to be taken into consideration when calculating the borrower's debt ratio as long as both of the following are true:

- The payments have been made on-time for the previous <u>12-month period.</u>
- The lender documents that the payments were made from the primary obligor's (i.e. the child in the above scenario) funds.

If the payments have not been made in a timely manner or the lender cannot document that they were made by the primary obligor, the minimum payment must be taken into consideration in the borrower's debt ratio. This same rule holds true for self-employed borrowers who have a co-signed debt appearing on their personal credit report, but the debt is actually paid on-time by the borrower's business using funds from the business.

c. Income

The two biggest things that lenders look for in income (and employment) are stability and consistency.

When calculating various ratios in order to determine whether a borrower qualifies for a loan, having proof of income is very important. In order for most kinds of income to count in the borrower's favor, lenders usually require that the income be verifiable over the previous <u>two years, and in many cases will take a two-year average of the income to qualify (especially for variable income such as overtime or bonus income).</u> If the borrower's income is declining, the lender will typically use the worst-case scenario in qualification.

In many cases, lenders will want to receive confirmation that income is likely to continue. For example, all income with an expiration date (child support, alimony, long-term disability programs for example) must be likely to continue for at least <u>three years after the loan closing</u>.

Non-Taxable Income: Grossing Up

Some income sources, such as permanent disability payments, Social Security benefits and child support, may be exempt from federal income taxes.

Most investors/governmental agencies allow the lender to calculate how much tax the borrower would pay if this income were taxable and add that figure to the gross amount received. This procedure is known as **grossing up**.

The allowable "gross up" factors range from 15% to 25%; in other words, the non-taxable income can be multiplied by <u>115% to 125%</u> to adjust it accordingly. The benchmark figure for conforming loans is 125%, and for government loans it is 115%.

Rental Income (Other Real Estate Owned)

If the borrower wishes to use rental income as a way of qualifying for a loan, the loan originator should obtain 1040 tax returns, complete with all schedules, including Schedule E.

Monthly income should be based on a <u>24-month average</u> of all Schedule E net rental income (gross income, less expenses, plus depreciation). If the resulting figure is positive, it can be used as qualifying income. If it is a negative figure, it must be used as a debt in the qualifying ratios.

If 1040 tax returns cannot be used to verify the rental income because the property was acquired since the borrower filed the previous year's tax returns, the loan originator may obtain copies of current lease agreements. Generally, a <u>25% vacancy/maintenance factor</u> should be subtracted from the monthly gross rent. Also subtract the property's mortgage payment (PITI). If the resulting figure is positive, it can be used as qualifying income. If it is a negative figure, it must be used as a debt in the qualifying ratios.

Unemployment Compensation

For applicants whose work is seasonal, unemployment income can be used as part of qualifying income. Some trades, such as fishing, construction and farm work, are seasonal with regular down time. During this time, most workers receive unemployment. If unemployment is part of the natural annual work cycle, then it may be included in qualifying income. The loan originator should obtain <u>two years' copies</u> of tax returns and average both the employment income and the unemployment income.

In general, unemployment compensation received due to layoffs or termination <u>cannot be used</u> as qualifying income.

Self-Employed Borrower

If an applicant is self-employed, the loan originator should obtain tax returns for the past <u>two years</u>.

In cases where tax returns are used to calculate income, the lender/investor will always require all pages of all schedules of the borrower's personal tax return. If the borrower has ownership interest in a partnership or corporation, the business tax returns may also be required.

Business Tax Returns

There are specific forms that should be reviewed when evaluating the income of a business owner. Examples of these forms include the following:

- Income from a sole proprietorship is found on the borrower's personal tax return (Schedule C of the 1040).
- Partnership income is reported on IRS form 1065.

- S-Corporation income is reported on IRS form 1120-S.

- C-Corporation income is reported on IRS form 1120.

Borrowers who are shareholders in an S-Corporation or members of a partnership will also receive a Schedule K-1. This is the schedule that ties the business returns and the personal returns together.

d. Credit Report

Credit reports must verify the information provided by the applicants on the loan application. Current open accounts, minimum monthly payments and current outstanding balances are provided in an easy-to-read format; public records and employment information are also set forth in the credit report.

If the applicants have derogatory credit, it will be reflected on the credit report. **Derogatory credit** means that the applicants have not paid their obligations on time and their creditors have reported the late payments to the credit bureaus or have filed judgments or other liens against the applicants.

There are three national credit bureaus (also called *consumer reporting agencies*) that receive this type of information from creditors:

- Equifax.

- TransUnion.

- Experian.

The three credit bureaus then supply the information to local credit reporting agencies who, in turn, supply it to lenders.

Derogatory Credit

If the applicant's credit report shows derogatory credit (such as late payments, current delinquencies, bad-debt write-offs, judgments, foreclosures or bankruptcies), the applicant must provide an explanation of each specific derogatory item in writing. Occasional or isolated late payments are understandable and often excusable. However, chronic patterns of late payments that demonstrate a disregard for meeting credit obligations can result in credit denial or a counteroffer on less favorable credit terms.

For serious derogatory credit events like foreclosures and bankruptcies, more documentation is required from the applicant to determine if the event was caused by financial mismanagement or because of some extenuating circumstance beyond the borrower's control. This has a direct impact on the length of time that must elapse before the borrower is eligible for financing (called the *seasoning period*). For example, both Fannie Mae and Freddie Mac require a seven-year waiting period after a completed foreclosure before the applicant is eligible for conforming financing. This number is reduced to three years for foreclosures that occurred as a result of extenuating circumstances. For *pre-foreclosure events* (a deed-in-lieu of a foreclosure or a short sale, for example), Fannie Mae requires a four-year waiting period, which can be reduced to two years with extenuating circumstances.

Bankruptcies are also viewed as major derogatory credit. The two most common types of bankruptcies that are seen in conjunction with an individual's mortgage loan application are Chapter 7 and Chapter 13. **Chapter 7 bankruptcy** is sometimes referred to as a *liquidation bankruptcy*, as the debtor may need to liquidate assets in certain circumstances to satisfy creditors. **Chapter 13 bankruptcy** is sometimes referred to as a "wage-earner plan" because the debtor is required to enter into a repayment plan that generally lasts <u>five years</u>. When the bankruptcy has been completed satisfactorily, it is "discharged." Unsuccessful Chapter 13 plans will result in the case being "dismissed," with the borrower still owing the debt. Fannie Mae and Freddie Mac both require a significant amount of time – called a *seasoning period* – to pass between the disposition of a Bankruptcy and the individual becoming eligible for a conforming mortgage loan. For example, Fannie Mae requires a four-year waiting period from the discharge of a Chapter 7. For a Chapter 13, the seasoning requirement is two years from discharge or four years from dismissal date. FHA is a bit more lenient, allowing a two-year seasoning period from a Chapter 7 discharge.

Credit Scores

The use of credit scores in conjunction with traditional credit reports is required by Fannie Mae, Freddie Mac and other investors. Each investor may have specific requirements and/or eligibility criteria for using credit scores in the underwriting process depending on the loan program. Each of the three national credit bureaus provides a credit score based on the information that has been reported to them. The scores are based on a statistical analysis of risk due to use of credit, numbers of open credit accounts, numbers of credit inquiries, derogatory credit (including bankruptcy and foreclosure) and other factors. Credit scores provide an underwriter with an initial assessment of risk.

Credit scores range from about 320 to 850 depending on the bureau. The higher the score, the better the credit. For Fannie Mae and Freddie Mac transactions, we use the middle score (numerically) as the risk indicator on the loan. If there are multiple applicants, we'll use the *lowest* of the middle scores to underwrite the loan. For applicants whose credit reports generate only two scores, we can use the lower of the two. The credit score used in underwriting analysis is called the *representative credit score* or *underwriting score*, depending upon the investor.

e. Qualifying Ratios (e.g., Housing, Debt-to-Income, Loan-to-Value)

In order to qualify for a mortgage loan, standard ratios are applied to the borrower's income and debts.

Housing Ratio (Front-End/Top Ratio)

As a benchmark, for loans being sold to Fannie Mae or Freddie Mac, the borrower's housing expense payment (also known as **PITI** – the total of monthly "P"rincipal, "I"nterest,"T"axes, and hazard, mortgage, and flood "I"nsurance payments – as well as homeowner's association fees when applicable) generally cannot exceed <u>28% of gross monthly income,</u>. This is referred to as the **housing ratio** or *housing expense ratio*. It is also referred to as either the *front-end ratio* or the *top ratio*. Be aware that unlike the debt-to-income ratio, this ratio is only concerned with the PITI on the applicant's primary residence. It does not include PITI for any additional mortgage loans that a borrower is still paying off. Also note that this is a benchmark ratio and can be exceeded in many cases if the applicant has positive characteristics (called **compensating factors**) to offset the higher housing ratio. Automated underwriting systems can assist in evaluating compensating factors.

Housing Ratio Calculation **= PITI on Primary Residence ÷ Gross Monthly Income**

Debt-to-Income Ratio (Back-End/Bottom Ratio)

The PITI plus all other monthly debts (including revolving debts, installment debts, alimony and/or child support) generally cannot exceed 36% of gross monthly income without compensating factors. This is referred to as the **total debt-to-income ratio**, the *back-end ratio*, the *bottom ratio* or the *total expense ratio*. When looking at other recurring debts, we typically use the payment showing on the credit report. Be aware that this ratio includes debts and legal obligations but generally does not include other forms of spending. For example, the ratio does NOT include utility payments, food bills, educational expenses (other than student loans), childcare expenses (other than child support payments), medical insurance premiums or entertainment expenses.

Total Expense **= All Recurring Monthly Debt ÷ Gross Monthly Income**

IMPORTANT: The borrower must qualify on BOTH ratios. Thus, an applicant who has a significant amount of non-housing debt will need to accept a lower housing payment to avoid exceeding the total DTI guideline. For example, assume a borrower's gross monthly income is $4,000 per month and the borrower has $850 in non-housing debt. To calculate the maximum *housing payment* the borrower can qualify for under FNMA/FHLMC guidelines, we must do two calculations:

1) $4,000 x .28 = $1,120

2) $4,000 x .36 = $1,440 - $850 = $590

The borrower must accept the LOWER of the two answers above ($590) as the maximum housing payment. Why? Because a housing payment amount over that number will push the total debt-to-income ratio over 36% given the other outstanding debt payments the borrower must make each month.

Computing Gross Income

The steps involved with calculating the various ratios will depend, to some extent, on the manner in which the borrower is paid. For example, there are different steps involved depending on whether the person is paid weekly, every other week or twice per month.

Paid Twice Per Month

If the borrower is paid twice a month (semimonthly —i.e., on the 15th and on the final day of each month), take the gross income on the semimonthly paycheck, multiply it by 24, and divide that result by 12 to determine the gross monthly income.

Paid Biweekly

If the borrower is paid every other week (biweekly), the gross biweekly paycheck should be multiplied by 26, then divided by 12 to find the monthly income.

Paid Weekly

If the borrower is paid weekly, the weekly gross pay should be multiplied by 52 weeks, then divided by 12 to find the monthly income.

Paid Hourly

If the borrower is paid on an hourly basis, the hourly rate should be multiplied by the number of hours worked per week to determine the weekly gross pay; then, the weekly gross pay is multiplied by 52 weeks, then divided by 12 to determine the monthly income. Any overtime hours that can be verified as continuous over a two-year period should be included at the appropriate overtime rate when making this calculation.

LTV, CLTV, HCLTV

The loan-to-value ratio (LTV) is determined by dividing the loan amount by the lower of (1) the purchase price or (2) the appraised value of the subject property.

LTV = **Loan Amount ÷ Property Value**

In some cases, if the loan-to-value ratio exceeds a certain amount, the borrower may be required to meet additional requirements in order to obtain the loan (e.g., mortgage insurance, tax escrows, insurance escrows).

Generally, as the risk on a loan increases, the loan-to-value for which the borrower is eligible decreases. This is the reason why owner-occupied properties (lower risk) can qualify at 95% LTV or more but investment properties (higher risk) are limited to 75% in many cases.

If there is more than one lien on a property, we must calculate what is referred to as **combined loan to value (CLTV),** also known as the *total loan to value (TLTV)*. This is done by adding the loan amount of the first lien plus the loan amount of the subordinate lien(s) and dividing that result by the purchase price or appraised value, whichever is less.

CLTV/TLTV = **(Loan Amount 1 + Loan Amount 2) ÷ Value**

In a case where there are multiple liens against a property and one of them is a home equity line of credit (HELOC) that is still in *draw period* (i.e., the borrower still has access to draw funds from the line of credit), we must calculate what is called **Home Equity Line of Credit Combined Loan-to-Value (HCLTV)**. This is done by adding the loan amount of the first lien plus the credit limit of the HELOC and dividing that result by the purchase price or appraised value, whichever is less.

HCLTV/HTLTV = **(Loan Amount 1 + HELOC Limit) ÷ Value**

For example: Jacob is purchasing a home for $100,000, and the property appraises for $105,000. Jacob will have two mortgage loans – the first lien will be $75,000 and the second lien will be $15,000.

LTV of the first mortgage: $75,000 loan amount ÷ $100,000 purchase price = 75% LTV

LTV of the second mortgage: $15,000 loan amount ÷ $100,000 purchase price = 15% LTV

CLTV/TLTV: $75,000 first mortgage + $15,000 second mortgage = $90,000 ÷ $100,000 purchase price = 90% CLTV

HCLTV/HTLTV: Now let's assume that in the above scenario, the second lien is actually a HELOC with a credit limit of $20,000. (Jacob is only drawing $15,000 at the closing, leaving an additional $5,000 available to draw at a later date.) To compute the HCLTV, we add the $75,000 first-lien balance plus the $20,000 HELOC credit limit to get $95,000. $95,000 ÷ 100,000 purchase price = 95% HCLTV.

Finally, please note that we only take into account the purchase price of the property for purchase transactions OR, in some cases, refinance transactions where the borrower has owned the property for fewer than 12 months. Purchase price does not factor into any refinance transaction where the borrower has owned the property for greater than <u>12 months</u>; in those cases, we use the appraised value to determine LTV/CLTV/HCLTV.

Occupancy

It is worth mentioning that, in order for a property to be considered owner-occupied, the borrower must move in within <u>60 days</u> of closing in order to avoid being in violation of the terms of the note and mortgage.

f. Ability-to-Repay Mortgage Rules

As was mentioned in a previous chapter, Dodd-Frank requires mortgage lenders to verify a borrower's ability to repay a loan before extending credit. In order to determine a borrower's ability to repay a loan, the following items must be included in the underwriting analysis:

- Credit history.

- Current and reasonably expected income.

- Current liabilities/obligations.

- Debt-to-income ratio or residual income.

- The monthly payment for any other mortgage(s) on the property.

- If the loan is an ARM or has negative amortization, the loan must be underwritten to the fully indexed rate for a fully amortizing loan.

Alternatively, a lender is presumed to be in compliance with the ability-to-repay requirements if the loan is a *qualified mortgage loan (QM)*.

The requirements for a QM are, in general:

- No negative amortization.

- No balloon payments (except for *small creditors*, defined by the CFPB as institutions that make no more than 500 first-lien mortgage transactions per year and have less than $2 billion in assets).

- Income and financial resources must be verified and documented.

- For ARMs - must be underwritten as a fully amortizing loan at the maximum interest rate that the loan can adjust to in the first five years.

- Maximum loan term of 30 years.

- Maximum back-end debt-to-income ratio of 43% (except for loans held in portfolio by small creditors, as defined above or for loans eligible for sale to government-sponsored enterprises such as Fannie Mae and Freddie Mac).

- A maximum of 3% of the loan amount in "points and fees."

Violations of the ability-to-repay provisions provide the consumer with a life-of-loan defense to foreclosure. In other words, mortgagors in foreclosure can assert that the lender did not properly verify their ability to repay the loan and seek damages as long as the loan remains in force. However, QM loans receive *safe-harbor* status and are deemed to comply with the ability-to-repay rules, thereby significantly reducing threat of legal action.

The ability-to-repay rules apply to all *consumer-purpose mortgages* except home-equity lines of credit (HELOCs), reverse mortgages, timeshare loans or temporary financing. Loans made for business purposes are also exempt from these requirements.

g. Tangible Net Benefit

Refinancing can be a good choice for many applicants, and there are many reasons to refinance a mortgage. For example, someone may be looking for a lower rate and mortgage payment or might be looking to pay off higher interest debt, such as credit cards (in which case, the possibility exists that the rate on the new mortgage loan may actually be higher than that on the existing loan). Often, people may want to shorten the term of their loan (i.e. go from a 30-year term to a 15-year term) or take cash out to help their children pay for college.

Whatever the reason for refinancing, borrowers must be receiving some sort of positive outcome by doing so, otherwise known as a *tangible net benefit*; that is, there must be facts about the new loan that make it in the interests of the applicant to proceed.

Often, we measure tangible net benefit through rate reduction, but there are other benefits as well, such as the cash-out or term change discussed above. One of the considerations that you should look at as a mortgage loan originator is the amount of time that it will take the applicant to recover the costs associated with the refinance through any payment savings. If the applicant is reducing payments by $20 a month but paying $3,000 in loan costs to do so, it will take the borrower 150 months to recoup the cost through savings. Considering the average loan life is five to seven years, one would be hard pressed to find a tangible net benefit in that loan.

Refinancing a loan with no tangible benefit to the borrower is called **loan flipping**, which is an abusive practice and considered loan fraud. Loan flipping is a form of **equity stripping** - a practice where the applicant's equity is taken away by a mortgage lender. Equity stripping can come in many forms, but in all cases is viewed as predatory lending and must be avoided.

2. Appraisals

The purpose of the property appraisal is to document that the property has sufficient value to support the mortgage debt.

Appraisal Methods

The appraiser uses three approaches in determining his or her *opinion of value* (appraisals are just that – opinions developed by a state licensed or certified appraiser):

- Sales comparison approach.
- Income approach.
- Cost approach.

Sales Comparison Approach

In the **sales comparison approach** (also called the *market data approach*), value is determined by looking at the recent sale price of similar properties. All comparable sales (*comparables* or *comps*) should reflect market activity for similar properties. According to Fannie Mae, the appraiser's opinion of value must be developed from at least three comparable sales that have closed within the past year (although six months or less is preferable) and located within one mile of the subject property (for urban and suburban properties). The comps should be in the same price range, with the same basic size and design, as the subject property. If the sales comps are not truly comparable to the subject property, a detailed explanation is required from the appraiser. Large dollar adjustments require an explanation from the appraiser. The sales comparison approach to value is the one most often used in mortgage lending.

Income Approach

For income-producing properties, the appraiser derives his/her opinion of value of the property by dividing the income from the property by a *cap rate* percentage determined to be appropriate for the subject property. In this manner, value is determined by assuming that an investor will demand a certain annual rate of return (equal to the cap rate) on the overall purchase price investment.

Cost Approach

In the **cost approach** to appraisal, the appraiser estimates the value of the property by calculating the cost of rebuilding the property in its current condition on the same site. In essence, this is the cost of materials and construction minus any depreciation, plus the value of the site (land).

Reconciliation

In the **reconciliation** stage of the appraisal, the appraiser arrives at the final opinion of value. The appraiser estimates the value of the property by considering the results of the three approaches explained earlier. The three values are not averaged because the appraiser will give more weight to the approach that is most consistent with the intended use of the property which, in mortgage lending, is generally the sales comparison approach.

Easements

An **easement** is a formal right granted to another party allowing them to traverse or access a given property. Utility companies are often granted easements to access a property to maintain their infrastructure, such as electrical wires or cell phone towers. When recorded on the title of a property, an easement will remain permanently and will survive any transfer of title of that property.

Encroachments

An **encroachment** is a structure or portion of a structure that extends over the boundary line of a property onto another parcel. For example, fences that are built to separate properties without the aid of a surveyor often are not built on the property line and end up encroaching on a neighbor's property.

Ethical Appraising

Effective May 1, 2009, Fannie Mae and Freddie Mac agreed to adhere to the Home Valuation Code of Conduct (HVCC) that sets forth specific requirements regarding the appraisal process.

The goal of the HVCC was to assure independence in the valuation process by eliminating coercive and manipulative practices by mortgage lenders and brokers in attempts to influence appraisal reports.

The HVCC prohibited real estate licensees and mortgage brokers (and their loan originators) from selecting appraisers. In fact, no one in the sales function at a lender or broker (i.e. a loan officer) may speak with an appraiser on a transaction.

Creditors must also separate the appraisal function from the loan production function (defined in the code as "those responsible for generating loan volume or approving loans") and prohibit contact between the mortgage loan originator (or any other loan production employee) and the appraiser. This has led to the widespread use of Appraisal Management Companies (AMCs) to provide appraisal reports. AMCs serve as a middleman or "firewall" between mortgage lenders/mortgage brokers and appraisers,

As a result of the Dodd-Frank law, the HVCC was eliminated. However, it was replaced with the *Fannie Mae and Freddie Mac Appraiser Independence Requirements (AIR)*, which are almost identical to the HVCC. Note that the AIR also apply to FHA and VA loans.

In a mortgage transaction, the appraiser is working for the lender, NOT the borrower or seller. The appraiser prepares the report and submits it to the lender, but it is the lender (through the underwriter) who is responsible for the accuracy of all appraisal reports. If there is any question in the underwriter's mind as to the appraiser's estimate of value or the logic used in arriving at that estimate, the underwriter will often ask either for an additional comparable sale to be added to the report or that the appraiser expand on his or her comments inside the report to address the issue. Although asking an appraiser for clarification or needed corrections is an acceptable practice (when done by a non-production employee), it is a violation of both the Truth in Lending Act and the AIR to try to influence the appraiser's opinion of value on a given property.

Appraisers should not ever accept an appraisal assignment that involves property in which they have ownership or any other conflict of interest (appraising a home in which their parents reside, for example).

Appraisal Forms

The standard appraisal form used to appraise single-family homes is called the **Uniform Residential Appraisal Report** or *URAR*. It is also known as the *1004* because it is Fannie Mae form number 1004.

The standard appraisal form used to appraise condominiums is form 1073.

Appraisers are also required to complete a *market conditions addendum* to the appraisal report on all loans sold to Fannie and Freddie. This addendum is known as the 1004MC.

3. Title Report

Title insurance is a type of insurance coverage that protects against defects in title that were not listed in a **title report** or abstract. The title report or abstract is a document typically prepared by an attorney or title company setting forth the condition of title. An owner's policy of title insurance does more than just set forth the condition of title and actually protects the owner from claims against the owner's ownership interest. A lender's policy of title insurance protects the lender from claims against the priority of the lien of the lender's mortgage.

Prior to closing, the lender will require that it determine satisfactory condition of title to the subject property. A *title search* is performed to determine any encumbrances or liens affecting the property by careful research regarding every known recorded document related to the current and prior ownership of the subject property. The search includes all public and court records of the county in which the property is located, including all property tax and assessment records.

In most cases, the title search is performed by a title insurance company (or an agent for the title insurance company), and the title insurance company will issue a title commitment for the subject property (also referred to as a *preliminary title report*, a *preliminary title commitment* or a *commitment for title insurance*).

Subordination

As we discussed elsewhere in this guide, the priority of a lender's lien on the property is determined by the age of that lien as measured by the date it was recorded in the public record in the county in which the property is located.

Occasionally, a borrower may have multiple liens on a property and lien priority may need to be altered through a legal agreement. For example, assume a borrower has two mortgages on a property and wishes to refinance only the existing first lien. By operation of law, the new mortgage loan would be in second lien position as it would be the newer of the two liens on the property. However, it's likely that the new lender would not be willing to make the loan to the borrower (and certainly not on the most favorable terms) if it were in second position. In this case, the lender funding the new loan can ask the existing lienholder – who has been occupying second position – to remain subordinate to the new lender's interest (that is, remain in second lien position even though the law would otherwise recognize that interest as superior to the new lender). If the existing second mortgage holder agrees, both parties would exercise a document called a *subordination agreement* that would then be recorded with the county upon the new loan closing to formally adjust the lien positions on the property.

4. Insurance: Hazard, Flood, and Mortgage

Depending on the risks confronting the lender and the borrower, receipt of a mortgage loan might be dependent upon the purchase of certain insurance policies.

Hazard Insurance

The borrower is required to maintain proper insurance to protect against possible loss or damage to the property that will be collateral for the mortgage. Insurance coverage may be for both dwelling and contents in case of fire, other damage, theft, liability for property damage and personal liability.

Mortgage lenders and investors require a certain amount of coverage for each residential dwelling from an acceptable insurance company. Typically, the property is required to be insured for the cost to rebuild it from scratch "as is" OR the loan amount, whichever is less. The easiest way to accomplish this in most states is to obtain *extended replacement cost coverage*.

The mortgagee clause of the hazard insurance policy must indicate that the lender's interest is properly covered at closing. Evidence of current hazard insurance coverage (typically a copy of the policy *declarations page*) will be required prior to closing.

If the loan-to-value ratio (LTV) is greater than 80%, a lender will typically require that the borrower pay 1/12 of the annual hazard insurance premium into escrow on a monthly basis as part of the monthly PITI payment. The lender then pays the hazard insurance company its premium on an annual basis from the escrowed funds.

Condominium homeowners associations are required to keep a *blanket policy* in effect that protects the entire structure. The hazard insurance premium for the blanket policy is included in the homeowners association dues paid monthly by condominium unit owners. Evidence of the association's blanket policy will be required at closing. Such evidence can usually be obtained by contacting the homeowners association representative or management agent for the condominium project.

Individual condominium unit owners are also required to purchase a special kind of contents coverage (sometimes called *HO-6 coverage* or *walls-in coverage*) to protect their furnishings and personal possessions and pay for restoration of the individual unit to its previous condition after a covered loss.

If required insurance is cancelled or not obtained, a lender can insure the property and force the borrower to pay for it. This insurance, known as **force-placed insurance,** has become controversial because it is often more expensive than what consumers can obtain on their own. Since it is designed to protect the lender's investment, it might lack the kinds of consumer-friendly features (such as sufficient coverage of personal liability and personal property) that a borrower might want.

As a result of the Dodd-Frank law, lenders must provide the borrower with two separate written notices in the 45-day period before establishing a force-placed policy and billing the borrower for it. These notices are designed to give the borrower ample time to reinstate their existing policy or find new coverage. The charges passed on to the borrower for this insurance must be reasonable.

Flood Insurance

Flood insurance is generally required by investors for any property with the principal structure situated in a Special Flood Hazard Area that has federally mandated flood insurance requirements – Zones A or V. If the property is in Zone A or V and flood insurance is available, then the borrower must obtain flood insurance for the benefit of the lender. Flood insurance must remain in effect for the life of the loan. Note that, if the property has land in a flood zone but the actual dwelling structure is not located in the special flood hazard area, no flood insurance is required.

In certain flood hazard areas, flood insurance may not be available because the community does not participate in the National Flood Insurance Program (NFIP). In those cases, loans on such properties would generally not be eligible for sale to secondary market investors.

The NFIP is administered by the Federal Emergency Management Agency (FEMA), and this agency is also responsible for maintaining the nationwide flood zone maps that are used to determine which zone a property occupies.

Mortgage Insurance

If the loan-to-value (LTV) of any conventional loan exceeds 80%, **private mortgage insurance (PMI)** is required. PMI protects the lender against losses that result from default by the borrower.

The amount of PMI premiums that will be due will depend on whether premiums are collected in one lump sum, on annual basis or on a monthly basis.

Single-Premium Plans

In a single-premium plan, the borrower pays one premium at closing, with no monthly premium thereafter.

To calculate the amount due at the closing on a single-premium mortgage insurance plan, you would take the loan amount and multiply it by the **MI factor**. The resulting dollar amount is what must be paid at closing.

In the world of mortgage insurance, a *factor* is a specialized term for insurance premium and is expressed as a percentage of the loan amount (i.e. a factor of 1.67 would be calculated as 1.67% or .0167 in decimal terms).

Generally speaking, the higher the coverage that is required by the investor on the loan and the higher the risk on the loan, the higher the factor that will need to be paid.

Single Premium = **Loan Amount x Factor**

Monthly Premium Plan

A monthly premium plan is the most frequently used payment plan option for mortgage insurance. In this type of plan, borrowers pay for mortgage insurance each month as part of the PITI house payment.

To calculate the amount due each month on a monthly premium plan, take the loan amount, multiply it by the factor, and divide the result by 12. For example, on a $150,000 loan with an MI factor of .72, the calculation would be: $150,000 x .72% (.0072) = $1080 ÷ 12 = $90/month.

Monthly Premium = (**Loan Amount x Factor**) ÷ 12

C. CLOSING

1. Settlement/Closing Agent

A closing (also referred to as *settlement*) can take place in a number of different locations depending upon the laws and customs of the state. For example, many states use title companies to handle closings. Some states – generally in the Western region of the country – use escrow companies, and still others may use attorney or real estate brokerage offices. The term *settlement agent* is a generic term that covers all bases.

The settlement agent acts on behalf of the lender to confirm that the borrower signs all of the loan documents and makes all other required closing deliveries (e.g., evidence of required insurance, adequate funds to close). The settlement agent is also involved in reviewing and approving any *power of attorney (POA)* that may be used at closing if a borrower cannot be present for some reason. If a POA is being used, the lender must also have approved its use in advance, and many lenders place strict limitations on such use. For example, a creditor generally requires that a borrower have a strong, sensible reason (such as being deployed for military service) to use a POA and may not allow them at all for certain transactions (such as cash-out refinances) due to the increased potential for fraud. Any power of attorney that is approved for use must be specific to the property and transaction in question and in force for only a limited period of time.

Finally, settlement agents are also required to provide the borrower the final Closing Disclosure (or HUD-1 Settlement Statement, as applicable) one day prior to settlement upon request. This disclosure is still subject to last-minute changes but must be presented with the best information available at the time of request.

2. Explanation of Fees

The loan originator should take responsibility for educating the borrower regarding the types of fees paid in connection with the mortgage loan. These fees should be described early in the origination process so the borrower will have a clear understanding of the following fees and any others paid at closing:

- Origination charges.
- Discount points.
- Closing costs.
- Prepayment penalties.

Origination Fee

An **origination fee** is a fee retained by the creditor and/or loan originator company (e.g. a mortgage broker) for the work involved in the evaluation, preparation and submission of a proposed mortgage loan. On the Loan Estimate and Closing Disclosure, we disclose origination charges in dollar amounts only, and they may be broken out into up to 13 individual charges in Box A. Origination charges are limited to 1% of the loan amount for VA loans.

Discount Points

Discount points are amounts charged by a creditor in order to increase its effective yield on the loan.

Discount fees are disclosed on the Loan Estimate and Closing Disclosure in Box A as both a dollar amount AND as a percentage of the loan amount. One discount point is equal to 1% of the total loan amount, although discount charges may also total to some fraction of a percentage of the loan amount (e.g. 1.274%).

From a borrower's perspective, discount points are paid to achieve a lower interest rate; without the payment of the discount points, the interest rate would be higher for the life of the loan.

Achieving a lower interest rate for the life of the loan by paying discount points is referred to as a *permanent buydown* of the rate. Achieving a lower interest rate for a short time at the beginning of the loan is called a *temporary buydown*, and the most common form of this is referred to as a *2-1 buydown* where the borrower's rate is reduced by 2% in the first year of the loan, 1% in the second year and then the actual rate is charged for the remainder of the loan term.

Discount points must be bona fide. That is, they must actually reduce the borrower's interest rate by an industry-standard amount to be legally recognized as a discount. A typical benchmark is that for each discount point paid in a permanent buydown, the borrower's rate is reduced by 1/8% to ¼%.

Closing Costs

Also referred to as *settlement costs*, **closing costs** are all of the costs related to closing except the prepaid or escrow items. Some examples of closing costs include:

- Origination charges.
- Discount points.
- Real estate sales commission.
- Attorney fees.
- Survey charge.
- Title insurance premiums.
- Agency closing fee (payable to title company).
- Appraisal fee.
- Credit report.
- Termite report cost.
- Loan amortization schedule cost.
- Recording fees.
- Document preparation fee.
- Mortgage insurance premiums.
- VA funding fee.
- Loan transfer or assumption fee.

By financing closing costs, the borrower reduces the amount of cash required at closing. On the other hand, by financing closing costs, the borrower incurs higher total costs because those costs bear interest over the life of the loan.

If the borrower prefers to reduce total costs (as opposed to upfront costs), it is always better to pay amounts up front instead of financing those amounts and incurring interest costs.

Prepayment Penalties

Some loans provide **prepayment penalties**, which are fees that must be paid by the borrower if the loan's principal is repaid in full prior to the loan's expiration.

The prepayment penalty is intended to discourage the borrower from repaying the loan early. When a loan is repaid early, the lender/investor loses the opportunity to continue earning interest on the principal amount for the balance of the intended life of the loan. The prepayment penalty must be disclosed as part of the Truth in Lending disclosure and on a separate disclosure.

The prepayment penalty is calculated by multiplying the outstanding principal amount of the loan by the penalty rate. For example, if a 30-year $200,000 loan has a prepayment penalty equal to 3% for the first 12 months of the loan, 2% for the second 12 months of the loan and 1% for the third 12 months of the loan, then:

- If the borrower repays the loan within the first 12 months, the prepayment penalty will equal 3% multiplied by the outstanding principal amount of the loan at the time of prepayment.

- If the borrower repays the loan during months 13 through 24, the prepayment penalty will equal 2% multiplied by the outstanding principal amount of the loan at the time of prepayment.

- If the borrower repays the loan during months 25 through 36, the prepayment penalty will equal 1% multiplied by the outstanding principal amount of the loan at the time of prepayment.

- If the borrower repays the loan during months 37 through 360, there will be no prepayment penalty.

3. Explanation of Documents

Prior to the closing, the lender's closing department prepares the closing documents and delivers them to the title company for execution by the borrower. The lender also delivers funds to the title company (either by check or wire transfer) for the closing. Closing documents include a promissory note and either a mortgage or deed of trust.

Promissory Note ("Note")

The **promissory note** is signed by the borrower and evidences the borrower's obligation to repay the debt to the lender. It contains all the material loan terms such as principal amount, interest rate, payment amount, prepayment penalty details (if any) and more. The note is not part of the public record and is not recorded with the county. When a loan is sold in the secondary market, it is the note that has value and is transferred between institutions. There is only one original note on any loan transaction.

Mortgage

The **mortgage** is signed by the borrower and creates a lien upon the subject property for the security of payment of the debt evidenced by the promissory note. In other words, if the applicant defaults on the note, the lender uses the terms of the mortgage to foreclose on the property. The borrower signing the mortgage is referred to as the *mortgagor*, and the lender receiving the mortgage is referred to as the *mortgagee*. It may be necessary to explain certain provisions included in the mortgage, such as the acceleration clause, the alienation clause and the defeasance clause.

The **acceleration clause** permits the lender to require the entire loan to be paid by the borrower upon the first instance of borrower default.

The **alienation clause** prohibits the borrower from transferring title to the mortgaged property without the consent of the lender. Any such transfer will cause default and permit acceleration of the loan.

The **defeasance clause** requires the lender to execute a release of lien or satisfaction of mortgage document upon full payment of the debt.

Deed of Trust

In a few states, a **deed of trust** (also called a *trust deed*) is used instead of a mortgage. The deed of trust may also be used to evidence security for the debt.

Under a deed of trust, the borrower actually conveys title to the secured property to a third-party trustee for the life of the loan. Upon repayment of the debt, the trustee executes a *reconveyance deed*, transferring title back to the borrower.

The mortgage or deed of trust (whichever is used) is recorded with the county in which the property is located in order to notify any interested person or party that the lender has a security interest in the property.

4. Funding

For a purchase transaction, once all required conditions are met, the loan funds are disbursed to the seller and other parties (e.g., title insurance company to pay for escrow fees and title insurance premiums, surveyor, other service providers) at the closing (sometimes referred to as *settlement*).

For refinances on owner-occupied primary residences, the loan funds are not disbursed to the borrower at the closing because the lender requires that the Truth in Lending Act three-business-day *right of rescission* period expire prior to disbursement/funding.

D. FINANCIAL CALCULATIONS USED IN MORTGAGE LENDING

1. Period Interest

Per-diem interest means the amount of daily interest payable under a loan. Loan originators need to calculate per-diem interest in order to determine the amount of interest payable by a borrower at closing.

A borrower's first monthly payment is typically due on the first day of the second month after closing. For example, if a loan closes on January 15, then the first monthly payment will be due on March 1.

Interest is payable in arrears, so (using the above example) the March 1 monthly payment will cover interest that accrued during the month of February.

At closing, the borrower will have to pay interest for the period from January 15 through January 31, since this interest will not be included in the March 1 monthly payment.

Per-diem interest is determined by first multiplying the principal amount of the loan by the interest rate to determine the annual amount of interest payable under the loan.

Next, that annual amount is divided by 360 days to determine the per-diem interest amount. (NOTE: Lenders typically calculate per-diem interest based on a 360-day year; when calculating per-diem interest, always divide by 360 days unless the lender instructs otherwise.)

Finally, the per-diem interest amount is multiplied by the number of days remaining in the month of closing, including the date of funding.

For example, assume that a loan with an original principal amount equal to $100,000 and an annual interest rate of 7% is funded on January 15. We must determine the amount of per-diem interest that will be payable by the borrower at closing.

- Total annual interest is equal to $7,000 ($100,000 x 7%).

- Per-diem interest is equal to $19.44 per day ($7,000 divided by 360 days).

- The total number of days for which per-diem interest is payable equals 17 days (January 15 through January 31 inclusive).

- The total amount of per-diem interest payable at closing equals $330.48 ($19.44 x 17 days).

2. Payments (Principal, Interest, Taxes, and Insurance; Mortgage Insurance, If Applicable)

Level monthly principal and interest payments are determined for the life of a fixed-rate loan based upon the amount of the loan, the interest rate and the length of the term of the loan.

Monthly payments may be derived on financial calculators by entering in the loan amount, interest rate and the term of the loan (whether in years or number of payments). In fact, any one of these four factors (i.e., monthly payment, loan amount, interest rate and loan term) can be determined by entering the other three factors into the financial calculator.

As discussed earlier, the interest portion of an amortized monthly payment decreases over the life of a loan; the principal portion of an amortized monthly payment increases over the life of a loan.

As principal is repaid, the amount of the borrower's **equity** (the value of the property less the amount of outstanding liens) increases.

Escrow Calculations

For most loans with a loan-to-value ratio above 80%, the lender will collect monthly **escrow payments** (also known as reserves or impounds), which are used by the lender to pay the property tax bill and hazard insurance premiums.

To determine the monthly property tax escrow payment required from the borrower, simply divide the total annual property tax bill by 12 months. The loan originator first may need to add together the amount of the two property tax installments in order to determine the total annual amount of property tax due.

To determine the monthly hazard insurance escrow payment required from the borrower, simply divide the annual hazard insurance premium by 12 months.

Lenders are permitted to collect and maintain no more than a <u>two-month</u> cushion (1/6 of a year) for property taxes in reserve.

To calculate the amount that must be deposited at closing for a property tax escrow reserve, the loan originator must first determine the monthly escrow payment. The loan originator can then determine the number of escrow payments that must be prepaid at closing in order to ensure that there is a sufficient balance in the escrow account when the upcoming property tax and/or property insurance bills are due. Finally, the creditor may add up to two additional monthly payments as a "cushion" to determine the amount that must be deposited at closing.

For example, consider the following scenario:

- The total annual property tax bill is $12,000.

- The property tax bill is paid in two installments due in June and September of each year.

- The loan closes (and funds) in January, meaning the first payment is due March 1.

Based on those facts, we can make the following determinations:

- The monthly escrow payment would be $1,000 per month ($12,000 divided by 12 months).

- When preparing for closing, we must look forward to determine how many payments the borrower will pay into escrow before the appropriate bills become due. Any shortage (plus the cushion) must be deposited into the account by the borrower at closing:

    o   We have six months of taxes due on June 1. By that time, the borrower will have paid three months of taxes into the escrow account (March, April and May; we cannot count June because of the grace period on that payment). That leaves a shortage of three months to cover the first installment.

    o   We have an additional six months of taxes due on September 1. The borrower will have paid three additional months of taxes into the account (June, July and August; we cannot count September for the same reason we could not count June above). That leaves an additional shortage of three months to cover the second installment.

    o   We also will collect two months of cushion payments.

As a result, the borrower will deposit a total of eight months' worth of impound payments into escrow, or in this case, $8,000 ($1,000 x 8).

Mortgage Insurance Calculations

Mortgage insurance premiums may be paid under various payment plans, as described earlier in these materials.

The loan originator must be able to calculate the amount of mortgage insurance premiums by multiplying the principal amount of the loan by a factor given for the PMI. That factor is always expressed as an annual premium rate.

For example, the loan originator may be informed that the PMI on a $200,000 conventional loan will be payable monthly at a rate of 0.75%. To determine the monthly premium, we multiply $200,000 by 0.75% to first determine the annual amount of PMI as $1,500. We then divide $1,500 by 12 months to determine the monthly PMI payment amount equal to $125 per month.

As another example, the loan originator may be informed that for a $120,000 FHA loan, the UFMIP will equal 1.75% and the monthly MIP will be payable at a rate of 0.85%. To calculate the UFMIP (the *upfront mortgage insurance premium*), we simply multiply $120,000 by 1.75%. As a result, the UFMIP is $2,100. To calculate the annual MIP (paid monthly), we first multiply $120,000 by 0.85% to determine the annual premium of $1,020. We then divide $1,020 by 12 months to determine that there will be a $85 MIP payable on a monthly basis.

3.   Down Payment

Generally, we consider the unfinanced portion of the purchase price to be the **down payment.** If we know the purchase price of the property and the loan-to-value ratio for the loan (see the next section below), then we can easily calculate the down payment.

For example, assume that the purchase price of a residence is $600,000. Also assume that the borrower's loan-to-value ratio will be 75%. This means that the amount of the loan equals $600,000 x 75%, or $450,000. Since the down payment equals the unfinanced portion of the purchase price, the down payment must equal $150,000 ($600,000 - $450,000).

If the borrower has already paid earnest money or some other amount that will be credited toward the purchase price, then the amount of cash required at closing will be reduced by any such amounts.

For instance, in the above example, the borrower has previously deposited $50,000 as earnest money with the seller's real estate broker. At closing, the borrower will be required to pay an additional $100,000 in order to close and purchase the property ($150,000 required down payment less $50,000 already paid as earnest money). The balance of the funds required to close will be paid by the lender advancing the loan proceeds.

4. Loan-to-Value (Loan-To-Value, Combined Loan-to-Value, Total Loan-to-Value)

Although we have covered loan-to-value ratios elsewhere in this study guide, they are important enough to be reviewed again.

LTV

LTV means *loan-to-value ratio*. The loan-to-value ratio is determined by dividing the principal amount of the loan by the lower of (1) the purchase price or (2) the appraised value of the subject property. As an example, consider a scenario in which all of the following are true:

- The contractual purchase price of a residence is $400,000.

- The appraised value of the residence is actually $380,000.

- The loan amount is $300,000.

Given the figures mentioned above, the loan-to-value ratio would be 78.9% ($300,000 divided by $380,000). We divided by $380,000 because we use the lower of the purchase price or appraised value to determine the LTV.

CLTV

CLTV means *combined loan-to-value ratio*. (This is also referred to as *TLTV* or *total loan-to-value ratio* for Freddie Mac loans.) The combined loan-to-value ratio is determined by dividing the sum of the outstanding principal amounts of the loan and all subordinate mortgage debt (i.e., second mortgage, third mortgage, etc.) by the lower of (1) the purchase price or (2) the appraised value of the subject property. For example, consider a scenario in which all of the following are true:

- The purchase price and appraised value of the property is $500,000.

- The loan amount is $400,000.

- The borrower also is borrowing $50,000 from a relative. This loan will be secured by a junior mortgage recorded after the first mortgage.

In this example, the LTV on the first mortgage is 80% ($400,000 divided by $500,000). The CLTV (or TLTV) is 90% ($450,000 divided by $500,000).

HCLTV

HCLTV (or HTLTV for Freddie Mac loans) means *home equity line of credit combined loan-to-value ratio*. The HCLTV/HTLTV is determined by dividing the sum of the outstanding principal amount of the loan and the maximum available balance of all subordinate mortgage debt (including any home equity line of credit [HELOC]) by the lower of (1) the purchase price or (2) the appraised value of the property.

For example, imagine a scenario in which all of the following are true:

- The purchase price and appraised value of the property is $800,000.

- The loan amount is $600,000.

- The borrower is also taking out a home equity line of credit that will allow her to borrow up to $100,000. The HELOC is to be secured by a mortgage recorded after the first mortgage. At closing, the borrower will immediately draw $50,000 from the line of credit in order to close the loan.

- The borrower also is borrowing $50,000 from a relative. This loan will be secured by a junior mortgage recorded after both of the other mortgages.

Based on those facts, we can arrive at the following calculations:

- The LTV is 75% ($600,000 divided by $800,000).

- The CLTV/TLTV is 87.50% (first mortgage of $600,000 plus HELOC drawn amount of $50,000 plus mortgage from relative of $50,000 divided by the purchase price of $800,000).

- The HCLTV/HTLTV is 93.75% ($750,000 divided by $800,000). We use $750,000 because the maximum amount of available indebtedness is $600,000 + $100,000 + $50,000. Even though the borrower has only borrowed $50,000 under the HELOC so far, we still include the entire $100,000 available balance in our HCLTV calculation.

5. Debt-to-Income Ratios

The borrower's total debt-to-income ratio is equal to the monthly PITI (principal, interest, taxes and insurance) plus all other monthly debts divided by the borrower's monthly income. For example, consider the following scenario:

- The borrower is paid every other week (biweekly) with a paycheck where the gross pay equals $2,000.

- The borrower's monthly principal and interest payment under an amortized loan equals $600.

- The borrower's annual property tax bill equals $2,400.

- The borrower's annual hazard insurance premium equals $900.

- The borrower has a monthly auto loan payment of $200.

- The borrower owes annual child support of $1,200.

To calculate the borrower's debt-to-income ratio, first we determine the total amount of the borrower's monthly PITI plus all other monthly debts. In this example, we'd calculate the monthly PITI plus other debts as follows:

- Monthly PITI is given as $600.

- Monthly property tax equals $200 ($2,400 divided by 12 months).

- Monthly insurance premiums equal $75 ($900 divided by 12 months).

- So, monthly PITI equals $875 ($600 + $200 + $75).

- Other monthly debts include the auto loan payment of $200 and the child support payment of $100 ($1,200 annual obligation divided by 12 months).

- So, total monthly PITI plus all other monthly debts equals $1,175 ($875 + $200 + $100).

Next, we calculate the borrower's monthly income.

- Gross biweekly income is given as $2,000.

- Annual income equals $52,000 ($2,000 x 26 paychecks in a year).

- Monthly income equals $4,333.33 ($52,000 divided by 12 months).

Now we can calculate the borrower's debt-to-income ratio:

- Debt-to-income ratio equals 27.1% ($1,175 total monthly debt divided by $4,333.33 gross monthly income).

- This debt-to-income ratio would comfortably satisfy Fannie Mae or Freddie Mac requirements that the borrower's debt-to-income ratio be no greater than 36%.

Note that the borrower's housing ratio would only use the PITI and would not take any other debts into account. For the above example, the borrower's housing ratio would equal 20.2% ($875 total PITI divided by $4,333.33 gross monthly income). This housing ratio would again satisfy Fannie Mae's requirements that the borrower's housing ratio be no greater than 28%.

Remember: For exam purposes, in order to be eligible for financing, the loan must qualify under BOTH debt-to-income ratios. Thus, if applicants have a substantial amount of non-housing-related debt, they could be forced to accept a lower housing payment than the benchmark. For example, in the conventional conforming scenario, if an individual's non-housing-related debt exceeds 8% of his/her income, that person could not undertake a housing payment of 28% of their income, because the total amount of debt would be over on the total DTI ratio. (36% - 28% = 8% spread between the benchmark front and back-end ratios.)

NOTE: Fannie Mae and Freddie Mac allow the underwriter to exclude monthly payments for any <u>installment</u> loan with fewer than 10 payments remaining from the debt ratio. This exception only applies to installment loans, not leases or revolving debt. Additionally, non-credit-related obligations, such as utility bills, health insurance, auto insurance, etc., are not included in the applicant's debt-to-income ratio.

6. <u>Temporary and Fixed Interest Rate Buy-Down (Discount Points)</u>

Discount points are amounts charged by a lender to the borrower or other party (e.g., builder, seller, father or mother, etc.) in order to reduce the interest rate on the loan.

One discount point is equal to 1% of the total loan amount and generally reduces the borrower's rate by 1/8% to ¼%. (This is a benchmark figure and can vary depending upon the current state of the secondary market.)

Achieving a lower interest rate for the life of the loan by paying discount points is referred to as a *permanent buydown* of the rate.

A temporary buydown occurs when the loan's interest rate is reduced for a temporary period of time, generally three years or less. This reduction in rate is subsidized, either by a fee paid to the bank OR in the form of a higher final interest rate than would have been charged in a loan without the temporary buydown. We discussed the 2-1 buydown a few paragraphs ago. An additional type of temporary buydown is a *3-2-1 buydown*:

- The interest rate is reduced by 3% for year one.

- The rate is reduced by 2% for year two.

- The rate would then be reduced only 1% for year three.

- The interest rate contained in the note would then return for year four through the end of the loan term in a fixed-rate scenario.

7. <u>Closing Costs and Prepaid Items</u>

Borrowers may be required to pay additional amounts beyond the purchase price at closing in order to reimburse the seller for prepaid expenses. For example, in some states, property taxes are paid in advance for the entire year. When the property is sold later in the year, the buyer will owe the seller for the amount of taxes attributable to the buyer's time of ownership and already paid by the seller. This amount will need to be credited to the seller at closing, and the borrower will be required to cover that additional amount, either through the borrower's own funds or through financing.

For example, consider the following scenario:

- Annual property taxes of $12,000 are payable in advance on January 1 of each year.

- The borrower will be closing on his acquisition of the property on July 1.

- At closing, the seller will receive a credit of $6,000 for prepaid property taxes.

  o Annual property taxes are $12,000.

  o Monthly property taxes equal $1,000 ($12,000 divided by 12 months).

  o The buyer is responsible for six months of property taxes for the year of closing (July 1 through December 31).

  o So, the buyer is responsible for $6,000 of property taxes ($1000 x 6 months) which will be credited to the seller at closing.

As a result, the borrower will owe $6,000 at closing in addition to the purchase price. Note that the above calculation is reversed for sates in which the property taxes are paid in arrears. In that case, the seller will owe the buyer a credit at closing for the taxes that have accrued during the time that the seller owned the property but will not be payable until after the buyer has taken title.

8. ARMs (e.g., Fully Indexed Rate)

As described earlier, adjustable-rate mortgages (ARMs) adjust interest rates at particular times during the life of the loan. A loan originator should be able to calculate the rate that will go into effect upon a certain adjustment date.

In order to calculate the rate, one must know the following values:

- The index rate at the date of adjustment.

- The margin that will be added to the index rate.

- Any interest rate adjustment cap, interest rate ceiling or interest rate floor that will be in effect at the adjustment date. The caps are referred to as the *initial cap*, the *periodic cap* and the *life cap* and are discussed in detail in Chapter Two of this guide.

The fully indexed rate is the rate determined by adding the index and the margin. The initial interest rate upon the making of the ARM is often lower than the fully indexed rate, as the lender provides an initial discount to the borrower in the form of a *teaser rate*. When calculating the rate at an adjustment date, always add the margin to the index rate as of the adjustment date; even though the index rate may be the same as it was at the date of the original loan, the rate may adjust because the *teaser rate* will cease. For example:

- At the making of a 3/1 ARM, the index rate is 3%. The margin is 2%. Even though the fully indexed rate would be 5%, the lender offers an initial "teaser rate" of 4% for the first three years of the loan.

- At the first adjustment date three years after the making of the loan, the index rate is still 3%. Now, the fully indexed rate of 5% (3% + 2%) will apply.

Knowing the Index

An index is simply a benchmark to which an ARM's rate is tied. A good loan originator needs to know the most common indexes in use in today's mortgage market. The most common indexes used in mortgage lending are described in Chapter Two of this guide.

9. Qualified Mortgage Monthly Payment Calculations

In order for a loan to meet the test to be a qualified mortgage (QM), the monthly payment for qualifying the borrower must be calculated based on the highest payment that will apply in the first five years of the loan. That qualifying payment (even if it is not the actual payment that the consumer will be required to make – such as on an ARM loan with a teaser rate) must result in a debt ratio that is no more than 43% unless otherwise exempt.

CHAPTER FOUR – ETHICS

A. ETHICAL ISSUES RELATED TO FEDERAL LAWS

1. Violations of Federal Law

As you have seen elsewhere in this guide, there are numerous federal laws that govern our actions as loan originators. While avoiding violations of law may seem like an easy thing to do, sometimes seemingly innocuous actions may cause unintentional violations. For example, when taking an application, the way that certain questions are phrased can get an unwitting loan officer into trouble.

Generally speaking, loan officers are advised to listen to their inner voice in all dealings with applicants and referral partners. If something seems questionable, it is wise to seek the advice of your manager or another trusted and knowledgeable source, such as an attorney. As with all actions that have ethical questions, a good rule of thumb is, "When in doubt, don't.'"

One of the things that MLOs and company owners must be aware of is the CFPB's focus on what has become known as **UDAAP** – Unfair, Deceptive or Abusive Acts or Practices. All entities that operate in the mortgage space are evaluated by regulators under this UDAAP standard and must operate free of practices such as misleading advertising, interfering with the consumer's ability to understand the transaction and/or concealing information from consumers that may result in them taking out a loan they cannot afford.

2. Prohibited Acts

RESPA

Lenders and loan originators must not compromise the interests of the borrower (or the investor) for the benefit of a referral source.

Even if a referral source is responsible for significant business opportunities, the beneficiary of those opportunities must report illegal or unethical activities committed by the referral source.

Under RESPA, referral sources cannot be compensated with kickbacks. It is important to note that a kickback need not be direct monetary compensation. Indeed, under RESPA, the provision of any *thing of value* in exchange for a referral (a donation to a referral source's favorite charity, for example) would be considered a kickback.

All parties to a real estate transaction must be very aware of potential violations of RESPA, as seemingly innocent business practices may in fact be violations of the law. For example, say a title company places a computer inside a mortgage lender's office. If that computer is solely used to transmit transactional data between the title company and the mortgage lender, this is an acceptable practice. HOWEVER, if the computer is used for other purposes in the mortgage lender's day-to-day operations, it could be a violation of RESPA because the title company could be construed as having provided that computer in return for the business given to it by the mortgage banker.

Similarly, if a mortgage broker and a real estate agent devise a joint advertisement that is published in the local paper and they split the cost of the advertisement on a pro-rated basis, it is an acceptable practice. If, however, the mortgage broker agrees to pay for the entire advertisement, or picks up a percentage greater than his or her participation warrants, that is a violation of RESPA because the broker has provided a "thing of value" (the ad) in exchange for the real estate agent referrals that it generates. Note in this example that, in order to be compliant with RESPA, the broker and real estate agent are required to pay exactly their share of the advertising cost. Thus, if 62% of the advertisement space featured the agent and 38% featured the broker, the agent must pay for 62% of the cost to the broker's 38%.

Gramm-Leach-Bliley Act

The Financial Modernization Act of 1999, also known as *The Gramm-Leach-Bliley Act* or *GLBA*, includes provisions to protect consumers' personal financial information held by financial institutions. (See the description of the GLBA earlier in Chapter One.)

The GLBA specifically prohibits **pretexting** (the use of false pretenses to obtain consumers' personal financial information). Loan originators seeking to expand their relationships with potential borrowers should always be forthright and honest about their motives with the prospective client. A loan originator should never seek information from a third party under false pretenses or by making fraudulent statements. This would include a fraud for convenience situation where the MLO has permission from the borrower to verify data with a third party, but that party requires that they speak directly with the borrower for permission. In that case, the mortgage professional would not be allowed to contact the third party and pretend to be the borrower to get the verification completed, even if the borrower knew of and approved the tactic.

3. Fairness in Lending

One of the biggest concerns of regulators, housing activists and industry in the present lending environment is making sure that all applicants have equal access to credit as required by fair lending law. It's important to note that equal access to credit is not synonymous with identical loan terms. In other words, as lenders, we are expected to take into account the various risk factors that determine how much borrowers may qualify for, the loan programs that they may be eligible to use and what interest rate they are charged. What is expected, however, is that similarly situated applicants receive similar loan terms without regard to protected class status, such as race, gender and religion. Thus, two applicants with similar credit profiles, similar down payment percentages, etc. should receive materially similar terms on a given loan product on the same day. Additionally, all individuals seeking information on or applying for credit should be treated equally. Thus, if one person is offered a beverage when coming into your office to speak with a MLO, ALL individuals should be offered a beverage in similar circumstances.

When looking for violations of fair lending law, regulators will compare terms given to borrowers with different demographic characteristics but similar financial situations to determine the risk for possible violations. Any discrepancies in loan structure (rate, total cost, etc.) should be directly attributable to a material fact on the loan application that is not related to prohibited basis information protected under the Fair Housing Act and ECOA.

Another key part of fairness in lending is ensuring that the borrower possesses a full and complete understanding of any potential conflicts of interest. For example, if a real estate agent will also be acting as a mortgage originator on the same transaction (permissible on conventional loans only, and only with investor approval), this must be fully disclosed to ***the applicant upfront.***

Working With Individuals With Disabilities and/or Limited English Proficiency

This is an area where there are a few federal laws (and many different state laws) that govern our behavior as MLOs. For example, disability is a protected class under the Fair Housing Act (prohibiting discrimination in all housing-related activities against those with disabilities), and the Americans With Disabilities Act (ADA) requires that we make reasonable accommodations to serve those with disabilities. While limited English proficiency isn't a protected class at the federal level on its own, treating those for whom English is a second language differently than native English speakers can certainly give rise to claims of discrimination based on race or national origin.

It's not always obvious to MLOs how best to serve the needs of these individuals, especially if originators are new to the business or don't have a lot of experience with such borrowers. Here are some examples of things you can do to put your clients at ease, facilitate transactions for everyone and avoid potential claims of discrimination:

- Treat people with disabilities identically to those without disabilities in terms of responsiveness and communication. Disabilities do not define the individual.

- Do not assume that an individual with disabilities needs assistance. For example, if you are working with borrowers who are using a walker, always ask if you can help them with anything before taking other action like grabbing their arm to steady them.

- If you are working with an individual who is using a prosthetic device and who offers the prosthetic in a handshake, shake the prosthetic just as naturally as you would the hand of an individual without a prosthetic.

- If a non-native English speaker has difficulty working through the financing process and/or the application, consider offering translation services through another employee at your firm who speaks the applicant's native language or through a third-party translation service.

- If you need to meet in person with an individual who uses a wheelchair and your office is not fully accessible, schedule a meeting in a place where the client has full accessibility and where transaction privacy can be maintained.

- If your client has a service animal, do not pet the animal or address it without first asking the individual.

- Never ask someone with a service animal about their disability. If you have doubts as to the validity of the service animal, the only permissible questions are, "Is this a service animal that is required due to a disability?" and "What tasks has the animal been trained to perform?"

- Companies should consider making their websites ADA-compliant for people with vision limitations; for example, implementing screen-reader technology and providing a method for individuals to adjust font size.

4. Fraud Detection

As a loan originator, you are the first line of defense against mortgage fraud. Fraud is a serious crime that is punishable by a fine of up to $1 million and 30 years in prison per count, yet it remains a large problem in the lending industry.

The definition of mortgage fraud is "causing a lender to fund or purchase a loan it may not have funded or purchased if it was made aware of all of the material facts." Fraud can take many forms – from altered documentation to false tax returns to failing to disclose debts on the loan application. One thing that all fraud has in common is intentional **misrepresentation**, which involves either a misstatement or omission of a fact that is important to the lender's credit decision.

There are two types of mortgage fraud: **fraud for property** (also called *fraud for housing*) and **fraud for profit**.

Fraud for property is more common and is typically perpetuated by borrowers. Fraud for property involves misrepresentation with the intent of gaining the property involved in the fraud scheme and, thus, is less likely to result in loan-level monetary loss to the creditor(s).

As its name insinuates, fraud for profit involves misrepresentation with the intent of gaining money through the affected transaction, is typically perpetuated by industry insiders and often involves more than one participant (such as a loan officer and an appraiser or attorney). Fraud for profit generally results in a large monetary loss for the creditor.

It is important to note that there is a difference between fraud and **negligence**, and that difference is intent. In order for a charge of fraud to be considered, the perpetuators must have knowledge that their actions are wrong and possess intent to deceive. Negligence – though it can still be a crime if serious enough – is unintentional misrepresentation.

5. Mortgage Fraud Categories and Red Flags

Asset and Liability Fraud

Bank statements and other asset documentation can often tip us off to potential misrepresentation on a loan. One of the biggest indicators that something may be amiss is a borrower whose asset position is out of line with his or her income. For example, an applicant who makes $40,000 a year but has $250,000 in non-retirement deposit accounts is worthy of underwriter scrutiny. This situation is NOT prima facie evidence of fraud, but an underwriter might ask the applicant to explain and document how those assets were accumulated (for example, proof of an inheritance if that is the explanation given). Failure to adequately explain or prove the source may be an indicator of an undisclosed loan or gift for down payment. Other tipoffs to possible asset or liability misrepresentation include:

- Borrower has a joint bank account with someone who is not a family member or a party to the transaction. This may indicate an asset-rental scheme or a straw buyer scenario.

- Alterations to bank statements or data integrity issues (such as the ending balance on one month's statement not matching the opening balance on the next month's statement) reflect poorly executed fraud-for-property attempts by the borrower.

- Transaction details on a bank statement may reveal undisclosed debt, so it's important to review statements in their entirety for recurring payments that don't correspond to debts showing on the 1003.

- The applicant's tax returns list a Schedule E deduction for rental property or a student loan interest deduction, but no real estate owned or student loans are listed on the application by the borrower.

Income and Employment Fraud

One of the most common types of borrower-perpetuated fraud is misrepresentation of income and/or employment. This can take many forms, from a paystub with altered earnings to wholly fictitious employment and earning documentation. Tipoffs that income or employment may be misrepresented include, but are certainly not limited to:

- Tax withholdings not commensurate with the gross income listed on the paystub and/or the gross income not corresponding with the net income after deductions.

- The check date listed on the stub does not correspond to the pay period for which it is supposed to cover.

- Gross earnings not commensurate with job title and/or length of time on job.

- Paycheck numbers are sequential across multiple pay periods.

- A completed verification of employment form is returned by the borrower instead of HR.

- Employer's address listed only as a P.O. Box and/or employer not located in a reverse directory search.

- Borrower's job title is generic, and the applicant cannot explain his/her duties when asked.

- Generic outgoing voicemail message on employer phone number.

Occupancy Fraud

Occupancy fraud has been a growing problem since the housing market crash of 2008. Applicants have many different reasons for misrepresenting occupancy. For example, a borrower who is purchasing an investment property may not have the larger down payment necessary to secure financing or may not want to pay the higher interest rates associated with non-owner-occupied financing. Applicants who do not have sufficient income to qualify for a home they wish to live in may indicate it is an investment property so they can use purported rental income from the property to help them qualify for the mortgage (this is often done in tandem with an undisclosed gift for all or part of the down-payment). Red flags for possible occupancy fraud include:

- Occupancy on the 1003 is listed as investment, but the borrower does not currently own a primary residence.

- Borrower claims he/she will be moving out of a single-family home and into a multi-unit property in the same area.

- The property is listed as a primary residence on the 1003, but the property insurance declarations page indicates it is a landlord's policy.

- Borrower is purchasing a property from a family member as a primary residence, and that property is currently in foreclosure.

- The borrower lists the occupancy as a second home, but the property is located in close proximity to their primary residence and is not in an area where second homes are common.

- Applicant is purchasing a home as a primary residence and is moving out of a larger home but retaining it as an investment property.

Keep in mind that the red flags listed above are just some of the many ways that potential misrepresentation may appear in a loan transaction. Also, the presence of red flags does not automatically mean that misrepresentation or fraud is occurring. The first step is to assess the situation by asking the applicant to explain or clarify any inconsistencies or questions that have arisen in the loan documentation. Under no circumstances should an MLO accuse the applicant of fraud without clear and concrete evidence and direction from company management. In many cases, the Bank Secrecy Act will require filing of a Suspicious Activity Report when certain misrepresentation exists on a file, and we will be prohibited from disclosing anything related to this to the borrower. A red flag is simply an indicator that further explanation is necessary; it is not proof positive that any wrongdoing is occurring.

What Do I Do When I Think a SAR Is Necessary?

ALL suspicious activity should be reported to the appropriate BSA compliance personnel per your company-specific anti-money laundering policy. The law requires companies to train all staff annually on BSA compliance, and you should be aware of what those processes and procedures are. When in doubt, err on the side of reporting issues; it is not for the MLO to decide whether the situation rises to the level of filing a SAR (that's what your BSA compliance officer is for), but nothing can be done without first being reported. It all starts with you.

6. Advertising

While mortgage professionals must be well-versed in the rules and regulations that govern our industry, this is typically not true for the consumers we serve. In fact, consumers often rely on published advertisements – whether in print or on the Internet – for information about the financing process. Thus, it is important for the information contained in these advertisements to be truthful and balanced.

As you have read elsewhere, the Truth in Lending Act has many rules for what must be advertised in different situations. Misleading advertising, offering rates that are not actually available, or any *bait-and-switch tactic* in which the lender offers a loan or cost structure that then changes at or prior to closing with no valid reason are examples of illegal advertising and can be considered predatory lending practices.

Remember that TILA requires all print advertisements containing an interest rate to also contain an annual percentage rate (APR) expressed in the same font and type-size as the interest rate. There are also other *trigger terms* that require disclosure of additional facts about the loan being advertised, as mentioned elsewhere in this guide.

Finally, the Fair Housing Act's advertising provisions require that advertisements be fair and inclusive. For example, if an advertisement contains pictures of people who are represented as customers of a real estate brokerage or mortgage lender, those people should be representative of society as a whole. In other words, different races, genders and familial statuses should be depicted in the ad, so as not to make someone viewing the ad feel unwelcome. Additionally, advertisements should not target people based on protected class status. Thus, advertising ARM loans only in predominately minority neighborhoods while advertising fixed-rate loans only in non-minority areas would not only be an unethical advertising practice but would also violate the Fair Housing Act.

7. Predatory Lending and Steering

Although many people equate the term "predatory lending" with "mortgage fraud," the two are not synonymous. Although it is very possible for both to be present in the same transaction, it is not always so. When we refer to predatory lending, we are talking about a wide range of unethical behaviors and abusive practices that can leave borrowers unable to pay the loans that they have received and/or unnecessarily take away the equity in their homes. Here are descriptions of some of the most egregious predatory lending practices:

- Excessive fees: Points and fees are costs not directly reflected in a mortgage's interest rate. Because these costs can be financed, they are easy to disguise or downplay. On predatory loans, fees often total more than 5% of the loan amount.

- Abusive prepayment penalties: Borrowers with higher-interest-rate loans have an incentive to refinance as soon as their situation improves. However, many subprime mortgages that were originated back in the days of the housing bubble carried a prepayment penalty (a fee for paying off a loan early). These are less common since passage of the Dodd-Frank Act, but they do still exist. Not all prepayment penalties are abusive, but one that is effective for more than three years and/or costs the consumer more than six months' interest would certainly fall into the predatory category.

- Loan flipping: This involves a lender refinancing a mortgage loan to generate fee income without providing any tangible net benefit to the borrower. Refinancing generates fee income to the lender, and these fees can quickly amount to thousands of dollars. Flipping can drain borrower equity and increase monthly payments -- sometimes on homes that were previously owned free and clear. Loan flipping is a form of *equity stripping,* in which applicants' equity is taken from them without cause or benefit.

Additionally, the practice of *steering* – discussed at length elsewhere in this book – is considered to be a predatory lending practice and is also a violation of the Truth in Lending Act as amended by Dodd-Frank.

B. ETHICAL BEHAVIOR RELATED TO LOAN ORIGINATION ACTIVITIES

1. Financial Responsibility

In mortgage lending, the term *financial responsibility* means that an individual has exhibited characteristics of being able to manage his/her own finances properly. This is an important concept and has been codified under the federal SAFE Act. For example, someone with a recent bankruptcy caused by financial mismanagement, or a pattern of delinquent credit accounts, may be judged unsuitable for licensure by the state(s) in which he or she wishes to do business. The thought behind this requirement is that people who will be advising others on financial matters should be well-versed in proper financial management in their own lives in order to be effective at their job.

Similarly, in a mortgage loan transaction, we as originators – assisted by underwriters – strive to determine whether our applicants have demonstrated an acceptable level of financial responsibility to qualify for the loan for which they have applied. We thoroughly review the applicant's credit report, bank statements and other documents to assist us in making this determination.

A key component of financial responsibility and consumer protection lies in looking for situations where monies from a closing are improperly distributed. For example, if one of the parties to a transaction directs the settlement agent to disburse funds to a third-party unexpectedly, that is something that needs to be addressed before the loan funds. For example, the borrower claims to be taking cash out of a property to pay off debt and the settlement agent is instructed to cut a check to a real estate brokerage; this could indicate that the consumer is actually in the process of purchasing another property that was not disclosed to the lender. In loans involving elderly borrowers, look for disbursements to home improvement contractors or other third parties that may indicate that the borrower is being taken advantage of; elder financial abuse is one of the most rapidly increasing crimes in the United States today.

2. Handling Consumer Complaints

Although good originators serve clients with honesty and integrity, treating each transaction as if it were their own, there will be the occasional consumer who is dissatisfied with the level of service received. As the saying goes, "You can't please all of the people all of the time" – even though that is our overarching goal as loan officers.

How one handles complaints when they do arise is often as much of a reflection on that individual's competence and character as is the number of complaints received. When faced with a consumer complaint, it is important to continue to act professionally, even if you feel the complaint is unjustified. Often, consumers are simply frustrated with a complex process that they feel they have no control over and are looking to have their fears addressed.

Regardless of the nature of the complaint, it is good practice to acknowledge the consumer's feelings (even if you don't agree with them), and communicate clearly about what is being done (or will be done) to address the situation. Many times, a simple explanation of what is happening and why will resolve the situation and stop it from being escalated to the point where the consumer will file the complaint directly with a regulator.

Sometimes, things do go wrong. In the case of a complaint that is justified, after acknowledging the issue, make sure to explain to the consumer what is being done to address it. In all cases, it is critical for a loan originator to be responsive and not attempt to ignore the situation, as that will escalate it. If you cannot resolve the complaint to the satisfaction of the consumer, seek assistance from your manager.

In any case, federal law requires all origination companies to maintain a record of all complaints received in a complaint log that can be made available to a state or CFPB examiner upon request. The log should include the facts of the complaint, the date received and its final disposition. If a regulator contacts your company about a complaint filed by a consumer on one of your loan files, you will likely need to work with your compliance department and/or management to assist in responding. All complaints received by the CFPB (and many state regulators) are forwarded to the company for a formal response. Needless to say, these should not be ignored.

Finally, when addressing complaints, keep in mind the principles of fair lending do apply. Your process for handling consumer complaints should be uniform without regard to the consumer's race, color, gender, religion or any other prohibited basis.

3. Company Compliance

Complying with federal and state mortgage laws is crucial for companies to stay in business and operate in a safe and sound manner. While ethical companies do everything in their power to remain compliant, sometimes there are breakdowns in the compliance management system that may result in violations of law. Because every company is expected to monitor their own compliance management system on a constant basis, it is likely that any such violations may be identified by the company itself well ahead of any regulator examination. In such cases, it may be tempting to correct the problem that caused the violations and attempt to conceal the truth of what occurred. However, this is not the proper course of action.

Regulators expect companies that have identified such violations to *self-report* them. That is, notify the regulatory body in question about what happened, what has been done to correct the situation with affected consumers and what procedures are being put in place to ensure the violations do not reoccur. Companies that self-report receive penalties that are much less harsh than those that attempt to conceal violations, only to have them uncovered in their next regulatory examination.

4. Relationships With Consumers, Your Company and Investors

Mortgage professionals are generally considered to have a **fiduciary relationship** with the consumers they serve. This means that they must put the well-being of their clients ahead of their own financial gain.

Fiduciaries must follow all lawful instructions given to them by their clients and must ensure that all confidential information received from the consumer remains private. Loan originators cannot seek to profit from information provided to them by their client, nor can they use that information in a manner that might harm the client. For example, loan originators working with a client on a purchase transaction cannot take the amount of an offer made on a property by the client and contact the real estate agent to make a slightly higher offer in the hopes of securing the property for themselves. That is unethical behavior and would violate the fiduciary relationship.

The loan officer's fiduciary duties can involve both legal and ethical questions, and violations of the fiduciary relationship can often be avoided by following the "golden rule:" Treat your clients as you would want to be treated if you were in their situation.

On the other hand, it's important to note that you have a responsibility to protect your company and/or the investor from misrepresentation as well. If a consumer tells you something that is material to the transaction, it is incumbent upon you to make sure that the underwriter on the file (and any other appropriate personnel) are notified of the situation even if the consumer does not wish for that to happen. For example, assume that you're working with a file where gift funds are going to be used for a down payment. You explain the gift letter requirement to the borrower, and he or she says, "I'll get my parents to sign it, but it won't be a big deal that they're actually going to make me pay the money back, right?" You clarify that, yes, gifts need to be actual gifts. The borrower then indicates that his/her parents won't provide the money unless it is to be paid back. You now have material knowledge that the so-called gift is actually an unsecured loan. That would not be an acceptable source of down payment in the vast majority of cases. Withholding that information from the underwriter is willful misrepresentation and you can now be considered complicit in a borrower scheme to defraud. The same would be true if you, for example, became aware that the borrower's employment has been terminated after the final verification of employment but before the closing actually occurs and you failed to inform the closer and underwriter.

Cybersecurity Issues

Today's mortgage industry is being victimized by bad actors who commit fraud or other criminal acts by exploiting vulnerabilities in our computer systems or through electronic communication. For example, one major wire fraud scheme that is prevalent today involves hacking into a real estate agent's email and monitoring communications on transactions in progress. Once a transaction gets close to closing, the criminal sends an email posing as the real estate broker or mortgage originator with fraudulent wiring instructions to the buyer of a property. If the scam is successful, the buyer will wire the balance of the cash required to close the transaction to the criminal instead of the settlement agent, and the money will be gone, often leaving the buyer/borrower with insufficient funds to consummate the transaction.

There are a few things you can do to mitigate the risk of a cybersecurity incident:

- Don't click on links or open file attachments in emails that you are not expecting.

- Even if you are expecting the message, always review the actual email address from which a message was sent before clicking links or opening attachments. (Fraudsters often impersonate actual people by using email addresses one letter off from the legitimate sender's account).

- Advise all borrowers to contact their agent, attorney or mortgage originator by phone before wiring funds. Confirm all wiring instructions personally before wiring – don't rely on email instructions alone.

- Use only authorized company email accounts to communicate. If this is impossible, set up two-factor authentication on all email accounts used to communicate professionally to confirm all logins are actually made by you.

- Do not share personal information on borrowers via email unless it is encrypted. (In addition to creating cybersecurity problems, such sharing also violates the Gramm Leach Bliley Act and potentially the Fair and Accurate Credit Transactions Act.)

5. Truth in Marketing and Advertising

In Chapter One of this guide, we thoroughly reviewed the Mortgage Acts and Practices advertising rule (also called the *MAP Rule*), implemented by the CFPB's Regulation N. From a legal perspective, this rule prohibits misrepresentation of any material facts when advertising loan products. Beyond legal mandates however, there are ethical issues at play as well. For example, when dealing with a loan product that may pose a higher default risk to a borrower – an ARM loan, for example – our marketing and advertising of that product should discuss the possible risks involved while also reviewing borrower benefits.

The key question when discussing truth in advertising is, "Does the potential applicant fully understand both the risks and rewards associated with the product?" This can only come with a balanced approach. Additionally, when advertising to consumers, it is good and ethical business practice to use simple terms to describe often complex financial topics. For example, you can say, "The loan's interest rate is subject to a variable index with a margin added to it," which the average consumer won't understand. Alternatively, you can say, "The interest rate can increase or decrease over time, which will have a direct impact on how much you pay each month." They're both accurate statements, but one of them is understandable by just about anyone.

6. Consumer Education

Consumers who fully understand the loan obligations that they are undertaking are far more likely to be successful homeowners than those who don't. Thus, the impact of consumer education cannot be understated.

This is another case where legal requirements and ethical considerations may differ. We know that Regulation Z requires all loan originators to provide a list of homeownership counseling organizations to all applicants within three business days of application on loans subject to TILA. While providing this required list satisfies your legal obligation, you still have an ethical obligation to evaluate whether the consumer understands the nature of their obligation throughout the origination process. If you have doubts about whether there is a thorough understanding, you can serve as a conduit for that education by explaining all of the disclosures provided to the consumer in plain language, taking the time to thoroughly review the promissory note that the applicant will be executing at closing and – just as with truth in advertising – provide balanced information on the risks associated with the loan product, contrasting those risks to the rewards that may be involved.

View the mortgage transaction much like a surgeon must view a complex medical procedure – ensure that your client is making his or her decision from a position of informed consent; that is, ensure that borrowers understand the nuances of the product involved. If, after a thorough and complete explanation, you still feel as if the they might not understand the loan, it may be smart to suggest that they book a counseling appointment with one of the agencies on the list provided or secure the services of an attorney or financial advisor to protect their interests.

7. General Business Ethics

Business ethics (or corporate ethics) is the set of moral rules that govern how businesses operate and how they treat their employees and customers. Owners of financial institutions, including mortgage banks and brokerages, need to clearly lay out their principles and ensure that their employees understand them and adhere to them in their day-to-day duties. One of the simplest ways to communicate your corporate beliefs to employees and vendors alike is through the use of a **code of ethics**. This is, in essence, a form of "company law" that clearly articulates company expectations of the people who represent it, with specific penalties for violating the code.

Responsive, consumer-oriented companies not only have a code of ethics, but also train their staff on a regular basis (monthly or quarterly) on what is contained in the code, taking time to address situations in which the code was effective in preventing consumer mistreatment and/or highlighting areas where staff may need more effective training.

Finally, as the business world evolves, it is wise to periodically review and update your company's code of ethics to ensure that you are addressing emerging concerns as well as those that are more established.

For a good example of a code of ethics developed specifically with mortgage loan origination in mind, review that of NAMB – The Association of Mortgage Professionals at the following Web address:

http://www.namb.org/images/namb/Ethics/Code_Of_Ethics.pdf.

CHAPTER FIVE –
UNIFORM STATE CONTENT

A. SAFE ACT AND CSBS/AARMR MODEL STATE LAW

In addition to being tested on their knowledge of federal laws and regulations, all students who enroll to take the National Component examination will be tested on *uniform state content*. The uniform state content is based in large part on material from the SAFE Act, federal regulations known as Regulation H and a model law that many states have adopted as a way to facilitate and strengthen their licensing requirements. This chapter is based on material from those sources.

1. State Mortgage Regulatory Agencies

The SAFE Act encouraged the establishment of a **Nationwide Multistate Licensing System and Registry (NMLS-R)** (also called the Nationwide Mortgage Licensing System). The establishment of the system and registry was facilitated in part by two national regulatory organizations: The Conference of State Banks Supervisors (CSBS) and the American Association of Residential Mortgage Regulators (AARMR).

The NMLS-R was created with the following purposes in mind:

- To provide uniform license applications and requirements for state-licensed loan originators.

- To provide a comprehensive licensing and supervisory database.

- To aggregate and improve the flow of information between regulators.

- To provide increased accountability and tracking of loan originators.

- To streamline the licensing process and reduce regulatory burden.

- To enhance consumer protections and support anti-fraud measures.

- To provide free information about loan originators to consumers.

- To establish a means by which loan originators are required to act in a consumer's best interest.

- To facilitate responsible behavior in the subprime mortgage marketplace.

- To facilitate the consumer complaint process.

Although fees may be charged to licensees and registrants to cover the costs of maintaining the NMLS-R, the public can't be charged for accessing the information in the system.

If a state chooses not to participate in the NMLS-R, the Consumer Financial Protection Bureau (CFPB) will establish and maintain a similar system for licensed loan originators in that state. Similarly, if the CFPB believes that the NMLS-R is not fulfilling its purposes, a new, similar entity can be created as a replacement. The CFPB is a relatively new regulatory agency (created under the Dodd-Frank Wall Street Reform and Consumer Protection Act) that oversees the implementation and enforcement of several financial laws.

The CFPB can also oversee the establishment of a licensing system if the state's way of licensing and regulating loan originators doesn't meet the standards found in the SAFE Act. Depending on your state, the agency that licenses loan originators and has regulatory authority over them might be the state's *Division of Banking, Division of Residential Finance, Department of Financial Institutions, Mortgage Regulatory Commission* or have some similar name.

Under the law, the entity that has authority over loan originators in a state must meet the standards listed below in order to avoid CFPB intervention:

- It has the authority to enforce the state's licensing law.

- It requires all state-licensed loan originators to register with the NMLS-R.

- It regularly reports enforcement actions and licensing violations to the NMLS-R.

- It has a process in place for loan originators to challenge the information being reported to the NMLS-R.

- It has a mechanism for assessing civil penalties against individuals who originate loans without a license.

- It requires loan originators to have either a minimum net worth or a surety bond, the value of which must reflect the aggregate dollar amount of the loans being originated. (Alternatively, the state authority can require payment into a recovery fund.) Note that originators can be covered by their company's bond – this is the most common practice.

After passage of the SAFE Act, a set of rules known as *Regulation H* was created by the CFPB in order to implement the law. Subpart B of Regulation H provides more details about required standards for state licensing authorities.

As a way of assisting state licensing authorities in the implementation of these standards, CSBS and AARMR created a model state law with suggested language. States that adopt requirements that are at least as strict as the model law are generally considered to be in compliance with the SAFE standards. (The requirements mentioned throughout this chapter are based on those found in the SAFE Act, Regulation H and the model law.)

a. Regulatory Authority

In addition to any authority already given under state or federal law, the SAFE Act gives the state licensing agency several important powers. For example, for the purposes of investigating violations or complaints, the agency can subject individual originators and their employers to examinations. As part of an examination, the agency can access books and records and conduct interviews with loan originators, officers, employees, principals, independent contractors, agents and customers of a licensee. Someone who is being examined or investigated by the agency can't knowingly withhold, destroy or compromise any information.

In the event that the CFPB must establish and maintain a licensing system for a state, it will obtain several of the powers being given by the SAFE Act to the states, including the power to subpoena, investigate and fine loan originators. The CFPB also has the power to subpoena in its role as a federal regulator for non-depositories.

Much of the regulatory authority provided by the SAFE Act is given to the states. Under the SAFE Act, a **state** is any state of the United States, the District of Columbia, any territory of the United States, Puerto Rico, Guam, American Samoa, the Trust Territory of the Pacific Islands, the Virgin Islands and the Northern Mariana Islands.

b. Responsibilities and Limitations

As you learned in the previous section, the state agency overseeing loan originator activities has several responsibilities. Some of those many responsibilities are listed below:

- Enforcing state licensing laws.

- Regularly reporting licensing violations to the NMLS-R.

- Assessing civil penalties against individuals who originate without a license.

Mortgage regulators generally have the power to demand information from loan originators in order to investigate and prevent wrongdoing. During a formal investigation, regulators can take possession of a loan originator's documents. However, unless there is a risk of the documents being compromised, the regulator must give the originator access to the documents so that normal business can be done.

2. State Law and Regulation Definitions

In order to do their jobs in compliance with state and federal laws, mortgage professionals must understand the definitions of several key terms. This section of the study guide contains important terminology from the SAFE Act, Regulation H and the model law from CSBS and AARMR.

All of these definitions will be explained later in greater detail and in fuller context. However, you can turn back to this section if you encounter a key term and need help remembering what it means.

- **Administrative and clerical tasks** are the receipt, collection and distribution of information that is common in the processing or underwriting of a loan in the mortgage business. The term is also used to describe communication that is designed to obtain common information from a consumer. In general, an individual who only performs administrative or clerical tasks and doesn't negotiate with or give advice to borrowers doesn't need a loan originator license.

- **The American Association of Residential Mortgage Regulators (AARMR)** is a national association of individuals who are charged with administering and regulating various aspects of residential mortgage lending. It played a major role in the formation of the NMLS-R and in the drafting of the model licensing law.

- An **application** is a request for a residential mortgage loan and includes the borrower-related information that lenders commonly use when considering the request. Someone who takes an application from a consumer is generally considered to be acting as a loan originator even when gathering application information over the phone or the Internet.

- **The Conference of State Bank Supervisors (CSBS)** is a national organization of state bank supervisors who are charged with ensuring that state banking institutions adhere to certain standards. The organization played a major role in the formation of the NMLS-R and in the drafting of the model licensing law.

- An **immediate family member** is a spouse, child, sibling, parent, grandparent or grandchild. An individual who only originates loans with or on behalf of an immediate family member doesn't need a loan originator license.

- An **independent contractor** is someone who performs mortgage-related duties and isn't supervised or directed by a licensed or registered loan originator. An independent contractor who otherwise only performs the same tasks as a loan processor or underwriter must still be licensed as a loan originator.

- A **loan originator** is someone who takes residential mortgage loan applications and offers or negotiates the terms of such loans in exchange for compensation or gain. Most loan originators must be licensed. Be aware that the term *loan originator* can refer to an individual or a company. In practice, the term *MLO* (or *mortgage loan originator*) is sometimes used to describe an individual who is a loan originator.

- A **loan processor or underwriter** is someone who is supervised by a licensed or registered loan originator and performs clerical or support duties. A loan processor or underwriter only needs to be licensed as a loan originator under certain circumstances, such as when performing work for more than one company at a time. However, loan processors and underwriters need to be supervised by licensed MLOs. This supervisory role must not be just in name only. The SAFE Act requires that there be an *actual nexus* between the unlicensed processor/underwriter and the supervisor who is licensed as an MLO.

- A **nontraditional mortgage product** is any mortgage product that isn't a 30-year, fixed-rate loan. In order to obtain and renew their licenses, loan originators must complete courses with an emphasis on nontraditional mortgage products.

- A **registered loan originator** is a loan originator who is registered with the NMLS-R and employed by a depository institution, a subsidiary of a depository institution or an institution regulated by the Farm Credit Association. A registered loan originator generally does not need to be licensed.

- A **residential mortgage loan** is any loan primarily for personal, family or household use that is secured by a mortgage, deed of trust or other equivalent security interest on a dwelling (or on real estate where a dwelling is being constructed or will be constructed). The requirements mentioned in this guide relate to the origination of residential mortgage loans. They do not necessarily apply to loans tied to commercial or industrial properties.

- A **state-licensed loan originator** is a loan originator who is licensed by his or her state, registered with the NMLS-R and isn't employed by entities mentioned in the definition of *registered loan originator*. If you are reading this study guide, you are likely planning on becoming (or have already become) a state-licensed loan originator.

- **State Regulatory Registry, LLC**, is a wholly owned subsidiary of CSBS that runs the NMLS-R.

- A **unique identifier** is a number or other identifier that is assigned to a loan originator by the NMLS-R in order to identify the person and track his or her conduct in the mortgage-lending business. The unique identifier must appear on various documents, including on advertisements.

3. License Law and Regulation

a. Persons Required to Be Licensed

Before we can address the kinds of individuals who need a loan originator license, we must address the activities that loan originators engage in. A loan originator is an individual who takes residential mortgage loan applications and either offers or negotiates the terms of a residential mortgage loan for compensation or gain. An individual is also acting as a loan originator if he or she presents himself or herself to the public as someone who can or will do those tasks.

To begin understanding who is and who isn't considered a loan originator, let's go over what it means to *take an application*. An application is a request for a residential mortgage loan and includes the borrower-related information that lenders commonly use when considering the request. You are considered to be taking an application if you receive one. It makes no difference whether the application is received directly from the borrower or indirectly from the borrower through a third party. You are also considered to be taking an application even if you are only entering the application information into an automated system and even if you lack authority to approve the applicant for a loan.

For the purpose of defining the term *loan originator*, the following actions DO NOT rise to the level of *taking an application*:

- Receiving an application in the mail and forwarding it to someone else without reviewing it.

- Explaining the content of an application to a borrower and where certain information should be noted.

- Giving a general description of the lending process without discussing particular loan products.

- Collecting basic identifying information from a borrower on behalf of a lender. (For example, taking the borrower's name, address and phone number over the phone or in a reception setting for the purpose of forwarding the information to a licensed loan originator for follow-up and/or setting an appointment for a licensed loan originator to contact the borrower in order to take an application.)

Now let's examine what it means to *offer* or *negotiate* the terms of a loan. You are offering or negotiating the terms of a loan if you are engaged in any of the following activities:

- Presenting terms to a borrower.

- Attempting to reach a mutual understanding with a borrower regarding loan terms.

- Recommending, referring or directing a borrower to a lender or a set of loan terms in accordance with an agreement with (or an incentive from) someone besides the borrower.

- Responding to a borrower's request for a different rate or different fees on a pending loan application by providing a revised offer (regardless of whether it's accepted).

Despite what the person might think, an individual IS offering or negotiating the terms of a loan in the following scenarios:

- The person presents loan terms before verification of loan data is complete.

- The mortgage loan offer being made is conditional.

- Other individuals will be responsible for completing the loan process.

- The person taking the application lacks the authority to negotiate the rate or loan terms.

- The person doesn't have the authority to bind the party who would be funding the loan (i.e., a mortgage broker).

- The person has a business card indicating that he or she originates residential mortgage loans. Holding oneself out to the public as a loan originator makes one a loan originator, even if no actual origination functions are being done.

For the purpose of defining the term *loan originator*, the following actions <u>DON'T</u> rise to the level of offering or negotiating loan terms:

- Giving general information in response to borrower queries. (General information includes information about terminology, lending policies and lending-related services.)

- Arranging the closing or other aspect of the loan process, as long as terms are only discussed for the purpose of verifying what's already been agreed to.

- Making an underwriting decision regarding whether a borrower qualifies for a loan.

- Explaining the steps a borrower must take in order to receive an offer for a loan.

- Communicating to the borrower that a loan offer has been sent (without providing other information about the offer).

- Offering or negotiating through a third-party loan originator without communicating with the borrower or holding oneself up to the public as a loan originator. (An example would be a seller offering financing to a borrower through a loan originator.)

Finally, for licensing/registration purposes, the loan being offered, negotiated or applied for must be a residential mortgage loan. A residential mortgage loan is any loan primarily for personal, family or household use that is secured by a mortgage, deed of trust or other equivalent security interest on a dwelling (or on real estate where a dwelling is being constructed or will be constructed). Commercial transactions are not covered by the SAFE Act but may be regulated separately by the states.

A loan originator must have a license, be registered with the NMLS-R or both. To determine whether a loan originator needs a license, we need to know the type of entity the originator works for. In general, a loan originator must be licensed if he or she is <u>not</u> an employee of the following entities:

- A depository institution.

- A depository institution's subsidiary that is regulated by a federal banking agency.

- An institution regulated by the Farm Credit Administration.

Individuals who are employed by the above are required to be registered.

Be aware that some requirements under the SAFE Act apply to companies as well as to individuals. For example, although some of the licensing requirements (such as the need to complete pre-license education) obviously are meant for actual persons and not business entities, a company that engages in loan origination generally must be licensed. Furthermore, sole proprietors need two licenses: one for themselves as individuals and one for their business. In practice, a person—but not a business—who is a loan originator is sometimes referred to as an *MLO* (or *mortgage loan originator*).

It is also important to know which individuals do not require a loan originator license. There are many exceptions to the licensing requirement.

Obviously, someone who is not considered a loan originator under the law is not required to have a loan originator license. In general, an individual is not a loan originator if the person only performs purely administrative or clerical tasks on behalf of a loan originator. Administrative or clerical tasks are the receipt, collection and distribution of information that is common in the processing or underwriting of a loan in the mortgage business. The term is also used to describe communication that is designed to obtain common information from a consumer (such as name, address, phone number and the purpose of the potential loan) in order to provide <u>general</u> information on loan products that the consumer <u>might</u> qualify for. (In other words, the individual is NOT presenting an offer of credit or discussing the particular details of the consumer's unique situation and how it would apply to those loan products.) However, a license is generally required when presenting an offer of credit and discussing the particular details of the consumer's unique situation and how the situation would apply to those loan products.

Individuals are also not loan originators if they are only performing real estate brokerage activities and have an appropriate real estate license. However, someone performing real estate brokerage activities is a loan originator and must be licensed if he or she is compensated by a lender (or lender's agent), a mortgage broker (or mortgage broker's agent), or a loan originator (or loan originator's agent) for residential loan origination activities.

Real estate brokerage activities involve offering or providing real estate services to the public. Real estate services are as follows:

- Acting as a real estate agent or real estate broker for a buyer, seller, lessor or lessee of real property.

- Bringing together parties who are interested in the sale, purchase, lease, rental or exchange of real property.

- Negotiating a real estate contract. (This doesn't include negotiations related to financing the transaction.)

- Engaging in any activity for which an individual must be licensed or registered as a real estate broker or real estate agent under applicable state law.

- Offering to engage in any of the activities listed above.

Loan processors and underwriters generally don't need a loan originator license if they are only performing clerical and support duties under the supervision of one licensed or registered company. A processor or underwriter who performs duties outside the direction or supervision of a single company is considered an *independent contractor* (regardless of the IRS definition of the term) and must have a loan originator license. If loan processors or underwriters are exempt from licensure because they work for only one licensed company, they must report to an individual who does hold a mortgage loan originator license. Thus, in practice, underwriting and processing managers almost always hold originator licenses – not because they use them to originate loans, but because they supervise operations members who are exempt from licensure. It's worthy of mentioning that there must be an **actual nexus** between unlicensed processors or underwriters and the licensed individual responsible for supervising them. This means they must have regular interaction, and the manager must be able to review the work if necessary and provide feedback and guidance as necessary.

For the purpose of the licensing exemption for loan processors and underwriters, clerical and support duties include the receipt, analysis collection or distribution of information that is commonly used for the processing and underwriting of a loan. They also include communicating with consumers in order to obtain this information.

Conversely, a loan processor or underwriter is going beyond the definition of clerical and support duties if the person is performing any of the following actions:

- Offering or negotiating loan rates or terms.

- Counseling consumers about loan rates or terms.

- Taking a residential loan application.

Finally, a loan originator license is not required for the following individuals:

- Someone who is engaged in loan-related activities in connection with a loan that will be secured by the person's own residence.

- Someone who is arranging business-purpose loans only. (NOTE: This does not mean that commercial loan licensing does not exist. Some states have separate licensing regimes for these originators; it is not, however, a federal requirement.)

- Someone who is offering or negotiating terms of a loan with or on behalf of an immediate family member. (An immediate family member can be a spouse, child, sibling, parent, grandparent or grandchild. The term includes stepparents, stepchildren, stepsiblings and adoptive relationships. It does NOT include aunts, uncles, cousins, etc.)

- Someone who is only involved in extensions of credit relating to timeshare plans.

- Someone who is engaging in loan-related activities in their official capacity at a government agency or housing finance agency. (Some states do not have this exemption if the individual is originating loans.)

- Someone who is engaged in loan-related activities as part of their employment at a non-profit organization. (This exemption applies if the loans being originated are "favorable to the borrower." Favorability will be based on whether the loan terms are consistent with those normally available through charities and public housing authorities.)

- Someone who is originating loans within the proper context of an attorney-client relationship if the person is an attorney and is not being compensated by a lender, mortgage broker or loan originator.

- Someone who is a registered loan originator. (A registered mortgage loan originator is a loan originator who is registered with the NMLS-R and is employed by a depository institution, a depository institution's subsidiary [if the subsidiary is regulated by a federal banking agency] or an institution regulated by the Farm Credit Administration.)

b. Licensee Qualifications and Application Process

In order to become licensed, a loan originator candidate must successfully complete a 20-hour pre-license course. The NMLS-R is responsible for approving courses and education providers.

At a minimum, the 20-hour pre-license course must satisfy the following rules regarding course topics and timing:

- Three hours of the course must focus on federal laws and federal regulations.

- Three hours of the course must focus on ethics topics. (Examples of ethics topics are fraud, consumer protection and fair lending issues.)

- Two hours of the course must focus on nontraditional mortgage products. (A nontraditional mortgage product is any mortgage product other than a 30-year, fixed-rate mortgage.)

Once pre-license education has been completed, a loan originator candidate must successfully complete a written exam developed by the NMLS-R. Candidates must answer at least 75% of the exam questions correctly. A candidate who fails the exam can retake it again with a 30-day gap between tests. If an applicant fails three consecutive times, a six-month waiting period is required before the applicant can test again, which resets the waiting cycle (i.e. if an applicant fails four times, the wait would be 30 days; a sixth failure would result in a six-month wait.)

Pre-license education credit expires three years after the course has been taken if the individual has not obtained a license and is not working as a federal registrant. Credit will not expire as long as an individual holds an active MLO license or federal registration but will expire if the individual allows that license or registration to lapse and does not reactivate it or get a new license within three years of leaving the industry.

License applicants must submit their identity, including fingerprints, to the NMLS-R. As part of this submission, applicants must submit to a series of criminal background and credit checks. The purpose of these checks is to verify that an applicant exhibits financial responsibility, character and general fitness to serve the public as a loan originator. An applicant who lacks these traits will not be issued a license.

If a loan originator's errors or misconduct result in negative financial consequences for consumers, there must be a safeguard in place to help facilitate the payment of compensation. States can work toward this requirement by choosing any of the following options:

- Require that loan originators maintain a net worth that is based on the dollar amount of their originated loans. (If this option is chosen, the loan originator might be able to substitute an employer's net worth.)

- Require that loan originators maintain a surety bond, the value of which is based on the dollar amount of their originated loans. (If this option is chosen, originators must file a new bond if money is ever recovered from one. Again, this requirement may be fulfilled at the company level as long as the bond covers the individual MLOs.)

- Require that loan originators pay into a state recovery fund.

Note that some of the options listed above can be satisfied by a licensed mortgage business on behalf of its individual loan originators.

Before originating any loans, a loan originator must be issued a unique identifier. A unique identifier is a number or other identifier that is assigned to a loan originator by the NMLS-R in order to identify the person and track his or her conduct in the mortgage-lending business. Once the unique identifier has been issued, the loan originator must include it on all applications, solicitations and advertisements, including business cards and websites.

To the greatest extent possible, states should use a loan originator's unique identifier in place of the person's Social Security number. However, the identifier can only be used by the states in order to fulfill the purposes of the SAFE Act and its rules.

c. Grounds For Denying a License

In order to become licensed, individuals must demonstrate financial responsibility in their own affairs. If background and credit checks reveal any of the following items, a candidate might not be considered financially responsible:

- Current outstanding judgments (other than those related to medical expenses).

- Tax liens or other government liens.

- Foreclosures within the past three years.

- A pattern of seriously delinquent accounts over the past three years.

Applicants will struggle to obtain a license if they have committed certain crimes. For example, no license can be issued if the candidate was convicted or pleaded guilty to a felony within the last seven years, unless the person was pardoned. A license can <u>never</u> be issued to someone who has <u>ever</u> been convicted of or pleaded guilty to a felony involving any of the following misdeeds, unless the person was pardoned:

- Fraud.

- Dishonesty.

- Breach of trust.

- Money laundering.

Similarly, a state can't issue a license to someone whose license was revoked in another state.

d. License Maintenance

Loan originator licenses must be renewed at least once each year. In order for a renewal to be possible, the licensee must continue to have met the license qualifications. (Those qualifications include, but aren't limited to, the ones previously mentioned regarding criminal history and financial responsibility.) The licensee can also be required to pay renewal fees.

In order to maintain and renew their license, loan originators must complete at least eight hours of continuing education each year. A loan originator who teaches a continuing education course can receive up to two hours of credit for every hour taught.

At a minimum, the eight hours of annual continuing education must consist of the following topics and timings:

- At least three hours must be instruction on federal law and federal regulations.

- At least two hours must be instruction on ethics topics. (Examples of ethics topics are fraud, consumer protection and fair lending issues.)

- At least two hours must be instruction on nontraditional mortgage products. (A nontraditional mortgage product is any mortgage product other than a 30-year, fixed-rate loan.)

Credit for completing a continuing education course will only be applied to the year in which the course is completed. The same course can't be completed more than once in the same year or in consecutive years. If a formerly licensed person wants to become licensed again, continuing education for the person's last year of licensure must be completed first. This is done through the completion of a *late CE* course.

Courses and education providers must be approved by the NMLS-R.

The renewal period for MLO licenses begins on November 1st each year and ends at midnight on December 31st. Failure to renew your license by the deadline will render it expired, and you will not be able to work. Some states allow for a late renewal period, which runs from January 1st through February 28th. In these states, failure to renew by that deadline will terminate the license, and a new license application will be necessary if the MLO wishes to originate loans again.

e. NMLS Requirements

The NMLS-R clearly has an important role in the licensing and regulation of loan originators. In summary, here are several general requirements that are related to the NMLS-R:

- State-licensed loan originators must register with the NMLS-R.

- Enforcement actions and licensing violations must be reported to the NMLS-R by the states.

- The unique identifier issued by the NMLS-R must appear on all of a licensee's advertisements, the promissory note, the mortgage, the loan application and on various other documents. Note that the NMLS unique identifier is used to facilitate regulator monitoring and tracking of loans originated by a given person or entity. The only other alternative was to use an MLO's Social Security Number in place of the unique identifier, but this proved to be an unworkable solution for many reasons.

- Education courses and education providers must be approved by the NMLS-R.

- License applicants must submit their identity, including fingerprints, to the NMLS-R.

- Licensees must submit *Mortgage Call Reports* to the NMLS-R. The Mortgage Call Report is a comprehensive and detailed report of all mortgage activity that has taken place in the previous quarter. It contains information on all transactions originated, closed, denied or in process.

- When licensees change employment, they are required to update their employment history information in the NMLS and request sponsorship from another licensed mortgage company (or federally regulated institution). Additionally, updates to address history must be made each time an MLO moves. Considering that the MLO will be certifying the accuracy of his or her NMLS record at each renewal (at a minimum), it is imperative that this information remains current.

f. Temporary Authority to Operate

As a result of the 2018 Economic Growth, Regulatory Reform and Consumer Protection Act, a new category of approved originator became effective on November 24, 2019. An MLO holding **Temporary Authority to Operate (TA)** is eligible to originate residential mortgage loans in a state in which he or she has an active application for licensure pending. This authority is granted under the federal SAFE Act, and individuals utilizing it are not actually licensed in the state unless and until the state has made the affirmative decision to approve a license after all its requirements have been satisfied. MLOs eligible for TA may legally originate loans in a state for no more than 120 days from the date on which the application for licensure was submitted.

The purpose of TA is to allow qualified licensed MLOs to begin working in a new state or qualified federally registered MLOs (working for a depository institution) to transition to a non-depository institution without having to wait to originate loans until all licensing requirements have been fulfilled. In order to be eligible for Temporary Authority, MLOs must:

- Have held a valid and active state license in at least one state for the entire 30-day period preceding the application for licensure in a new state; **OR**

- Have been a federally registered MLO working for a depository institution for the entire 12-month period preceding the application for licensure.

Assuming the length of experience requirements are met, the MLO will be granted Temporary Authority within 48 hours of applying for licensure in a new state, provided all of the following conditions are met:

- The criminal background check does not reveal any disqualifying felony or misdemeanor convictions barring the individual from licensure in the state in which the individual is applying.

- The individual has not had a MLO license application denied or a license suspended or revoked in any jurisdiction.

- The MLO has not been subject to a cease and desist order or other disciplinary action.

A state may withhold TA approval for seven additional days (for a total of nine days) if more information is needed from an applicant about an item appearing on the background check report. Provided the state does not issue an intent to deny the license application within the initial window described, MLOs meeting the experience requirements will automatically receive TA as long as they have an active sponsorship with a licensed mortgage originator company inside of NMLS. The MLO now has the balance of the 120-day period to complete any outstanding education and testing requirements and authorize a credit report to be pulled as part of the character and fitness evaluation. Temporary authority will end when any of the following events occur:

- The MLO withdraws the license application.

- The state denies or issues an intent to deny the license application.

- The 120-day period expires, and the license application is not complete (there are still outstanding testing, education or other state requirements). If the application is complete in NMLS, TA can continue until the state makes a decision on the application.

- The state issues an MLO license to the applicant.

4. Compliance

a. Prohibited Conduct and Practices

The model law from CSBS and AARMR lists several activities that a loan originator is not allowed to engage in. A licensee can be disciplined for any of the following acts:

- Attempting to defraud borrowers, lenders or any person.

- Engaging in any unfair or deceptive practice.

- Soliciting or entering into a contract that allows the loan originator to earn a fee or commission even if no loan is obtained.

- Soliciting, advertising or entering into a contract for specific interest rates, points or other financing terms that aren't actually available.

- Failing to make disclosures as required by state or federal law.

- Failing to comply with state or federal laws, rules or regulations.

- Making false or deceptive statements or representations.

- Negligently making any false statement or intentionally omitting facts in connection with information that is being filed with a government agency or the NMLS-R or an investigation being conducted by one of these entities.

- Making any payment, threat or promise to any person in order to influence their independent judgment regarding a residential mortgage loan.

- Making any payment, threat or promise to any appraiser in order to influence their independent judgment regarding a property's value.

- Collecting, charging or attempting to receive illegal fees.

- Requiring or causing a borrower to obtain property insurance in an amount greater than the property's replacement cost.

- Failing to account for money belonging to someone as part of a residential mortgage transaction.

According to the model law, a loan originator who commits a licensing violation or engages in a prohibited activity can be fined up to $25,000 per offense.

b. Required Conduct

Loan originators are required to exhibit good character, financial responsibility and general fitness to serve the public. Once a unique identifier has been issued to them, they must include it on all of their applications, solicitations and advertisements. Licensees should also engage in proper record-keeping procedures and maintain well-secured copies of all disclosures and loan documents. This includes documents that are distributed in paper or electronic formats.

A licensee must be sure not to commit any of the prohibited actions listed in the previous section.

c. Advertising

All advertising must include a loan originator's unique identifier. In addition to traditional forms of advertising, this requirement also applies to business cards and websites.

Advertising must be free of fraud, deception or intentional misrepresentations. Optional language within the state model law specifically prohibits bait-and-switch tactics, in which advertised loan terms aren't actually available.

PRACTICE EXAM A

Test your mortgage knowledge by taking the following practice exam. Answer keys for all three practice exams are provided in a later section of the study guide.

1. If a consumer believes that information on a credit report is inaccurate, what must the credit bureau do?
   A. Notify any lender of the alleged discrepancy.
   B. Confirm and remove inaccurate information within 30 days.
   C. Provide a credit score at no charge.
   D. Prevent creditors from accessing the report.

2. A lender that is transferring the servicing of a loan to another lender must provide the Servicing Transfer Disclosure within what timeframe?
   A. 3 business days before the transfer
   B. 3 business days after the transfer
   C. 15 business days before the transfer
   D. 15 business days after the transfer

3. Although some exceptions apply, in general, overtime income should be _____ in order to be used for qualifying purposes.
   A. averaged over the past 18 months
   B. averaged over the past 2 years
   C. used as a compensating factor only
   D. received for more than 1 year

4. Under RESPA, when is it acceptable for a property seller to condition a sale on the buyer's use of a specific title company?
   A. When full disclosure is provided
   B. Under no circumstances
   C. When the property contains more than one dwelling unit
   D. When the loan amount exceeds the conforming loan limit

5. If consumers disputes an item on their credit report that they believe to be inaccurate, the dispute must be investigated by the bureau(s) and any inaccurate, incomplete or unverifiable information must be removed within:
   A. 15 days.
   B. 30 days.
   C. 45 days.
   D. 60 days.

6. What is the maximum length of time that Temporary Authority will allow an eligible MLO to legally originate mortgage loans while completing the licensing requirements in a given state?
   A. 120 days
   B. 45 days
   C. 90 days
   D. 180 days

7. In certain flood hazard areas, flood insurance may not be available because:
    A. individuals cannot afford it.
    B. the community does not participate in the National Flood Insurance Program.
    C. the National Flood Insurance Program has rejected the community for lack of funds.
    D. the community has not flooded within the last five years.

8. The document that determines the sales price for real property is called the:
    A. appraisal report.
    B. commitment letter.
    C. purchase and sale agreement.
    D. Truth in Lending disclosure.

9. Before the MLO Compensation rule took effect, mortgage brokers were often able to increase their compensation by providing borrowers with a higher interest rate than that for which they qualified. Such compensation was referred to as:
    A. lender-paid compensation.
    B. service-release premium.
    C. double-dipping.
    D. yield-spread premium.

10. If a loan is neither insured nor guaranteed by the Federal Government, it is referred to as a/an:
    A. FHA loan.
    B. HELOC.
    C. conforming loan.
    D. conventional loan.

11. Which federal agency is responsible for writing and promulgating rules under Regulation X?
    A. CFPB
    B. HUD
    C. FTC
    D. None of the answers

12. Which factor must be considered when evaluating a borrower's ability to repay a mortgage loan?
    A. The borrower's debt-to-income ratio
    B. The borrower's plans to start a family
    C. The lender's desire to retain servicing
    D. The borrower's ancestry

13. PMI protects:
    A. the public.
    B. the mortgagor.
    C. the mortgagee.
    D. the seller.

14. Which of the following is typically not required in a gift letter?
    A. A statement that the money is not a loan
    B. The donor's relationship to the recipient
    C. The amount of the gift
    D. The donor's Social Security number

15. Which type of mortgage loan lets the borrower make regular monthly payments for a period of time and then requires one larger payment upon maturity?
    A. Jumbo loan
    B. Balloon loan
    C. Alt-A loan
    D. Subprime loan

16. Molly O'Callaghan walks in to a creditor's office to apply for a loan at 9:00 AM. She is greeted promptly and offered a cup of coffee before being directed to a loan officer. At 3:30 PM, Quoc-Huy Nguyen enters the same office. The receptionist is busy and does not greet him for five minutes. After introducing himself, Quoc-Huy is directed to a couch to wait for a loan officer, which takes an additional five minutes. During this time, he is not offered a beverage. This is an example of:
    A. an acceptable practice.
    B. overt discrimination.
    C. disparate treatment.
    D. disparate impact.

17. Which of the following loans is subject to RESPA's disclosure requirements?
    A. A loan secured by vacant land
    B. A loan secured by commercial property
    C. A loan secured by a residential property on a 29-acre lot
    D. A loan secured by a four-unit residential property

18. A borrower has applied for a $296,000 loan with an interest rate of 6.25%, a term of 30 years with a loan-to-value ratio of 65%. Assuming that the loan funds on May 22, how much per-diem interest will be collected at closing as shown on the Closing Disclosure?
    A. $334.03
    B. $513.90
    C. $506.85
    D. $329.45

19. If a borrower paid $12,000 in discount points on a $600,000 loan, how many points did he pay?
    A. 2 points
    B. 5 points
    C. 12 points
    D. 20 points

20. Five business days prior to closing, the creditor sends its figures to the settlement agent to prepare the borrower's closing disclosure. The settlement agent delivers the Closing Disclosure to the borrower two business days prior to closing and there is a tolerance violation. Under TRID, who will be held liable for the errors in documentation and process?
    A. The creditor
    B. The settlement agent
    C. The loan officer
    D. The notary public who witnessed the signing

21. If the loan-to-value ratio on an FHA-insured 30-year loan exceeds 90% at origination, how long will the applicant be required to pay the FHA annual MIP (paid monthly)?
    A. 7 years
    B. 11 years
    C. Until the loan reaches 78% LTV
    D. For the life of the loan

22. When a Mortgage Loan Originator issues a Loan Estimate to an applicant, which of the following fees is not subject to any tolerance check between the LE and the final charges as shown on the Closing Disclosure?
    A. The borrower's hazard insruance premiums
    B. The origination fee
    C. Any borrower-paid transfer tax associated with the purchase of a property
    D. The title charges, including any settlement fee

23. Negative amortization results when:
    A. the term of a loan is less than 20 years.
    B. the minimum payment made is less than the amount of interest accrued on the loan in a given period.
    C. an ARM interest rate adjusts downward.
    D. a 15-year balloon loan has an interest rate above 8%.

24. A loan officer meets with a client at 9:00 AM to take an application. When the client arrives, the MLO welcomes her warmly, shakes her hand and offers a cup of coffee. During the meeting, the client decides that she is not ready to own a home and does not follow through with the loan application. The MLO had counted on this loan application to reach a volume bonus for the month. An hour later, an existing client comes into the office to see the same MLO and drop off a document. The MLO greets the client and shakes his hand, but does not offer a cup of coffee. Which of the following statements is TRUE regarding this series of events?
    A. The actions of the MLO do not raise any potential issues.
    B. The actions of the MLO could give rise to a claim of overt discrimination.
    C. The actions of the MLO could give rise to a claim of disparate treatment.
    D. The actions of the MLO could give rise to a claim of disparate impact.

25. The Nefarians are applying to purchase a new single-family home in a better school district. They are selling their current residence and using the proceeds from the sale as a down payment on their new residence. Because of some surprise last-minute inspection issues on the sale of their home, they have to spend more money than originally planned, making them short on funds to purchase the new property. In order to overcome this issue, they take a cash advance on their credit card and transfer it to a relative who then transfers it back to the Nefarians, disguising the unallowable funds from the cash advance as a legitimate gift. The Nefarians have committed:
    A. identity fraud.
    B. fraud for housing.
    C. fraud for profit.
    D. occupancy fraud.

26. Peter is purchasing a home for $300,000 and the home appraises for $306,000. Peter is making a down-payment of 10%. Fannie Mae will purchase this loan from the bank and requires mortgage insurance. Peter elects the monthly-premium option. The mortgage policy has coverage of 25% and a factor of 0.67; what will Peter's monthly mortgage insurance premium be?
    A. $62.50
    B. $63.75
    C. $150.75
    D. $153.77

27. FHA's maximum loan limits:
    A. are the same throughout every state.
    B. are variable by county.
    C. are higher than jumbo loan amounts.
    D. are determined by a survey of average annual income for households with 4 persons in a given area.

28. Cindy Client applied with Leonard Loanofficer to finance the purchase of her first home. Cindy was originally interested in a 30-year, fixed-rate loan to keep her payments low enough that she could continue to put money into savings each month. As the transaction progressed, Leonard kept encouraging Cindy to go with a 15-year, fixed-rate product. After much prodding from Leonard, Cindy agreed to take the 15-year loan. After closing, Cindy found out through a mutual friend that Leonard was paid almost double on the 15-year loan than he would have been on the 30. Which of the following unethical practices might Leonard be guilty of?
    A. Loan flipping
    B. Equity stripping
    C. Steering
    D. Shunting

29. A borrower's ability to repay a loan is referred to as:
    A. commitment
    B. capacity
    C. consideration
    D. credit

30. Under the Dodd-Frank Act, which of the following methods of compensation would be legal?
    A. An MLO is paid a base salary on a bi-weekly basis
    B. An MLO who is not also an owner of the company is given stock options in the company when a loan results in at least $5,000 gross profit.
    C. An MLO is paid 1% of the loan amount for all FHA ARM loans over $150,000 and 1.5% of the loan amount for FHA Fixed rate loans under $150,000.
    D. An MLO receives a $50 gas card in addition to her base compensation, but only for loans where the interest rate provided to the borrower is at least 0.5% higher than the base rate.

31. Financial institutions are required to develop a _____ that describes the procedures they take to protect consumer financial information.
    A. video presentation on security
    B. secure web site
    C. written information security plan
    D. regular security newsletter

32. What is the formula for calculating the housing ("top" or "front-end") ratio?
    A. Index plus margin
    B. Monthly PITI divided by gross monthly income
    C. Gross monthly income divided by monthly PITI
    D. All recurring monthly debts divided by gross monthly income

33. A subordinate loan is best described as:
    A. a second mortgage.
    B. a first mortgage.
    C. a loan with lower lien priority.
    D. a loan with higher lien priority.

34. The practice of denying loan applications in a particular neighborhood without considering individual applicant qualifications is called:
    A. steering.
    B. redlining.
    C. blockbusting.
    D. disparate impact.

35. During the processing of a loan, the processor needs to obtain a verification of deposit (VOD) from the borrower's bank. The borrower has signed a form authorizing this, but the bank wants independent confirmation from the applicant to release the information. The applicant is on vacation in Mali, so the MLO calls the bank to authorize the release, posing as the applicant and providing the necessary information to confirm identity. The VOD is completed and the loan closes on time. Which of the following statements is most accurate?
    A. The borrower had signed an authorization for this purpose and would want the loan to close in a timely fashion, so this action is permissible.
    B. The bank's policy to require additional confirmation to release data after the borrower had signed an authorization form is unreasonable.
    C. The mortgage loan originator acted in an unethical manner and also violated federal law.
    D. The originator's decision was unethical but not technically illegal and is reasonable given the circumstances.

36. Bill is an attorney who does title work and real estate closings. Bill has been receiving referrals from ABC Mortgage Lenders for a long time and, because of this relationship, provides all of the employees of ABC with special discounts on legal services. Which of the following statements is TRUE?
    A. Bill is employing a legal and ethical strategy to grow his business.
    B. Bill has provided ABC employees with a kickback, which violates RESPA.
    C. ABC is not permitted to refer any business to attorneys for any reason.
    D. This is an allowable practice because Bill is not providing services at no charge.

37. A mortgage broker company takes a loan application and issues a Loan Estimate. Who is ultimately responsible for the accuracy of that estimate and its proper delivery?
    A. The mortgage broker company
    B. The loan officer
    C. The title company
    D. The creditor funding the transaction

38. In general, auto leases with how many remaining payments can be excluded from liabilities when attempting to qualify a borrower?
    A. 15 or less
    B. 12 or less
    C. 10 or less
    D. This type of debt can never be excluded.

39. Which of the following is true of FHA loans?
    A. They insure the lender against borrower default.
    B. They provide a government-backed guarantee.
    C. They require no down payment.
    D. They can be used to purchase commercial properties.

40. Before the Dodd-Frank Act was passed, CSBS, AARMR and NACCA tried to address the effect of payment shock to the borrower on an ARM loan with a teaser rate, high margin and prepayment penalties by issuing which of the following guidance?
    A. Regulation BB
    B. Risky Loan Advisory Directive
    C. Minimum ARM Requirement Rule
    D. Subprime Statement

41. Which of the following statements in an advertisement would not trigger the need to provide disclosure of any additional loan terms?
    A. "Today's APR is 3.42%."
    B. "We have rates from 2.5%."
    C. "Principal and interest payments start at $525."
    D. "This is a 30-year fixed rate loan."

42. What does the lender's closing department do prior to closing a loan?
    A. Issues a revised Closing Disclosure to correct all loan officer errors made on the Loan Estimate
    B. Closes all pertinent questions from underwriting on referred files
    C. Prepares and delivers final documents to the title company
    D. Prepares the bill of sale

43. Which of the following compensation arrangements would violate the CFPB's MLO Compensation rule?
    A. The MLO is paid commission based on individual loan profitability.
    B. The MLO is paid a base salary.
    C. The MLO is paid commission based on a percentage of the loan amount.
    D. The MLO is paid a salary plus a bonus based on total funded dollar volume for the month.

44. An individual performing only _____ does not need to be licensed as an MLO if he or she works for only one company.
    A. qualifying activities
    B. automated underwriting services
    C. administrative or clerical tasks
    D. origination assistance functions

45. Which of the following is part of a loan's annual percentage rate?
    A. Hazard insurance premiums
    B. Appraisal fee
    C. Discount points
    D. Title insurance premiums

46. Which of the following would be permitted under the FNMA/FHLMC appraiser independence requirements?
    A. A loan officer calling an appraiser and asking for a verbal range of values for a property
    B. A bank's appraisal desk requesting a list of comparable properties from an appraiser who will not end up receiving the actual order for the appraisal on that property
    C. The processing manager at a mortgage company setting his expectation of value with an appraiser before sending an appraisal order to that appraiser
    D. A bank withholding payment to an appraiser because the indicated value on a report was less than required to complete a transaction

47. In order to be considered an "affiliated business" under RESPA, joint ownership exceeding _____ in a settlement service provider is required.
    A. 5%
    B. 10%
    C. 1%
    D. 7%

48. An applicant's loan application has been cleared-to-close by an underwriter. On the morning of closing, the MLO learns that one of the applicants was laid-off by his employer the previous day. What action should the MLO take?
    A. The MLO should take no action. The loan was cleared-to-close before the job loss occurred, so it is immaterial to the transaction.
    B. The MLO should call the borrower's employer and verify the lay-off occurred.
    C. The MLO should inform his/her manager of the situation, call the borrower and explain that the loan must be re-qualified with only the income of the remaining applicant(s) and ensure that the settlement agent and any attorneys involved are notified and the closing postponed.
    D. The MLO should immediately re-pull the applicant's credit report to see if the change in employment is reported. If it is not, the MLO should allow the closing to proceed.

49. A mortgage broker:
    A. retains servicing, uses its own funds, and is a lender.
    B. does not retain servicing, but does use its own funds and is a lender.
    C. does not retain servicing, does not use its own funds, but is a lender.
    D. does not retain servicing, does not use its own funds, and is not a lender.

50. Today is Monday, December 10, and you are at the closing table with your borrower and the settlement agent. Your borrower is closing an owner-occupied cash-out refinance transaction. Your borrower is concerned about the date that he can pick up his proceeds check. What is the earliest that the lender will fund the loan and allow disbursement of funds?
    A. Tuesday, December 11
    B. Wednesday, December 12
    C. Thursday, December 13
    D. Friday, December 14

51. Unlicensed processors and underwriters working for a state-licensed mortgage bank must be supervised by an individual who holds a valid Mortgage Loan Originator license. When examining the licensed company for compliance with the SAFE Act, regulators will look for a/an _____ between the processor or underwriter and their licensed supervisor.
    A. actual nexus
    B. general affiliation
    C. longstanding friendship
    D. organization chart reporting relationship

52. In the Sales Comparison or Market Value Approach, comparables on an appraisal should be closed sales and:
    A. be exactly the same as the subject property.
    B. include a wide range of home styles.
    C. be the same basic size and design as the subject property.
    D. always have been sold within the last two weeks.

53. A borrower earns $2,500 per month. The borrower leases an automobile for $100 per month and owes $800 in monthly child support. Given a $950 monthly mortgage payment, what would the borrower's debt-to-income ratio be?
    A. 36%
    B. 38%
    C. 70%
    D. 74%

54. A borrower with gross monthly income of $2,567 per month applying for a loan with a PITI of $567.87 and total other long-term obligations of $456.00 would have a monthly debt-to-income ("bottom" or "back-end") qualifying ratio of:
    A. 17.90%
    B. 39.90%
    C. 49.40%
    D. 22.10%

55. One of the best ways that companies can communicate their corporate beliefs to vendors and employees is through development and distribution of a/an:
    A. employee handbook.
    B. code of ethics.
    C. disciplinary policy.
    D. notice of core principles.

56. The Nationwide Multistate Licensing System and Registry (NMLS-R) was created for all of the following purposes EXCEPT:
    A. To provide uniform license applications and requirements for state-licensed loan originators.
    B. To provide increased accountability and tracking of loan originators.
    C. To provide low-cost information about loan originators to consumers.
    D. To streamline the licensing process and reduce regulatory burden.

57. Pursuant to the Equal Credit Opportunity Act (ECOA), notification of action taken must be provided to the applicant within which of the following time frames?
    A. 180 days after notifying the applicant of a counteroffer if applicant does not expressly accept or use the credit offered
    B. 60 days after taking adverse action on an incomplete application or an existing account
    C. 60 days after receiving an application by mail
    D. 30 days after receiving a completed application

58. When can a loan originator call a consumer whose phone number is in the Do Not Call Registry?
    A. When there is an established business relationship between them
    B. When the discussion relates to services that would clearly benefit the consumer
    C. When the consumer's phone number is obtained from an affiliated business
    D. Any time during normal business hours

59. All of the following are considered to be an immediate family member EXCEPT:
    A. spouse.
    B. sibling.
    C. aunt.
    D. grandparent.

60. The applicant estimates the value of the property at $275,000, but the appraised value comes in at $250,000. How long after receiving the appraisal does the creditor have to issue a revised Loan Estimate to the borrower?
    A. 1 business day
    B. 3 business days
    C. 5 business days
    D. This is not a valid changed circumstance.

61. Which of the following is the estimated total cost of credit over the life of the loan?
    A. Origination fee
    B. Settlement costs
    C. Annual percentage rate
    D. Discount point

62. In a VA loan a down payment is not required, but a funding fee is required and:
    A. is always equal to 1% of the loan amount.
    B. cannot be financed as part of the loan.
    C. the percentage amount can vary based on the veteran's circumstances.
    D. is always equal to 2% of the loan amount.

63. Which of the following would you NOT expect to see in a fraud for property scam?
    A. Altered paystubs to show more income
    B. An artificially inflated appraisal
    C. A fake verification of employment
    D. Tampering with bank statements to show more funds available than are actually in the account

64. What is the minimum number of continuing education hours that Mortgage Loan Originators need to complete during each renewal period under FEDERAL law?
    A. Six
    B. Eight
    C. 10
    D. 12

65. A licensee helps a homeowner refinance even though there is no tangible benefit to the homeowner. This is an example of:
    A. redlining.
    B. loan flipping.
    C. non-QM lending
    D. deed scamming.

PRACTICE EXAM B

Test your mortgage knowledge by taking the following practice exam. Answer keys for all three practice exams are provided in a later section of the study guide.

1. What is the term for the number that the NMLS-R assigns to a loan originator that identifies the person and allows the NMLS-R to track that person's conduct?
   A. Social Security number
   B. Unique identifier number
   C. Loan originator number
   D. Loan originator license number

2. The term for the rate on an ARM loan that is lower than the fully-indexed rate at the time of closing is:
   A. bought-down rate.
   B. teaser rate.
   C. fully indexed rate.
   D. margin rate.

3. The use of overtime or bonus income in total qualifying income:
   A. can be included by adding 100% of each year's overtime and bonus total to the income received for that year.
   B. must be based on the average over two years, and the employer must verify that such income is expected to continue to be earned by the borrower.
   C. is never allowed.
   D. is only allowed on conventional loans.

4. In general, what must a borrower do to avoid having late payments reported to a credit bureau?
   A. Pay within 30 days of the due date.
   B. Pay within 15 days of any grace period.
   C. Contact the lender within 90 days of the due date.
   D. Pay back the entire balance of the loan within 120 days of the due date.

5. The purpose of the property appraisal is to:
   A. set the market price of a property.
   B. determine the gross rent multiplier.
   C. determine the actual income a property will produce.
   D. assess the adequacy of collateral for a mortgage transaction.

6. Under Regulation Z, which of the following disclosures is required to be provided within three business days of loan application on all adjustable-rate mortgages?
   A. Servicing transfer statement
   B. CHARM booklet
   C. Closing disclosure
   D. "When your home is on the line" disclosure

7. To estimate value under the cost approach, the appraiser:
    A. calculates the cost of construction minus any depreciation, plus the value of the land.
    B. compares similar type properties and averages the sale prices.
    C. calculates cost by an equalization factor.
    D. calculates the building's list price plus any "tear-down" costs.

8. Which practice is illegal under the MLO Compensation rule?
    A. A mortgage broker company receives compensation from a lender on a transaction.
    B. A mortgage banking firm pays a commission to its MLOs for a closed loan.
    C. A mortgage broker company receives compensation from both the creditor and the consumer on a transaction that is then used to pay a commission to the MLO.
    D. A mortgage bank receives a dividend check from a title company in which it has an ownership interest.

9. When used in an advertisement, which of the following is not a "trigger term" that would require additional disclosures?
    A. APR
    B. The interest rate
    C. Number of payments
    D. The amount of down payment required

10. Achieving a lower interest rate for the life of the loan by paying discount points is referred to as a/an:
    A. prepayment direct option.
    B. permanent buydown.
    C. amortization buydown.
    D. lock-in control period.

11. What is the only fee that can be charged prior to providing a Loan Estimate to the borrower?
    A. Credit report fee
    B. Origination fee
    C. Appraisal fee
    D. Discount point

12. Which term is used to describe the arbitrary denial of loan applications in certain geographic areas without considering an individual's qualifications?
    A. Steering
    B. Loan flipping
    C. Redlining
    D. Equity stripping

13. If a borrower is improperly required to use a specific title company or settlement agent, the maximum penalty to the violator is equal to _____ the amount of the improperly required fee.
    A. 2 times
    B. 3 times
    C. 5 times
    D. 10 times

14. According to Guidance on Non-Traditional Mortgage Product Risk, which of the following should not be over-weighted in an analysis of borrower repayment capacity?
    A. Liquid assets
    B. Credit scores
    C. Income verification
    D. Liability analysis

15. Prepayment penalties on residential mortgages, when allowed by law, are limited to a maximum of _____ of the unpaid principal balance in the first year of the loan.
    A. 1%
    B. 5%
    C. 2.5%
    D. 3%

16. Under the Red Flags Rule, the FTC requires all mortgage lenders to have written policies and procedures in place to address which of the following?
    A. Occupancy fraud
    B. Incorrect income calculations
    C. Identity theft
    D. Secondary market risk

17. For purposes of delivering the Closing Disclosure, a "business day" is defined as:
    A. any day the lender's office is open for business.
    B. every day except Sundays.
    C. any day except Sundays and federal holidays.
    D. all days except Independence Day, Christmas and New Year's Day.

18. As they relate to permissible actions by someone other than a loan originator, which of the following is not considered to be "general information"?
    A. Terminology
    B. Loan terms
    C. Lending policies
    D. Borrower identifying information

19. How should loan originators approach the issues of home ownership and renting?
    A. The loan originator should assume that home ownership is beneficial to a borrower.
    B. The loan originator should take time to understand a borrower's preferences.
    C. The loan originator should avoid these topics due to conflicts of interest.
    D. The loan originator should become dually licensed as a leasing agent.

20. What must condominium associations do with respect to property insurance?
    A. They must insure each unit in the amount of the separate unit's purchase price.
    B. They do nothing, each individual condominium owner is responsible for its own unit.
    C. They are required to keep a "blanket" policy that protects the entire structure.
    D. The common areas only require insurance.

21. A $200,000 interest-only loan has an interest rate of 6%. What is the monthly interest-only payment?
    A. $100
    B. $1,000
    C. $3,333
    D. $10,000

22. Which of the following is not a violation of Section 8 of Regulation X?
    A. An insurance company providing a free vacation to the mortgage professional who generates the largest number of new client referrals for quotes
    B. A mortgage company using an affiliated title company to pass-through title orders to a third-party company for processing
    C. A mortgage company providing a complimentary bottle of wine and gift certificate for a home-furnishings store to its clients at closing
    D. A mortgage professional paying all of the costs for a joint newspaper advertisement with a real estate agent

23. Someone who performs unsupervised mortgage-related duties is called a/an:
    A. loan originator.
    B. loan processor.
    C. independent contractor.
    D. registered loan originator.

24. Tony's Mortgage Emporium has a 25% ownership interest in Totally Tubular Title. Tony's loan officers often refer business to the affiliated title company on refinance transactions. This practice is legal as long as the applicant is not REQUIRED to use the title company and the Affiliated Business Arrangement Disclosure (AfBA) is provided to the borrower:
    A. within three business days of application.
    B. at closing.
    C. before the referral to the title company is actually made.
    D. three weeks from the first Wednesday after application if the moon is a waxing gibbous.

25. Which of the following would be the largest factor in determining the maximum amount for a VA loan?
    A. The property's location
    B. The property's value
    C. The payment schedule
    D. The property's replacement cost

26. The secondary market is where:
    A. mortgage loans are originated.
    B. borrowers can find the best rates.
    C. existing mortgage loans are bought and sold.
    D. overseas loans are originated.

27. At which website can consumers obtain the copy of their credit report that the credit bureaus are required to provide once per year at no charge?
    A. freecreditreport.com
    B. mycreditreport.com
    C. annualcreditreport.com
    D. getyourcredit.gov

28. 95% is generally the maximum loan-to-value ratio on a purchase transaction for which of the following loan programs?
    A. Conforming
    B. FHA
    C. VA
    D. USDA

29. Creditors must retain all Loan Estimates for a period of at least _____ after a loan closes:
    A. 24 months
    B. 5 years
    C. 1 year
    D. 3 years

30. A borrower has the following minimum payments due monthly:
Mortgage PITI - $1100, Auto loan with 12 payments remaining - $350, Auto lease with 3 payments remaining - $250, Electric bill - $110, Gas bill - $80, Student loan with 92 payments remaining - $60, Visa credit card - $50. Given this data, what amount would the underwriter use to calculate the borrower's total debt ratio in a conventional conforming loan?
    A. $1810
    B. $2000
    C. $1560
    D. $900

31. Under the Equal Credit Opportunity Act, which of the following is not a protected class/prohibited characteristic?
    A. Race
    B. National origin
    C. Religion
    D. Handicap

32. Who is ultimately responsible for ensuring that the appraisal used by a lender for underwriting a loan is accurate?
    A. The lender
    B. The borrower
    C. The appraiser
    D. The borrower's real estate agent

33. Of the terms listed, which is the best description of a 2-1 loan?
    A. A buydown loan
    B. An ARM loan
    C. A growing equity mortgage
    D. A reverse mortgage

34. According to which regulation can an escrow account have a cushion in an amount equal to 1/6th of the yearly taxes and property insurance cost?
    A. Regulation Z
    B. Regulation X
    C. Regulation C
    D. Regulation B

35. A reverse mortgage is a type of mortgage where:
    A. the payments are more frequent and reduce the principal balance at a faster rate.
    B. payments are amortized over 30 years, but the full principal balance is due at the end of a much shorter period.
    C. the lender may make periodic payments to the borrower.
    D. the amortization begins at a fixed rate and converts to an adjustable-rate mortgage.

36. A real estate agent and mortgage loan originator can advertise their services jointly as long as:
    A. the real estate professional pays the full cost of the ad.
    B. each professional pays a cost proportional to their amount of space in the ad.
    C. the mortgage professional pays the full cost of the ad.
    D. real estate agents and mortgage professionals can never advertise together.

37. What is accomplished through a permanent buydown?
    A. The seller agrees to accept less money for the property.
    B. The lender agrees to reduce the interest rate on the loan.
    C. The borrower agrees to pay more in interest in exchange for lower fees.
    D. The borrower agrees to pay less in interest in exchange for higher PMI premiums.

38. Under Regulation X, how often are lenders required to send borrowers with escrow accounts a summary statement of the account balance and transactions?
    A. At closing and every 6 months
    B. Only at closing
    C. At closing and every month
    D. At closing and every year

39. When a borrower's regular payments on a loan result in an increase of the principal balance:
    A. the loan is a reverse mortgage.
    B. negative amortization occurs.
    C. the borrower's rate cap has ended.
    D. positive amortization occurs.

40. Which of the following debts could be excluded from the borrower's total debt ratio (DTI) at the discretion of the underwriter for a mortgage loan being sold to Fannie Mae?
    A. An auto lease with 6 payments remaining
    B. An installment loan for a boat with 8 payments remaining
    C. A deferred student loan
    D. A revolving credit card account with an outstanding balance less than 20% of the available credit limit.

41. A borrower has a loan with an outstanding principal balance of $350,000, an interest rate of 7.375%, a principal and interest payment of $2,693 with a 2% prepayment penalty in effect. If the borrower pays off the loan today, what would be the amount of the prepayment penalty?
    A. $53.86
    B. $7,000
    C. $514.50
    D. $7,500

42. Under FEDERAL law, which of the following actions taken on an application would not require a written notice to the applicant?
    A. The application is approved.
    B. The application is denied.
    C. The creditor issues a counteroffer to the applicant.
    D. The file is incomplete and the creditor needs more information to decision the file.

43. Before a loan originator candidate is licensed, how many hours of pre-license ethics training must she or he complete?
    A. 20 hours
    B. 10 hours
    C. 3 hours
    D. 2 hours

44. A "Cap" is a feature of an adjustable rate mortgage that:
    A. prevents negative amortization.
    B. can be used to limit the interest rate increase or decrease.
    C. increases the amount of the payment due from the borrower.
    D. shortens the term of the loan.

45. A loan originator feels that a property is under-valued and pays an appraiser $500 to change his or her opinion about the property's value. When the activity is discovered, what might happen?
    A. Nothing; it is common for appraisers to accept small amounts of money.
    B. Nothing; payments of less than $1,000 do not constitute a prohibited activity.
    C. The loan originator could be fined up to $25,000 per offense.
    D. The NMLS-R will revoke the appraiser's license.

46. Borrowers have contracted to purchase their first home, and they come to you to apply for a mortgage loan. You run an analysis of their qualifications and are able to get them approved for a 30-year, fixed-rate loan at 5.5% with a PITI payment of $1750. The borrowers tell you that is a higher payment than they are comfortable with. How do you proceed?
    A. Review the borrowers' monthly expenses and point out that they can easily afford the payment with a few lifestyle changes.
    B. Tell the borrowers that, since the loan has been approved by automated underwriting, they should have no problem making the payment.
    C. Have an open discussion with the borrowers about their affordability concerns, keeping an open mind to cancelling the transaction.
    D. Cancel the loan and retain any application fee charged to the borrowers.

47. The servicing of Jim's mortgage loan is being transferred from one servicer to another. If Jim makes a mistake and sends his mortgage payment to the OLD servicer instead of the new servicer, the old servicer is required by law to accept the payment and forward it on to the new servicer for at least _____ after closing.
    A. 30 days
    B. 90 days
    C. 180 days
    D. 60 days

48. Under HMDA's Regulation C, creditors subject to data collection and reporting requirements must maintain a _____, which is essentially a log of applications.
    A. File Sheet Document (FSD)
    B. Loan Delivery Report (LDR)
    C. Loan Application Register (LAR)
    D. Mortgage Loan Origination Log (MLOL)

49. In describing an ARM loan with caps of 5/1/6, which of the following statements is accurate?
    A. The initial interest rate on the loan is 5%.
    B. The highest that the interest rate on the loan can be is 6%.
    C. At the first adjustment period, the interest rate will only adjust to 5%.
    D. At the first adjustment period, the interest rate may not increase more than 5% over the initial rate.

50. Which of the following terms can be used to describe a balloon loan?
    A. Partially amortizing loan
    B. Fully amortizing loan
    C. Negatively amortizing loan
    D. ARM loan

51. As a result of the Dodd-Frank Act, what must lenders do in regard to insurance?
    A. Refer borrowers to a property insurance company upon request.
    B. Provide information about the risks of not having flood insurance.
    C. Give notice to borrowers before billing them for force-placed insurance.
    D. Require that credit life insurance be purchased through an affiliated service provider.

52. Which of the following documents/disclosures would NOT need to be provided to an applicant who is applying for a five-year ARM loan to refinance a primary residence?
    A. ARM Disclosure
    B. Loan Estimate
    C. CHARM Booklet
    D. Your Home Loan Toolkit

53. Form 1004 is also known as the:
    A. Uniform Loan Application for Reverse Mortgages.
    B. Uniform Residential Appraisal Report.
    C. Uniform Residential Loan Application.
    D. IRS Personal Income Tax Return.

54. What is the federally mandated rescission period (after closing) on a refinance transaction for a borrower's second home?
    A. 3 business days
    B. 5 business days
    C. 1 business day
    D. There is no right of rescission.

55. The Federal Home Loan Bank System (FHLB) provides:
    A. residential mortgage loans directly to qualified borrowers.
    B. federal loan guarantees to member lenders.
    C. liquidity to community banks and other depository institutions.
    D. free appraisals for FHA-approved residential mortgage loans.

56. After the initial Loan Estimate has been sent to the applicant, when is the earliest that a mortgage loan transaction can close?
    A. 3 business days after receipt
    B. 7 business days after receipt
    C. The day the borrower indicates intent to proceed
    D. 15 days after receipt

57. Under the SAFE Act, a state licensing authority may act in all of the following ways EXCEPT:
    A. Examine an individual mortgage loan originator's books.
    B. Retain and destroy a loan originator's documents.
    C. Enforce state licensing law.
    D. Conduct interviews with a loan originator's customers.

58. An individual comes into your office accompanied by a dog that you suspect is a pet and not a service animal. Your company does not allow pets on the premises. Which of the following actions is acceptable?
    A. Explain the company's no-pet policy and nicely ask the person to leave.
    B. Ask the person what tasks the dog has been trained to perform and the nature of the disability that requires a service animal.
    C. Ask the individual if the dog is required due to a disability and what tasks it has been trained to perform.
    D. Pet the dog and offer it some water if it looks thirsty.

59. A lender gave a borrower an ARM with a 3% introductory rate. At the time, the index associated with the ARM was at 2%, and the lender's margin for the loan is also 2%. The ARM has a 3% initial and periodic cap. The loan has reached its first adjusment period, but the index value has not changed. What is the new interest rate that will be imposed on the borrower?
    A. 2%
    B. 3%
    C. 4%
    D. 5%

60. Referrals are a significant source for business opportunities in the mortgage industry and are allowable:
    A. in the form of a "kickback."
    B. only between loan originators.
    C. as long as nothing of value changes hands in exchange for the referral.
    D. if placed through the loan originators' referral network.

61. In general, how many years of a borrower's income must be verified?
    A. 1
    B. 2
    C. 3
    D. 5

62. A lender that funds loans originated through a mortgage broker is referred to as a/an:
    A. wholesale lender.
    B. below-market lender.
    C. retail lender.
    D. courageous lender.

63. If you formally grant another person or company the right to access or traverse your property and record that right of access in the public record, you have provided that person or company a/an:
    A. right of access.
    B. easement.
    C. Encroachment.
    D. zoning exception.

64. When an appraiser is performing a valuation for a residential mortgage transaction, for whom is he or she working?
    A. The buyer
    B. The seller
    C. The real estate brokers
    D. The creditor

65. When a borrower fails to maintain adequate insurance coverage on a property, the lender/servicer is allowed to purchase insurance to protect its interest and charge the borrower for the cost of the policy. This is called "force-placing" of insurance. The borrower must receive at least two separate written notices within the _____ window before force-placement occurs.
    A. 15-day
    B. 30-day
    C. 45-day
    D. 60-day

PRACTICE EXAM C

Test your mortgage knowledge by taking the following practice exam. Answer keys for all three practice exams are provided in a later section of the study guide.

1. A loan originator may access a consumer's credit report for which of the following purposes?
    A. To help a consumer determine the credit obligations of a former spouse
    B. To determine a consumer's eligibilty for loan products
    C. To help a real estate agent pre-screen a tenant for a rental property
    D. To verify marital status, national origin and other demographic information

2. What income generally can not be used as qualifying income?
    A. Trust income
    B. Child support income
    C. Part-time work income with the minimum of a two-year history
    D. Unemployment income

3. Which of the following is a conventional loan?
    A. FHA loan
    B. USDA loan
    C. Assumable VA loan
    D. Private loan sold to Fannie Mae

4. What is the maximum fine for providing an illegal kickback under Section 8 of RESPA?
    A. $10,000
    B. $50,000
    C. $100,000
    D. $1,000,000

5. PMI:
    A. protects the borrower in the event of death or disability, and is paid by the borrower.
    B. protects the borrower against property defects which are the responsibility of the seller or builder, and is paid by the seller or builder.
    C. protects the lender in case of default by the borrower, and is paid by the borrower.
    D. protects the lender in the event of fire and/or theft, and is paid by the borrower.

6. Your borrower has an annual gross income of $60,000. According to Fannie Mae and Freddie Mac guidelines, what is the maximum amount the borrower can spend per month on debt service payments, including housing expense, without compensating factors?
    A. $1,400
    B. $1,800
    C. $2,150
    D. $2,250

7. Fifteen days of "per diem" interest on a new loan amount of $175,000 with an interest rate of 7% would equal:
   A. $581.86
   B. $1,163.75
   C. $503.42
   D. $510.42

8. The purchase price of a home is $300,000, and the appraised value is $250,000. If the amount of mortgage loan is $225,000, what is the loan-to-value ratio?
   A. 80%
   B. 75%
   C. 84%
   D. 90%

9. What happens when a routine background check reveals that a loan originator candidate has had his or her license revoked in another state?
   A. The applicant can re-apply for a license after two years.
   B. The state can require the applicant to obtain a surety bond.
   C. The applicant can demonstrate an adequate net worth to cover the dollar amount of his or her originated loans.
   D. The state can never issue a license to the applicant.

10. Which of the following documents is prepared by the lender's closing department in connection with a closing?
    A. Warranty deed
    B. Promissory note
    C. Bill of sale
    D. Surveyor's special report

11. FHA qualifying ratios and underwriting standards:
    A. can be relaxed if the buyer has a large down payment
    B. are strictly held at 31% and 43%.
    C. conform to conventional standards.
    D. must be reviewed by HUD for each loan.

12. Before opening a new mortgage account for a consumer, creditors are required to verify the individual's identity and ensure that the person is not on the OFAC list of known or suspected terrorists, drug traffickers and money launderers. Under which federal law are these processes required?
    A. TILA
    B. USA PATRIOT Act
    C. RESPA
    D. Gramm-Leach-Bliley Act

13. Which of the following loans is characterized by a short maturity period (usually six to nine months), interest-only payments on the outstanding balance and multiple draws?
    A. Fixed-rate loan
    B. Graduated payment mortgage
    C. Home-equity loan
    D. Construction loan

14. Which of the following fees or charges is included in the finance charge?
    A. Escrow deposits
    B. Appraisal fees
    C. Pest inspection fees
    D. Mortgage insurance premiums

15. If you are someone who tells a borrower that you can negotiate the terms of a residential mortgage loan, you are acting as a/an:
    A. loan originator.
    B. independent contractor.
    C. loan underwriter.
    D. loan processor

16. In general, an installment loan with how many remaining payments can be excluded from liabilities when attempting to qualify a borrower?
    A. 15 or less
    B. 12 or less
    C. 10 or less
    D. This type of debt can never be excluded.

17. Which of the following fees cannot increase by more than 10% between the Loan Estimate and Closing Disclosure?
    A. Transfer taxes
    B. Loan origination charges
    C. Credit report fee
    D. Title insurance charges

18. In general, what percentage of the loan amount do borrowers pay for each discount point?
    A. 1/8%
    B. 1%
    C. 1.50%
    D. 2%

19. A seller's attorney is acting as the issuing agent for an owner's title insurance policy in a purchase transaction. The buyer elects to obtain the lender's title insurance policy from that attorney as well. Instead of paying in cash, the attorney and buyer agree that the buyer will provide the attorney with a luxury box at an upcoming baseball game instead. Who has violated RESPA?
    A. The borrower
    B. The attorney
    C. Both the borrower and the attorney
    D. Neither the borrower nor the attorney

20. A loan originator should do more for the borrower than just fill out forms. The loan originator must act as a source of information:
    A. who predicts the direction of interest rates.
    B. who knows the different investor loan programs and analyzes the borrower's circumstances and aligns the borrower with appropriate loan products.
    C. regarding expenses the borrower may incur to close the loan, such as homeowners insurance rates.
    D. regarding the borrower's selection of home improvements.

21. In the application process, which responsibility belongs to the consumer?
    A. Ordering the appraisal
    B. Entering personal information into the lender's atuomated underwriting system
    C. Providing accurate and truthful information to the loan originator
    D. Taking care to influence the outcome of an independent appraisal

22. Paying money in advance to subsidize the monthly payments for an intial period of years is called a:
    A. permanent buydown.
    B. temporary buydown.
    C. mortgage insurance premium.
    D. home equity line of credit.

23. A borrower owning a property located in a Special Flood Hazard Area:
    A. will not be able to obtain FHA financing.
    B. will not be able to obtain a conventional loan.
    C. will require flood insurance for the benefit of the lender.
    D. will require private mortgage insurance for the benefit of the lender.

24. Your clients are purchasing a home for $320,000 and will be making a 10% down payment. They have elected a monthly premium plan for the required mortgage insurance. 25% coverage is required by the investor, and the PMI company has provided you with a factor of 0.45% for this policy. How much will the borrower pay each month for mortgage insurance after the loan closes?
    A. $60.00
    B. $120.00
    C. $66.67
    D. $108.00

25. Under TRID, the Home Loan Toolkit is required to be presented to the borrower on which type(s) of transactions?
    A. All mortgage loan transactions
    B. Purchase money loan transactions
    C. Refinance transactions
    D. Reverse mortgage transactions

26. Where are existing mortgage loans bought and sold?
    A. The secondary market
    B. The subprime mortgage market
    C. The nontraditional mortgage market
    D. The non-conforming mortgage market

27. A borrower is closing on a 3/1 ARM with 2/2/6 caps. The start rate on the loan is 4.0%, the loan is based off the 1-year LIBOR index and the margin is 2.5%. The index value at the time of closing is 2.0% and has fluctuated between 1.5% and 3.0% for the past 10 years. Given the above scenario, what interest rate will the borrower pay in the 30th month on this loan if the index value at that time is 2.375%?
    A. 4.50%
    B. 4.00%
    C. 10.00%
    D. 4.88%

28. Which of the following characteristics is protected under the Fair Housing Act but not protected under the Equal Credit Opportunity Act?
    A. Race
    B. Color
    C. National origin
    D. Familial status

29. Which of the following features would ensure that the loan in question could never achieve Qualified Mortgage (QM) status?
    A. An adjustable rate
    B. A prepayment penalty
    C. Negative amortization
    D. Full documentation of income and assets

30. Who must a mortgage broker use to order an appraisal for transactions covered by the appraiser independence requirements?
    A. ATM
    B. FHA
    C. AMC
    D. Any local appraiser

31. Which of the following statements is true about a loan originator?
    A. A loan originator must always be licensed.
    B. A loan originator may be an individual or a company.
    C. A loan originator completes applications only in person.
    D. A loan originator is paid by the loan applicant.

32. Which of the following is often done by a loan processor?
    A. Making product recommendations to loan applicants
    B. Referring consumers to third-party service providers
    C. Verifying information on loan applications
    D. Assisting in making the credit decision

33. According to the Fair Credit Reporting Act, all consumers are entitled to one free copy of their credit report each year. Which website is maintained by the credit bureaus to allow consumers to access these legally-mandated reports?
    A. FreeCreditReport.com
    B. GetMyCreditReport.com
    C. AnnualCreditReport.com
    D. CreditKarma.com

34. The Equal Credit Opportunity Act (ECOA) prohibits discrimination in the granting of all types of credit on the basis of:
    A. specific criteria determined annually by the Secretary of Housing and Urban Development, the U.S. Attorney General and the shareholders of Fannie Mae.
    B. employment history, prior bankruptcy, foreclosure, missed loan payments and availability of verifiable cash.
    C. credit scores, automated underwriting determinations, verifications of employment, verifications of deposit and existence of notes receivable income.
    D. race, color, religion, national origin, sex, marital status, legal age, receipt of income from public assistance benefits and the fact the applicant has exercised any right, in good faith, under the consumer credit protection act.

35. Which activity is NOT part of servicing the loan?
    A. Funding the loan
    B. Handling borrower inquiries
    C. Collecting payments
    D. Providing disclosures

36. How many months of property taxes and homeowners insurance can a lender hold in a borrower's escrow account above and beyond the amount required to pay the bills when due?
    A. 1 month
    B. 6 months
    C. 2 months
    D. 3 months

37. Under the E-SIGN Act, in order for electronic signatures to be binding and carry the same weight as wet-signed documents, a creditor must:
    A. verify the identity of consumers signing electronically.
    B. obtain consent from the consumer to use electronic signatures before presenting any documents for electronic signature.
    C. have established procedures for a consumer to withdraw consent
    D. All of these.

38. What is the calculation for determining the amount due at closing for a single-premium mortgage insurance plan?
    A. Loan amount multiplied by MI factor
    B. MI factor divided by loan amount
    C. MI factor multiplied by 12
    D. MI factor multiplied by number of months in the loan term

39. The appraiser uses which of the following standard approaches during a valuation analysis?
    A. Cost approach
    B. Sales comparison approach
    C. Income approach
    D. All of the above

40. Which of the following borrowers would be the most likely candidate for a USDA loan?
    A. A veteran hoping to make no down payment
    B. A high-income farmer hoping to purchase rural property
    C. A moderate-income borrower in an area with less than 35,000 people
    D. A low-income family in an urban area

41. In mortgage lending, "steering" refers to the practice of:
    A. directing an applicant to a loan product to increase the originator's compensation.
    B. refusing to make mortgage loans in a certain area based on its demographic makeup.
    C. telling applicants the best strategies to qualify for a home loan.
    D. delaying a closing to allow the interest rate lock to expire and charge the borrower more.

42. What is the minimum down payment for an FHA purchase loan?
    A. 0%
    B. 3.5%
    C. 5%
    D. 10%

43. What are "seasoned" funds?
    A. Funds on deposit for at least 3 months
    B. Newly deposited funds
    C. Gift funds
    D. Funds deposited under the grandfather rule

44. Which of the following is the primary federal regulator for mortgage banks and mortgage brokers licensed by the states?
    A. CFPB
    B. HUD
    C. FDIC
    D. FHFA

45. Expressed as a percentage of the base loan amount, how much is the Upfront Mortgage Insurance Premium (UFMIP) on standard forward FHA loans?
    A. 0.85%
    B. 1.25%
    C. 1.75%
    D. 2.25%

46. Which of the following IRS forms would you request from a borrower who is a partner in a partnership?
    A. 1120S
    B. 1065
    C. 8821
    D. 2706

47. FEMA is responsible for overseeing the:
    A. NFIP.
    B. PMI.
    C. AIR / HVCC.
    D. CRA.

48. Which of the following is a characteristic of a fully amortizing loan?
    A. The payment due does not cover all the interest owed.
    B. The balance is not fully extinguished at the end of the loan term.
    C. The balance is fully extinguished at the end of the loan term.
    D. The interest rate is based on the fully indexed rate.

49. When an individual identifies information on a credit report that is incomplete or inaccurate and reports it to a credit reporting agency, the agency:
    A. does not need to investigate.
    B. only needs to investigate if the consumer pays a fee.
    C. must investigate unless the dispute is frivolous.
    D. will require that the individual file a police report.

50. Which of the following actions would be permissable under Regulation B due to special carve-out provisions?
    A. Marketing a 0.25% interest-rate discount to newly-married couples
    B. Offering a loan product with special repayment features only to senior citizens
    C. Providing special pricing to members of one race if you can statistically prove that they have a lower homeownership rate than other races
    D. Advertising a special closing cost reduction in a church circular and restricting that deal to members of that religion only

51. Flood insurance is required when:
    A. any portion of a property is in a special flood hazard area.
    B. the entire property is located in a special flood hazard area.
    C. a dwelling/structure on the property is located in a special flood hazard area.
    D. FEMA tells the lender that they will require it.

52. In an automated underwriting system, if a loan is "referred." it means:
    A. it is being sent to another loan officer.
    B. it is completely denied.
    C. it is not qualified.
    D. it needs a complete underwriting procedure to be completed.

53. Which of the following items would be an acceptable gift for a mortgage broker to provide his/her clients at the closing of their first home?
    A. A $40 bottle of wine
    B. A $100 gift card to a furniture store
    C. A bouquet of flowers
    D. Any of these items would be acceptable.

54. The purpose of a professional home inspection is:
    A. to obtain a valuation of the property.
    B. to help the seller disguise obvious defects in the property.
    C. to help the seller rescind the sale of the property.
    D. to help disclose any defects in the property.

55. A purchase transaction is 48 hours from the scheduled closing, and the borrower receives an email from the settlement agent with wiring instructions. What should the borrower do?
    A. Go to the bank in person and request a wire within 8 business hours to ensure an on-time closing.
    B. Refuse to wire funds and instead obtain a cashier's check in the amount requested to bring to closing.
    C. Call the settlement agent or real esate agent at a known phone number to confirm the instructions are legitimate.
    D. Reply to the email asking the settlement agent to confirm the loan number on the file.

56. Dave Developer purchases 10 homes in need of repair that have been condemned by the local housing authority. He makes minor cosmetic repairs on them to make it appear as though they are in satisfactory shape, but in reality the homes still have major structural defects. Dave markets the properties at a value that far exceeds their actual worth and offers the low-income buyers an incentive to use Larry Loanofficer at Shady Bank. Larry and Dave are working with April Appraiser and have paid her a cash bonus to ensure that the structural defects are not reflected on her reports. This is an example of:
    A. identity fraud.
    B. fraud for housing.
    C. fraud for profit.
    D. occupancy fraud.

57. The Dodd-Frank Act added to TILA the requirement that prepayment penalties must not extend beyond the first three years. According to the language of the Act, what is the maximum prepayment penalty in the second year of a loan?
    A. 0.50%
    B. 1%
    C. 2%
    D. 3%

58. This entity exists in the secondary market and provides a guarantee to investors purchasing certain mortgage bonds secured by government loans:
    A. Fannie Mae (FNMA)
    B. Ginnie Mae (GNMA)
    C. Penny Mac (PNMC)
    D. Sallie Mae (SLMA)

59. A conventional loan made to an individual with marginal credit history that is not eligible for sale to the GSEs is also called a:
    A. predatory loan.
    B. high-cost loan.
    C. subprime loan.
    D. high-risk loan

60. A lender has set a minimum credit score of 680 for conventional loans in order to mitigate its default risk. The same lender's minimum FICO score for FHA loans is 620 to accommodate the goals of the FHA loan program. In analyzing the lender's HMDA data, the regulator determines that a significantly higher percentage of minority borrowers received FHA loans than did non-minority borrowers. Which of the following statements is accurate?
    A. Since the intent of the FICO policies were non-discriminatory, there can be no allegation of discrimination.
    B. There is a potential cause of action against the lender for overt discrimination.
    C. There is a potential cause of action against the lender for disparate treatment.
    D. There is a potential cause of action against the lender for disparate impact.

61. Automated underwriting systems can be used for:
    A. conventional loans only.
    B. conventional, jumbo, FHA, VA and USDA loans.
    C. FHA loans with HUD approval.
    D. VA loans with the government's approval.

62. After a loan has consummated, how long must creditors retain a copy of the Loan Estimate(s) under FEDERAL law?
    A. 3 years
    B. 5 years
    C. 10 years
    D. For the life of the loan

63. The tasks of maintaining databases regarding money laundering and terrorist funding activities, facilitating communication between law enforcement and financial institutions in money laundering investigations and processing Suspicious Activity Reports falls to:
    A. the Consumer Financial Protection Bureau.
    B. FinCEN.
    C. the Department of Justice.
    D. the Federal Bureau of Investigation.

64. Under the USA Patriot Act, which of the following are the acceptable methods of verifying a customer's identity?
    A. Physical and virtual
    B. In-person and video
    C. Documentary and non-documentary
    D. Photo and non-photo

65. On a $230,000 FHA loan with a term of 30 years and a loan-to-value ratio of 92% at origination, what will be the annual MIP factor that the borrower must pay?
    A. 0.70%
    B. 0.80%
    C. 0.85%
    D. 1.00%

PRACTICE EXAM ANSWER KEYS

Practice Exam A

1. B	11. A	21. D	31. C	41. A	51. A	61. C
2. C	12. A	22. A	32. B	42. C	52. C	62. C
3. B	13. C	23. B	33. C	43. A	53. D	63. B
4. B	14. D	24. C	34. B	44. C	54. B	64. B
5. B	15. B	25. B	35. C	45. C	55. B	65. B
6. A	16. C	26. C	36. B	46. B	56. C	
7. B	17. D	27. B	37. D	47. C	57. D	
8. C	18. B	28. C	38. D	48. C	58. A	
9. D	19. A	29. B	39. A	49. D	59. C	
10. D	20. A	30. A	40. D	50. D	60. B	

Practice Exam B

1. B	11. A	21. B	31. D	41. B	51. C	61. B
2. B	12. C	22. C	32. A	42. A	52. D	62. A
3. B	13. B	23. C	33. A	43. C	53. B	63. B
4. A	14. B	24. C	34. B	44. B	54. D	64. D
5. D	15. D	25. B	35. C	45. C	55. C	65. C
6. B	16. C	26. C	36. B	46. C	56. B	
7. A	17. C	27. C	37. B	47. D	57. B	
8. C	18. B	28. A	38. D	48. C	58. C	
9. A	19. B	29. D	39. B	49. D	59. C	
10. B	20. C	30. A	40. B	50. A	60. C	

Practice Exam C

1. B	11. A	21. C	31. B	41. A	51. C	61. B
2. D	12. B	22. B	32. C	42. B	52. D	62. A
3. D	13. D	23. C	33. C	43. A	53. D	63. B
4. A	14. D	24. D	34. D	44. A	54. D	64. C
5. C	15. A	25. B	35. A	45. C	55. C	65. B
6. B	16. C	26. A	36. C	46. B	56. C	
7. D	17. D	27. B	37. D	47. A	57. C	
8. D	18. B	28. D	38. A	48. C	58. B	
9. D	19. D	29. C	39. D	49. C	59. C	
10. B	20. B	30. C	40. C	50. B	60. D	

GLOSSARY

Acceleration clause: A portion of a lending agreement that forces the borrower to repay the entire loan upon the first instance of borrower default.

Actual nexus: A term in the SAFE Act that describes the relationship that must exist between unlicensed loan processors or underwriters and the licensed MLO who is responsible for supervising them. The individual with the license must perform actual oversight and be available to provide feedback and answer questions as necessary. In other words, the manager/employee relationship cannot be merely symbolic.

Adjustable-rate mortgage (ARM): A type of mortgage instrument in which the interest rate periodically adjusts up or down according to a specific index and pre-determined margin. ARM transactions require the creditor to provide borrowers with a special ARM disclosure as well as a CHARM booklet.

Adjustment period: The amount of time during which a new interest rate will be in effect for an adjustable-rate mortgage. New adjustment periods might occur after several months, every year or every few years.

Administrative and clerical tasks: The receipt, collection and distribution of information that is common in the processing or underwriting of a loan in the mortgage business. The term is also used to describe communication that is designed to obtain common information from a consumer. In general, an individual who only performs administrative or clerical tasks and doesn't negotiate with or give advice to borrowers doesn't need a loan originator license.

Adverse action: An unfavorable credit decision rendered against a consumer made on the basis of information contained on the credit application. If a lender takes adverse action against an applicant, the lender must notify the applicant in writing. If the adverse action is taken as a result of information contained on the credit report, the notice must also provide the name, address and toll-free phone number of the credit bureau that supplied the information.

Affiliated Business Arrangement Disclosure (AfBA): A document that informs mortgage applicants of any service providers that may be used in the loan transaction that are affiliated with the lender. It must be provided to the borrower no later than the time the referral to the affiliated business is made and is required when there is greater than a 1% common ownership in the affiliated settlement service business. If the lender requires the use of an affiliated provider (such as for a flood certification), then the disclosure must be given at application.

Alienation clause: A portion of a lending agreement that prohibits the borrower from transferring title to the mortgaged property without the consent of the lender.

Alt-A loans: Loans in which the borrower represents too much risk to meet the underwriting standards for a conforming loan but is not risky enough to be considered *subprime*.

American Association of Residential Mortgage Regulators (AARMR): A national association of individuals who are charged with administering and regulating various aspects of residential mortgage lending. It played a major role in the formation of the NMLS-R and in the drafting of the model licensing law.

Annual percentage rate (APR): A measurement of the total cost of the credit, expressed as an annual rate. The APR includes specific costs of financing paid at the time of closing and/or over the term of the loan. It includes all items that are included in the finance charge, such as interest, discount points, mortgage insurance premiums and administrative fees.

Application: A request for a residential mortgage loan and includes the borrower-related information that lenders commonly use when considering the request. Someone who takes an application from a consumer is generally considered to be acting as a loan originator even when gathering application information over the phone or Internet.

ARM Disclosure: A disclosure required to be presented to the applicant within three days of application on any ARM loan. This disclosure provides the applicant with information about the specific ARM product for which they are applying, such as a historical index value.

Assumable: A term used to describe a loan in which a new borrower can take over the payments of an existing borrower.

Balloon mortgage: A type of fixed-rate mortgage loan with monthly payments based on a 30-year amortization schedule, setting a maturity date for a shorter period of time – usually five, seven, 10 or 15 years. This allows the borrower to make lower monthly payments for that shorter period of time, with a large payment of the full remaining principal balance and interest due at the maturity date.

Bank Secrecy Act (BSA): A federal law requiring that financial institutions take steps to prevent and report cases of money laundering.

Bridge loan: A short-term balloon loan that is paid back either through the sale of the current property or through a subsequent mortgage loan. It is commonly used when borrowers are buying a new home but still haven't sold their current residence.

Business day: Depending on the law in question, either any date on which the creditor is open to the public for carrying on substantially all of the creditor's business functions (when providing the initial Loan Estimate and any disclosures required under RESPA) OR any day except Sunday and federal holidays (when providing the Closing Disclosure and other disclosures required under TILA EXCEPT the Loan Estimate). Many mortgage-related disclosures must be provided to consumers within a certain number of business days.

Capacity: In mortgage lending, the borrower's ability to repay the loan (and service other debts and obligations) based upon sufficient income.

Capital: In mortgage lending, the borrower's ability to make a down payment, pay for closing costs and fund any escrows or reserves required at closing.

Certificate of Reasonable Value (CRV): A document issued by the VA that establishes the value of a property to be secured with a VA-guaranteed loan.

Changed circumstance: A material event or piece of information that is discovered after the issuance of a Loan Estimate and has an impact on either the borrower's settlement costs or the borrower's eligibility for a loan. A changed circumstance allows a loan originator to reissue the Loan Estimate to reset applicable tolerances.

Chapter 7 bankruptcy: A common kind of bankruptcy in which a borrower might need to liquidate assets in order to satisfy creditors.

Chapter 13 bankruptcy: A common kind of bankruptcy in which a borrower might need to enter into a repayment plan with his or her creditors.

Character: In mortgage lending, the borrower's willingness to repay the debt.

CHARM (Consumer Handbook on Adjustable Rate Mortgages) booklet: A booklet about adjustable-rate mortgages that is issued by the Federal Reserve. It must be provided within three business days of application if the loan is an adjustable-rate mortgage.

Closing costs: Also called *settlement costs*, all of the costs related to closing except the prepaid or escrow items. Examples of closing costs are the origination fee, discount points, real estate sales commission, attorney fees, survey charges, title insurance premiums, agency closing fees, appraisal fees, credit report fees, termite report fees, recording fees, mortgage insurance premiums, loan transfer or assumption fees and more.

Closing Disclosure: A disclosure that provides a final accounting of the closing costs associated with the transaction, as well as information about the cost of the credit itself (such as the loan's APR). Required to be provided to the borrower within three business days of application under Regulation Z, the Closing Disclosure is part of the TILA-RESPA Integrated Disclosure rule and replaced the HUD-1 Settlement Statement for most transactions.

Code of ethics: A policy statement and written guidelines that reflect the ethical principles of the company and how its employees are supposed to act when dealing with customers and/or each other. It should contain clear and enforceable consequences for violations.

Collateral: In mortgage lending, the value of the property mortgaged as security for the loan.

Combined loan-to-value ratio (CLTV): The figure that is found by adding the loan amount of the first lien plus the loan amount of any subordinate lien(s) and dividing that result by the purchase price or appraised value, whichever is less.

Commercial bank: A financial institution organized to accumulate funds primarily through time and demand deposits and to make these funds available to finance the nation's commerce and industry.

Compensating factors: Positive characteristics about a borrower that might help to offset some negative information on the borrower's application. For example, a high credit score might be a compensating factor for a borrower who has a high debt-to-income ratio.

Conference of State Bank Supervisors (CSBS): A national organization of state bank supervisors who are charged with ensuring that state banking institutions adhere to certain standards. The organization played a major role in the formation of the NMLS-R and in the drafting of the model licensing law.

Conforming loans: Loans that can be sold to Fannie Mae and Freddie Mac.

Construction loan: A loan intended to facilitate the new construction of improvements at a property. Typically, a construction lender will require a low loan-to-value ratio and only release funds as it receives evidence of actual completion of construction. Most construction loans provide for interest-only repayment and a requirement to pay off the principal balance within a limited time period following completion of construction.

Consumer Financial Protection Bureau (CFPB): A federal regulator created under authority of the Dodd-Frank Act. This agency is housed under and funded directly by the Federal Reserve and has been tasked with rulemaking for and enforcement of the majority of U.S. mortgage laws.

Consumer reporting agencies: Organizations that allow lenders to report and gather information about a borrower's credit history. This is the legal term for what are generally referred to as *credit bureaus*. The three major consumer reporting agencies are Equifax, Experian and TransUnion.

Contingent liability: A liability that may be incurred as the result of a future action. A good example of this in a mortgage transaction is the debt that is produced when a person has co-signed for another person's debt (like a student loan) but the actual payments are being made by the other person (known as the *primary obligor*). Such liabilities do NOT have to be taken into consideration when calculating the borrower's debt ratio if the payments have been made on-time for the previous 12-month period by the primary obligor.

Conventional loan: Any loan that is not insured or guaranteed by the federal government.

Cost approach: A method of appraisal in which the appraiser estimates the value of the property by calculating the cost of construction minus any depreciation, plus the value of the site (land).

Credit: In mortgage lending, the amount of a borrower's outstanding debt.

Credit freeze: An action by a consumer that makes his or her credit report inaccessible to a lender until it is lifted.

Credit union: A financial institution operating somewhat differently than other thrift institutions. After deducting operating expenses and reserves, credit unions return their earnings to their members.

Customer Identification Program: A written program for determining the identity of individuals who wish to open accounts at a financial institution, as required by the USA PATRIOT Act.

Deed of trust: An arrangement by which the borrower actually conveys title to the secured property to a third-party trustee for the life of the loan. Upon repayment of the debt, the trustee transfers title back to the borrower. In some states, a deed of trust is used as a substitute for a mortgage.

Defeasance clause: A portion of a lending agreement that requires the lender to execute a release of lien or satisfaction of mortgage document upon full payment of the debt.

Derogatory credit: The result of not paying obligations on time. A borrower's derogatory credit might be reported to a credit bureau or might lead to a judgment being filed against the borrower.

Desktop Underwriter (DU): An automated underwriting system (AUS) maintained by Fannie Mae.

Discount points: Amounts charged by a lender to the borrower or seller in order to increase the lender's effective yield on the loan. One discount point is equal to 1% of the total loan amount. An industry-standard benchmark is that for each discount point paid, the lender increases its yield on the loan by 1/8% to ¼%. From a borrower's perspective, discount points are paid to achieve a lower interest rate; without the payment of the discount points, the interest rate would be higher for the life of the loan.

Disparate impact: A method of identifying discrimination through statistical analysis. Disparate impact claims occur when a seemingly neutral (non-discriminatory) policy is implemented to achieve a neutral result but ends up having a disproportionately negative impact on a protected class.

Disparate treatment: A method of identifying illegal discrimination. Occurs when two people (or groups of people) are treated differently based on membership in a protected class. For example, offering coffee to one visitor to your office but not to another; should those people be of different races, genders, ethnicities, etc., disparate treatment may have occurred.

Dodd-Frank Act: A federal law that addresses several aspects of mortgage lending and other financial regulatory matters. It created the Consumer Financial Protection Bureau (CFPB) and amended many other mortgage-related laws.

Down payment: The portion of a property's purchase price that won't be financed as part of the mortgage loan.

Dual compensation: A prohibited act under the CFPB's Loan Originator Compensation Rule, this refers to a broker receiving compensation from multiple parties (such as the lender AND the borrower) on the same transaction.

Dwelling: A residential structure that contains one to four units, whether or not that structure is attached to real property. This includes a condominium unit, cooperative unit, mobile home and trailer (if it is used as a residence).

Easement: Formal right to traverse or use real property without ownership or possession. Often granted to utility companies so that they may maintain infrastructure located on a property. Recorded with the county in which the property is located, easements will appear on the title report and, in certain limited circumstances, may raise questions from an underwriter or attorney.

Encroachment: A fixture, such as a fence, that crosses the boundary line of one property onto another. It can create adverse possession issues and a cloud on the property's title.

Equal Credit Opportunity Act (ECOA): A federal law prohibiting discrimination in the granting of credit. Creditors cannot discriminate on the basis of race, color, religion, national origin, sex, marital status, age, receipt of income from public assistance programs or the fact that an applicant has exercised his or her rights under the Consumer Credit Protection Act. It is implemented by Regulation B.

Equitable right of redemption: The ability to avoid a foreclosure prior to, or at the time of, a judicial sale of a property.

Equity: The value of the property minus any mortgage debt.

Equity stripping: A practice whereby the applicant's equity is taken away by a mortgage lender. Equity stripping can come in many forms, but in all cases is viewed as predatory lending and must be avoided.

Escrow payments: Funds used by the lender to pay the property tax bill and hazard insurance premiums.

Extenuating circumstances: Events beyond a person's control that may have a temporary negative impact on his/her credit history. Death of a close family member or an unexpected job loss are examples of extenuating circumstances that may be taken into account during the underwriting process.

Fair Credit Reporting Act: A federal law regulating the users and use of consumer credit information. Parts of the law are now implemented and enforced by the Consumer Financial Protection Bureau, but parts of it remain with the Federal Trade Commission.

Fannie Mae: The common name for the *Federal National Mortgage Association*, which is a government-sponsored enterprise that acts as a quasi-governmental agency for the purpose of creating a secondary market for mortgages. It purchases loans on the secondary market and turns groups of loans into mortgage-backed securities (MBS) through the securitization process.

Federal Home Loan Bank (FHLB) system: A system of GSEs owned by over 8,000 community financial institutions. It provides advances to financial institutions in order for those institutions to make residential mortgage loans.

Federally related mortgage loan: A purchase or refinance loan (other than a temporary loan) that that is secured by a first or subordinate lien on residential property upon which a one-to-four family structure or manufactured home is located or is to be constructed with the proceeds of the loan. Further, the loan must be made by a lender, creditor or dealer OR made or insured by the federal government OR intended for sale to or pooling by FNMA, FHLMC or GNMA.

FHA loans: Government-insured loans that are issued by HUD-approved primary lenders. They are for one-to-four-family-unit dwellings and require at least a 3.5% down payment. They also require the payment of mortgage insurance premiums. In general, a maximum housing ratio of 31% and a maximum debt-to-income ratio of 43% are required, too.

Fiduciary relationship: A relationship between financial professionals, such as mortgage loan originators, and the consumers they are doing business with. Fiduciary duties require originators to place the consumer's best financial interests ahead of their own.

Finance charge: The total cost of the loan in dollars, including interest, points, mortgage insurance, administrative fees or any other charge paid directly or indirectly by the consumer and imposed by the lender in connection with making the loan. The finance charge does not include deposits into escrow accounts, appraisal fees or pest inspection fees. An individual charge is a finance charge (and therefore affects the APR) if that charge is directly related to the extension of credit itself. A simple test is to determine if a fee would be paid in an all-cash transaction with no credit involved. If the answer is yes, then the fee is NOT a finance charge. If the answer is no, then the fee IS a finance charge. For example, if an individual were to purchase a house with cash instead of a loan, that person would still likely get an appraisal to determine whether the price to be paid is reasonable. Therefore, appraisal fees are NOT included in the finance charge.

Financing contingency date: In real estate transactions, the contractually determined date by which the buyer's financing must be in place.

Fixed-rate mortgage: A type of mortgage loan in which the interest rate and payments remain the same for the life of the loan. It is the opposite of an adjustable-rate mortgage.

Floating rate: A mortgage interest rate that has not been locked and is being allowed to move (or "float") with the market. Floating the rate will benefit the borrower if interest rates drop between the time of application and closing and will be a detriment if interest rates increase. The floating rate is ultimately locked-in sometime prior to closing.

Force-placed insurance: Property insurance that is purchased by a lender when an owner's insurance is cancelled or not properly obtained. Lenders must provide notice before billing a borrower for force-placed insurance. The charges passed on to the borrower for this insurance must be reasonable.

Foreclosure: A proceeding to extinguish all rights, title and interest of the owner of a property in order to sell the property and satisfy a lien against it. Foreclosures are initiated by lenders when borrowers fail to make payments.

Fraud alerts: A notice indicating that an issue pertaining to a credit file must be addressed and cleared before extending credit to a borrower. Fraud alerts are intended to prevent identity theft.

Fraud for profit: A willful misrepresentation of material facts on a mortgage loan application with the intent of gaining money through the transaction. This type of fraud is more likely to be committed by industry professionals/insiders and result in more damage to the victimized creditor(s).

Fraud for property: Also called *fraud for housing*, this is a willful misrepresentation of material facts on a loan application with the intent of gaining property. This type of fraud is more likely to be perpetuated by borrowers and result in less damage to the creditor(s) involved because the loan is typically paid in a timely manner.

Freddie Mac: The common name for the *Federal Home Loan Mortgage Corporation*, which is a government-sponsored enterprise that was intended to provide a secondary market for mortgages originated by savings and loan associations and create competition to Fannie Mae. Like Fannie Mae, Freddie Mac also issues mortgage-backed securities (MBS).

Fully indexed rate: The amount of interest that is calculated by adding the index to the margin. Unless caps prevent it, the fully indexed rate becomes an ARM's interest rate at the start of each adjustment period.

Ginnie Mae: A government-sponsored enterprise that guarantees interest payments on MBS pools made up of only government-insured or government-guaranteed mortgages (such as FHA, VA and USDA loans).

Good Faith Estimate (GFE): This disclosure, required under Regulation X, has been replaced by the Closing Disclosure for most mortgage loans. It contains information on the known or anticipated fees, charges or settlement costs that the mortgage applicant is likely to incur at the settlement (closing) of the loan. It must be delivered within three business days of receiving or preparing an application on loans that do not use the TRID disclosures.

Government-sponsored enterprise (GSE): A quasi-governmental agency. Fannie Mae and Freddie Mac are examples of GSEs.

Gramm-Leach-Bliley Act (GLBA): A federal law that includes provisions to protect consumers' personal financial information held by financial institutions. Some of the issues pertaining to GLBA compliance include financial privacy rules, safeguard rules and pretexting rules.

Grossing up: Calculating how much tax the borrower would pay if this income were taxable and then adding that figure to the gross amount received. This is commonly done when non-taxable income is used to qualify a borrower.

High-cost mortgage loan: A mortgage loan with an annual percentage rate exceeding the Average Prime Offer Rate (APOR) by more than 6.5% for a first-lien transaction or 8.5% for a second-lien transaction OR a mortgage loan with total points and fees exceeding 5% of the loan amount. ALL high-cost loans must be compliant with the Home Ownership and Equity Protection Act (HOEPA).

Home equity line of credit (HELOC): A revolving mortgage loan that allows the borrower to take advances at his/her discretion up to an approved limit that represents a percentage of the borrower's equity in a property.

Home Equity Line of Credit Combined Loan-to-Value (HCLTV): The figure found by adding the loan amount of the first lien plus the credit limit of the home equity line of credit (HELOC) and dividing that result by the purchase price or appraised value, whichever is less. This is calculated when a borrower wants to obtain multiple mortgage loans for the same property and at least one of the loans is a home-equity line of credit (HELOC).

Home Loan Toolkit: A booklet that provides consumers information on shopping for a home loan, common closing costs and reading required disclosures like the Loan Estimate and Closing Disclosure. This booklet is published by the CFPB and must be provided to the applicant within three business days of application on purchase transactions according to TILA/Regulation Z.

Home Mortgage Disclosure Act (HMDA): A federal law written as a response to public concerns that lenders were redlining. Requires creditors to track demographic data on applications and lending activity and report that data to the federal government on an annual basis.

Home Ownership and Equity Protection Act (HOEPA): A federal law that sets rules for high-cost loans. A loan that is subject to HOEPA cannot feature a balloon payment, negative amortization or a prepayment penalty and cannot be refinanced within one year by the original creditor (other creditors may refinance the loan) unless doing so is "clearly in the best interests of the borrower."

Homeowners Protection Act (HPA): A federal law requiring that private mortgage insurance be automatically cancelled when the loan-to value ratio (LTV) on an owner-occupied single-family residence reaches 78% or less of the original value of the property. Borrowers have the ability to request cancellation of mortgage insurance when loan-to-value reaches 80% of the appraised value.

Housing ratio: The sum of monthly principal, interest, taxes and insurance divided by the borrower's gross monthly income. For some loans, such as those sold to Freddie Mac, the housing ratio cannot exceed 28% without compensating factors. The ratio is sometimes called the *front-end ratio* or the *top ratio*.

Identity theft: A fraud, committed or attempted, using the identifying information of another person without authority. Many businesses are required to implement a program that detects and prevents identity theft.

Identity theft prevention program: A written program designed to detect the warning signs of identity theft in day-to-day operations. Businesses defined as *financial institutions* under the Fair and Accurate Credit Transactions Act's Red Flags Rule are required to implement this kind of program. Because of the broadness of the definition, all mortgage brokerages and mortgage banks are covered by it.

Immediate family member: A spouse, child, sibling, parent, grandparent or grandchild. An individual who only originates loans with or on behalf of an immediate family member doesn't need a loan originator license.

Independent contractor: Someone who performs mortgage-related duties and isn't supervised or directed by a licensed or registered loan originator. An independent contractor who otherwise only performs the same tasks as a loan processor or underwriter must still be licensed as a loan originator.

Index: An economic measurement that is used to make periodic interest adjustments for an adjustable-rate mortgage. The index plus the margin equals the fully indexed rate.

Initial cap: A rate cap that applies only to the first rate adjustment period and indicates the number of percentage points that a rate may increase over the introductory rate.

Initial Escrow Statement: A required summary of payments into and disbursals from a borrower's escrow account that is provided at closing.

Intent to proceed: An indication by a potential borrower that he or she is interested in moving forward with a mortgage transaction after delivery of the Loan Estimate. The intent to proceed might be provided orally in a face-to-face or phone conversation or in some written format. However, a creditor cannot interpret a borrower's silence as an intent to proceed with the transaction. In general, no fees (other than a fee to obtain a credit report) can be charged to a consumer until there is an intent to proceed.

Interest-only loan: A fixed-rate mortgage that allows the borrower to pay only the interest due on the mortgage for a period of years, after which the loan becomes fully amortizing.

Introductory rate: An initial rate for an adjustable-rate mortgage that is often lower than the fully indexed rate. The introductory rate will often expire after anywhere from a few months to a few years.

Judicial foreclosure: A method of foreclosure that requires court action in order to complete the process. Typically found in states that use the mortgage document as the security instrument.

Jumbo loans: Loans for amounts that are greater than the standards of Fannie Mae and Freddie Mac.

Kickback: Something of value that is given in exchange for a referral. Kickbacks are prohibited by RESPA.

Legitimate business need: One circumstance under which a lender can receive a consumer's credit information from a credit bureau. The disclosure must relate to a business transaction that was initiated by the consumer or must be intended to help a creditor review an account in order to determine whether a consumer continues to meet the terms of that account.

Lender-paid compensation (LPC): Compensation paid by a lender to a mortgage broker for originating a loan funded by that lender. This compensation is different from the old yield-spread premium (YSP) in that it does not vary based on the terms or conditions of a loan. Typically, LPC is paid as a percentage of the loan amount and does not vary from transaction to transaction in a given lender/broker relationship.

Life cap: A rate cap that sets a maximum number of percentage points that the rate can increase over the start rate for the life of the loan.

Life expectancy set-aside: An account, similar to an escrow account, that must be created if a borrower with a reverse mortgage cannot prove an ability to pay future property taxes and insurance premiums.

Loan Application Register (LAR): A log of applications taken by a creditor. Required to be kept up to date and provided to the federal government once per year under the Home Mortgage Disclosure Act (HMDA).

Loan Estimate: A disclosure containing information on settlement costs and the cost of credit itself. Required to be provided to the applicant within three business days of application under Regulation Z, the Loan Estimate is part of the TILA-RESPA Integrated Disclosure rule that replaced the Good Faith Estimate and Truth in Lending disclosure for most mortgage loans.

Loan flipping: An abusive practice in which a loan is refinanced without any tangible net benefit for the borrower. A form of equity stripping.

Loan originator: Someone who takes residential mortgage loan applications and offers or negotiates the terms of such loans in exchange for compensation or gain. Most loan originators must be licensed. Be aware that the term *loan originator* can refer to an individual or a company. In practice, the term *MLO* (or *mortgage loan originator*) is sometimes used to describe an individual who is a loan originator.

Loan processor or underwriter: In the context of the SAFE Act, this is someone who is supervised by a state-licensed or federally registered lending institution and who performs clerical or support duties. Loan processors and underwriters do not typically need to hold loan originator licenses unless they are performing duties for more than one company at a time.

Loan Product Advisor (LPA): An automated underwriting system (AUS) maintained by Freddie Mac.

Loan-to-value ratio (LTV): The loan amount divided by the lesser of the purchase price or appraised value of the property. The higher the loan-to-value ratio on a given loan, the less investment from the applicant in the form of a down payment is required.

Mailbox rule: If disclosures such as the Loan Estimate and Closing Disclosure are mailed to the applicant, they are deemed received on the third business day after they are placed in the mail.

Margin: The number that a lender adds to an index to determine the interest rate of an ARM. The margin never changes during the life of the loan.

MI factor: Another word for the premium on a mortgage insurance policy. It can be paid monthly, annually or in a lump sum.

Misrepresentation: A characteristic of mortgage fraud and negligence, this involves a misstatement or omission of a material fact on a loan application. A fact is considered to be material if knowledge of that fact would have caused a lender to consider a different outcome on a credit application.

Money laundering: Bringing illegally obtained funds into and out of the financial system in a manner that evades law enforcement. Under the Bank Secrecy Act, many businesses, including non-depository mortgage banks and mortgage brokers, must implement a program that detects and prevents money laundering.

Monthly MIP: The monthly charge for FHA mortgage insurance. It is calculated by multiplying the base loan amount by a factor, then dividing by 12. The borrower pays the MIP as part of the monthly mortgage payment, along with principal, interest, taxes and insurance (PITI).

Mortgage: A document that creates a lien upon the subject property for the security of payment of the debt.

Mortgage-backed securities (MBS): Pooled mortgages that have been converted into bonds and sold to the public.

Mortgage banker: An individual, firm or corporation that originates and sells loans secured by mortgages on real property. Mortgage bankers may occasionally service loans, although that tends not to be their primary function. Some states actually require a separate license or endorsement to allow a mortgage banker to engage in the act of servicing loans.

Mortgage broker: A firm or individual that, for a commission, matches borrowers and lenders. A mortgage broker does not retain servicing, does not use its own funds and is not a lender.

Mortgage Loan Servicing Disclosure: A notice regarding the lender's practices of transferring or retaining the servicing of the loan. It must be provided to the borrower within three days of the loan application.

National Do Not Call Registry: A list of phone numbers that cannot be called for telemarketing purposes. Sellers of goods or services (including loan origination services) are required to search the registry every 31 days and delete from their call lists phone numbers that are in the registry.

Nationwide Multistate Licensing System and Registry (NMLS-R): A licensing system and registry that was established in connection with the SAFE Act.

Negative amortization: The result of an interest payment being less than the amount of interest actually due. The difference between what is paid and what is due is added back to the loan principal. In effect, this can force the borrower to make longer payments (or make bigger payments) later in order to retire the debt.

Negligence: Unintentional misrepresentation on a loan application. The difference between negligence and fraud is that negligence does not involve intent on the part of the perpetrator(s), though it may still be a crime if it is serious enough.

Non-conforming loans: Loans that do not satisfy requirements of Fannie Mae and Freddie Mac and cannot be sold to those GSEs.

Non-judicial foreclosure: A form of foreclosure that only requires administrative actions rather than the involvement of a court. Typically found in states that use the trust deed as the security instrument.

Nontraditional mortgage product: Any mortgage product that isn't a 30-year, fixed-rate loan. In order to obtain and renew their licenses, loan originators must complete courses with an emphasis on nontraditional mortgage products.

Notice of Escrow Analysis: A required summary of payments into and disbursals from a borrower's escrow account. It must be provided to the borrower every year.

Novation: The process of releasing one borrower from a lending agreement and substituting a new borrower.

Opt-out right: A consumer's right, under the Privacy Rule of the Gramm-Leach-Bliley Act, to limit some sharing of his or her financial information.

Origination fee: A fee or charge for the work involved in the evaluation, preparation and submission of a proposed mortgage loan. The origination fee is limited to 1% of the loan amount for FHA and VA loans.

Overt discrimination: A method of identifying illegal discrimination. Occurs when a business has a known policy that refuses to serve, or provides different levels of service to, members of a protected class based solely on their membership in the protected class (i.e., refusing service to Hispanic borrowers).

Per-diem interest: The amount of daily interest payable under a loan. Per-diem interest is determined by first multiplying the principal amount of the loan by the interest rate to determine the annual amount of interest payable under the loan. Next, that annual amount is divided by 360 days to determine the per-diem interest amount. Finally, the per-diem interest amount is multiplied by the number of days remaining in the month of closing, including the date of closing.

Periodic cap: A rate cap that applies to all subsequent adjustment periods and indicates the number of percentage points that a rate may increase or decrease from the rate that was in effect prior to the adjustment.

PITI: The monthly sum of principal, interest, taxes and insurance owed by the borrower. For some loans, such as those sold to Freddie Mac, the monthly PITI cannot exceed 28% of the borrower's gross monthly income.

Positive amortization: The payment of a debt with equal periodic installments of both principal and interest, so that a loan will be paid off at the end of a specific period of time.

Prepayment penalties: Fees that must be paid by the borrower if the loan's principal is repaid in full prior to the loan's expiration. Many loans in today's market cannot have prepayment penalties that last more than three years or that are greater than 3% during the loan's first year, 2% during the loan's second year and 1% during the loan's third year.

Pretexting: The use of false pretenses in order to obtain consumers' personal financial information. It is prohibited by the Gramm-Leach-Bliley Act.

Privacy policies: Required under the Privacy Rule of the Gramm-Leach-Bliley Act, these are written documents that detail the financial institution's practices for collection of non-public personal information about customers and with whom that information is shared. A privacy policy must be provided to your customers when they first become your customers, annually for as long as they remain your customers and anytime the policy changes for as long as they remain your customers. A short-form version of the policy must be readily available to consumers (not customers) in a place like the company website.

Private mortgage insurance (PMI): Insurance that protects the lender against losses that result from default by the borrower. It is required when the loan-to-value ratio is greater than 80% and must be cancelled when the loan-to-value ratio is equal to or less than 78%. Other kinds of mortgage insurance (not PMI) are used for FHA and VA loans.

Processor: An individual who performs clerical duties for a lender or mortgage broker, including ordering independent verifications of employment, income and assets, preparing a loan for underwriting and assisting in clearing of any underwriting conditions.

Promissory note: A document that evidences the borrower's obligation to repay the debt to the lender. Unlike the mortgage, the promissory note does not state that the property will be used as collateral in order to obtain the loan.

Qualified mortgage (QM): One type of mortgage loan defined in the Dodd-Frank Act. If a loan is a qualified mortgage, the lender is presumed to have complied with the Dodd-Frank's ability-to-repay requirements.

Rate cap: A limitation on the amount an interest rate may increase or decrease either at the adjustment date or over the lifetime of the loan. Sometimes referred to as an *adjustment cap*, a rate cap can dictate how much a rate can increase during the loan's first adjustment period, during each adjustment period or during the entire life of the loan.

Rate floor: The lowest interest rate to which an ARM may adjust.

Rate lock: An agreement between the borrower and lender for a specified period of time in which the lender will keep a specific interest rate, loan fee and discount points available for the borrower. Some lenders charge a fee for locking a rate at application.

Rate lock fee: An amount charged by a lender to dissuade a borrower from switching to a different lender in the event of a decrease in market interest rates before closing.

Real estate contract: A written contract between a buyer and seller of real property, setting forth the price and the terms of the sale. This contractual agreement contains all the terms and conditions upon which the seller agrees to sell and the buyer agrees to buy.

Real Estate Settlement Procedures Act (RESPA): A federal law that allows borrowers to receive pertinent and timely disclosure regarding the nature and costs of the real estate settlement (closing) process. The law also protects consumers against abusive practices (such as kickbacks) and places limitations on the use of reserve accounts. It is implemented by Regulation X.

Reconciliation: The process by which an appraiser examines several estimates of value and bases the property's final estimate of value on the intended use of the property.

Red flags: Warning signs of a particular activity. Many businesses are required to have programs that detect the red flags of identity theft and money laundering.

Redemption period: A period of time in which the borrower may pay off the loan in full in order to avoid a foreclosure sale of the property.

Redlining: The arbitrary denial of real estate loan applications in certain geographic areas without considering individual applicant qualification. Concerns about redlining prompted the passage of the Home Mortgage Disclosure Act (HMDA).

Refinance transactions: Loan transactions in which one mortgage loan is satisfied and replaced by another mortgage loan. Refinance transactions on an owner-occupied primary residence give borrowers a three-day right of rescision.

Registered loan originator: A loan originator who is registered with the NMLS-R and employed by a depository institution, a subsidiary of a depository institution or an institution regulated by the Farm Credit Association. A registered loan originator generally does not need to be licensed.

Regulation B: The federal regulation that implements the Equal Credit Opportunity Act (ECOA). Rules from this regulation are enforced by the Consumer Financial Protection Bureau.

Regulation C: The federal regulation that implements HMDA. The Consumer Financial Protection Bureau has primary rulemaking and enforcement authority over this regulation.

Regulation X: The document containing the rules for implementing the Real Estate Settlement Procedures Act (RESPA). The rules are enforced by the Consumer Financial Protection Bureau.

Regulation Z: The federal regulation that implements the Truth in Lending Act (TILA). Rulemaking and enforcement power under TILA are handled by the Consumer Financial Protection Bureau.

Reserves: A borrower's remaining liquid assets after the closing of a real estate transaction.

Residential mortgage loan: Any loan primarily for personal, family or household use that is secured by a mortgage, deed of trust or other equivalent security interest on a dwelling (or on real estate where a dwelling is being constructed or will be constructed). The requirements mentioned in this guide relate to the origination of residential mortgage loans. They do not necessarily apply to loans tied to commercial or industrial properties.

Residual income: The amount of income that a borrower will have left after taxes, debt payments and childcare expenses to purchase necessities such as food or gasoline.

Retail lending: Direct lending to borrowers (as opposed to lending that is facilitated by a broker).

Reverse mortgage: A mortgage loan in which the lender makes periodic payments at a fixed rate to the borrower using the borrower's equity in the home as security. This is often used to provide income to retirees or elderly borrowers based upon their existing home equity. Typically, no repayment is required until the property is sold or the borrower is deceased.

Right of rescission: The borrower's right to cancel certain refinance transactions. Under the Truth in Lending Act, this right lasts for three business days, not including Sundays or legal holidays.

Sales comparison approach: A method of appraisal in which value is determined by looking at the recent sale price of similar properties.

Seasoned funds: Funds that have been in the account for a minimum period of time. Many lenders will require that money intended for a down payment or closing costs come from seasoned funds.

Secondary market: The sector of the economy where existing mortgage loans (and the right to collect borrower payments) are bought and sold. This market provides liquidity for lenders and creates standardization in regard to credit requirements, loan types and loan documents.

Securitization: The pooling of multiple loans into single investment vehicles.

Service release premium: An amount paid by an investor to a mortgage banker in exchange for the right to service (collect payments on) the loan after closing.

Servicer: The party collecting payments from borrowers. Servicing can be handled by the original lender or by a third party.

Servicing: The process of collecting the principal, interest and escrow account payments on the loan. Servicing may be done by the lender or transferred to another party.

Servicing Transfer Disclosure: A document informing the borrower that servicing of a loan has been transferred to another entity. It must be provided to the borrower no later than 15 days before servicing rights are transferred to a new institution.

Settlement service business: Any service provided in connection with a real estate settlement including, but not limited to: title searches, title examinations, the provision of title certificates, title insurance, services rendered by an attorney, document preparation, property surveys, credit reports, appraisals, pest and fungus inspections, services rendered by a real estate agent or broker, the origination of a federally related mortgage loan (and all related activities) and the handling of processing and closing of settlement.

State: In regard to the SAFE Act, any state of the United States, the District of Columbia, any territory of the United States, Puerto Rico, Guam, American Samoa, the Trust Territory of the Pacific Islands, the Virgin Islands and the Northern Mariana Islands.

State-licensed loan originator: A loan originator who is licensed by his or her state, registered with the NMLS-R and isn't employed by entities mentioned in the definition of *registered loan originator*. If you are reading this study guide, you are likely planning on becoming (or have already become) a state-licensed loan originator.

State Regulatory Registry, LLC: A wholly owned subsidiary of CSBS that runs the NMLS-R.

Statutory right of redemption: The ability to cure a foreclosure even after a judicial sale has occurred.

Steering: Directing a borrower to a given loan or loan product to increase compensation when that loan is not in the consumer's interest. This is prohibited by the Dodd-Frank Act.

Subordinate financing: Loans secured by subordinate liens.

Subordinate lien: Any mortgage or other lien that has priority lower than that of the first mortgage. Such a lien is also referred to as a *junior lien*.

Subprime loan: A loan in which the borrower represents too high of a risk for it to be sold to Fannie Mae or Freddie Mac.

Suspicious activity reports (SARs): Reports that must be filed with the Treasury Department whenever a person engages in suspicious aggregate transactions of $5,000 or more. These reports are required by the Bank Secrecy Act.

Table-funded transaction: A settlement at which a loan is funded by a contemporaneous advance of loan funds and an assignment of the loan to the person advancing the funds. A table-funded transaction is not a secondary market transaction.

Teaser rate: For an ARM, an introductory interest rate that is lower than the fully indexed rate at the time of closing.

Temporary Authority to Operate (TA): A status granted to established originators applying for licensure in additional states or to those transitioning from a federally registered originator to a state-licensed originator. Allows the individual to legally originate residential mortgage loans without holding an actual state license for up to 120 days while fulfilling all licensing obligations imposed by the state in which an MLO license application is pending.

Thrift: Sometimes known as a savings and loan, a mutual or stock association chartered and regulated by the Office of the Comptroller of the Currency. Traditionally, deposits are invested in residential mortgage loans.

TILA/RESPA Integrated Disclosures (TRID): A new disclosure regime, implemented by the CFPB in accordance with a Dodd-Frank Act mandate, that combined the old Good Faith Estimate, Truth in Lending Disclosure and HUD-1 Settlement Statement into two new disclosures: the Loan Estimate (LE) and the Closing Disclosure (CD). The TRID disclosures are used for the vast majority of loans today and provide consumers critical information to help them shop for the best home loan and ensure that their fees do not increase beyond permitted tolerance amounts between origination and closing.

Title insurance: A type of insurance coverage that protects against defects in title that were not listed in a title report or abstract. Separate coverage exists for owners and lenders. Owners' policies are typically issued each time property is sold, covering the buyer. Lenders' policies are typically required each time a new mortgage loan is closed, including refinance transactions.

Title report: A document typically prepared by an attorney setting forth the condition of title. Title insurance can be purchased to protect the lender or the owner from defects in title that were not found in the title report.

Total debt-to-income ratio: Monthly principal, interest, taxes and insurance payments plus other debts (such as credit card debt, installment loan payments, alimony and child-support payments) divided by the borrower's gross monthly income. However, the ratio doesn't include other expenses, such as utility payments, food bills, educational expenses (other than student loans), childcare expenses (other than child support payments), medical insurance premiums or entertainment expenses. For most loans, the debt-to-income ratio cannot exceed 36%. It is sometimes known as the *back-end ratio* or the *bottom ratio*.

Total interest percentage (TIP): The total amount of interest paid over the life of the loan expressed as a percentage of the loan amount. It appears on both the Loan Estimate and Closing Disclosure.

Treble damages: The maximum penalty allowed under RESPA for requiring a buyer/borrower to use a specific title company: three times the amount of the title fees assessed to the borrower.

Trigger terms: Items in an advertisement that automatically require the disclosure of other items in the same advertisement. Trigger terms are the amount or percentage of down payment, the number of payments or period of repayment, the amount of any payment and the amount of any finance charge.

Truth in Lending Act (TILA): A federal law designed to promote the informed use of consumer credit (i.e., credit to a consumer primarily for personal, family or household purposes) by requiring disclosure about its terms and cost. It does not apply to loans for commercial or business purposes. It is implemented by Regulation Z.

UDAAP: *Unfair, deceptive or abusive acts or practices*. Industry regulators apply a UDAAP standard when examining mortgage companies to ensure that entities operating in the mortgage space are doing so free of practices (such as deceptive advertising) that may cause harm to the applicant.

Underwriter: The individual responsible for reviewing an application (including all related documentation) evaluating the strength of the application (often in conjunction with findings from an automated underwriting system) and issuing a credit decision.

Uniform Residential Appraisal Report (URAR): The most common form used by appraisers to appraise a single-family home. Also called the *1004*.

Uniform Residential Loan Application (URLA): The common application form for residential mortgage loans. It is also known as the *1003*.

Uniform Settlement Statement: A form containing a complete list of the actual settlement costs (not an estimate) that will be charged at the closing. Also known as the *HUD-1*, this disclosure has been replaced by the Closing Disclosure for most mortgage loans.

Unique identifier: A number or other identifier that is assigned to a loan originator by the NMLS-R in order to identify the person and track his or her conduct in the mortgage-lending business. The unique identifier must appear on various documents, including on advertisements.

Upfront mortgage insurance premium (UFMIP): A one-time cost of FHA mortgage insurance that is paid at closing. It is calculated by multiplying the loan amount by a factor.

VA entitlement: The portion of a VA loan that is guaranteed by the government.

VA funding fee: An amount paid by a veteran in order to help defray the costs of the VA loan program. The size of the fee will depend on several factors, including the loan-to-value ratio, the purpose of the loan, the veteran's status and the number of times the veteran has obtained a VA loan.

VA loans: Government-guaranteed loans that are made to owner-occupant veterans by private lenders, such as banks, thrifts and mortgage companies.

Verification of deposit (VOD): Third-party verification of a borrower's bank statements, typically gathered by a loan processor.

Verification of employment (VOE): Third-party verification of a borrower's employment, typically gathered by a loan processor from an employer.

Veteran: A person who is currently serving in the U.S. Army, Navy, Air Force, Marine Corps, or Coast Guard, or who has been discharged from those services and has served a sufficient amount of time to be eligible for the VA mortgage program.

Warehouse line of credit: A line of credit commonly used by mortgage bankers to fund loans.

Wholesale lenders: Entities that purchase and sell loans which have been originated by third parties. Wholesale lenders may purchase loans with the intent to package the loans for sale to secondary market investors; or they may purchase loans in order to service the loans themselves.

Yield spread premium: An amount paid by an investor to a lender or mortgage broker at closing to compensate the loan originator for making a loan at an interest rate that is higher than the interest rate which the investor would have accepted for that loan. This type of compensation was made illegal under the Dodd-Frank Act and the MLO Compensation Rule under TILA.

QUICK REFERENCE CHARTS AND LINKS

A. Disclosure Requirements and Timeline

DISCLOSURE	LAW	REGULATION	TIMELINE
Loan Estimate	TILA	Z	Within three business days of application. (Day of application is "Day Zero" with Day one being the first business day after the application is taken.)
CHARM booklet	TILA	Z	Within three business days of application. (ARM transactions only.)
Mortgage Loan Servicing Disclosure	RESPA	X	Within three business days of application.
CFPB's *Home Loan Toolkit*	RESPA and TILA	X and Z	Within three business days of application. (Purchases only.)
Right of Rescission Disclosure (two copies to each title holder)	TILA	Z	Generally given at closing but must be provided in all cases before the three-day rescission right begins. (Owner-occupied refinances only.)
Closing Disclosure	TILA	Z	At least three business days prior to closing.
Initial Escrow Account Disclosure	RESPA	X	Within 45 days after the closing date, though generally done at closing.
List of HUD-Approved Counseling Providers	HOEPA (TILA)	Z	List must contain the 10 counselors closest to the borrower. Due

			within 3 business days of application.
Annual Escrow Account Disclosure	RESPA	X	Once per year.
Servicing Transfer Statement	RESPA	X	At least 15 days before servicing is transferred.
Affiliated Business Arrangement Disclosure (AfBA)	RESPA	X	When the referral is made to the business, UNLESS a lender requires the use of a certain provider - then it must be done at application.
Privacy Policy Notice	Gramm-Leach-Bliley	N/A	1) At first contact. 2) Once per year (for as long as the person remains your customer). 3) When it changes (as long as the person remains your customer).

B. Triggering Events and Timeline

EVENT	LAW	REGULATION	TIMELINE
Borrower makes a servicing complaint	RESPA	X	Servicer must respond within five days and resolve within 30 days in most circumstances.
Calling a client on the Do Not Call list	Do Not Call	N/A	You have 18 months from the last transaction date to call a client on the list.
Calling a non-client who has contacted you about a service	Do Not Call	N/A	You have three months from the date of last inquiry to call a client on the list.

Notifying a borrower of action taken on a loan	ECOA	B	Must notify within 30 days from application date.
Derogatory credit – late pays	FCRA	V	Must be removed from bureau after seven years.
Derogatory credit – bankruptcies	FCRA	V	Must be removed after 10 years.
Derogatory credit – unpaid tax liens	FCRA	V	Remain indefinitely.

C. Maximum Penalties and Implementing/Enforcing Agencies

LAW	AGENCY	MAXIMUM PENALTY
RESPA	CFPB	$10,000 and up to one year in prison. Requiring a specific title company - up to treble damages (three times the cost of the service) in private lawsuits plus the RESPA violation penalty.
TILA	CFPB	$5,000 per day for a single violation. $25,000 per day for reckless violations. $1,000,000 per day for knowingly violating the TRID rules.
ECOA	CFPB	$10,000 plus actual damages for individual actions. $500,000 or 1% of net worth for class actions.
Fair Housing Act	HUD	$16,000 first violation / $37,500 if previous violation within five years / $65,000 if two or more violations within seven years. Any additional private civil lawsuit must be filed within two years.
Mortgage fraud prosecuted under federal fraud statutes	FBI investigates DOJ prosecutes	30 years in prison and up to $1,000,000 in fines plus actual and punitive damages.
Do Not Call	FTC	Max fine of $42,530 *per violation.*

D. Benchmark Debt-to-Income Ratios (Front / Back)

Fannie Mae / Freddie Mac (Conforming)	28% / 36%
FHA	31% / 43%
VA	None / 41% (AND residual income test)
USDA Rural Development	29% / 41%

E. Loan Estimate Fees and Tolerances

LE Box and Title	Fees Disclosed	Tolerance Applied
Box A: Origination Charges	Discount points Origination charges (itemized)	Zero tolerance
Box B: Services you cannot shop for	Appraisal, credit report, tax service, flood cert, FHA upfront MIP, etc.	Zero tolerance
Box C: Services you can shop for	Title search, closing fee, lender's title policy, pest inspection, survey, etc.	10% aggregate tolerance when using a vendor on the creditor's list. Unlimited tolerance if borrower selects alternate vendor.
Box E: Taxes and other government fees	Recording fees and transfer taxes.	Recording fees: 10% tolerance Transfer taxes: Zero tolerance
Box F: Prepaids	First year homeowner's insurance premium, prepaid/per-diem interest, property tax bill that has been released for payment.	Unlimited tolerance
Box G: Initial Escrow Payment at Closing	Impounds to start escrow account plus allowable cushion: property taxes, property insurance, mortgage insurance (monthly).	Unlimited tolerance
Box H: Other	Items not required by lender but that may be obtained: often owner's title policy, but sometimes not used.	Unlimited tolerance

F. Helpful Links and Reference Tools

- Consumer Financial Protection Bureau regulatory implementation page (information on mortgage rules implemented by the CFPB): https://www.consumerfinance.gov/policy-compliance/guidance/

- Fannie Mae Selling Guide (Fannie Mae's guidelines, policies and procedures): https://www.fanniemae.com/content/guide/selling/index.html

- Freddie Mac Seller/Servicer Guide (Freddie Mac's guidelines, policies and procedures): http://www.freddiemac.com/singlefamily/guide/

- HUD Handbook 4000.1 (FHA guidelines, policies and procedures): http://portal.hud.gov/hudportal/HUD?src=/program_offices/housing/sfh/handbook_4000-1

- Uniform Residential Appraisal Report (Form 1004): https://www.fanniemae.com/content/guide_form/1004.pdf

- Uniform Residential Loan Application (Form 1003): https://www.fanniemae.com/content/guide_form/1003irev.pdf

Made in the USA
Columbia, SC
12 May 2021